E–Banking Management:
Issues, Solutions, and Strategies

Mahmood Shah
Lancashire Business School, University of Central Lancashire, UK

Steve Clarke
University of Hull, UK

 **INFORMATION SCIENCE REFERENCE**

Hershey · New York

Director of Editorial Content:	Kristin Klinger
Senior Managing Editor:	Jamie Snavely
Managing Editor:	Jeff Ash
Assistant Managing Editor:	Carole Coulson
Typesetter:	Jeff Ash
Cover Design:	Lisa Tosheff
Printed at:	Yurchak Printing Inc.

Published in the United States of America by
Information Science Reference (an imprint of IGI Global)
701 E. Chocolate Avenue
Hershey PA 17033
Tel: 717-533-8845
Fax: 717-533-8661
E-mail: cust@igi-global.com
Web site: http://www.igi-global.com/reference

and in the United Kingdom by
Information Science Reference (an imprint of IGI Global)
3 Henrietta Street
Covent Garden
London WC2E 8LU
Tel: 44 20 7240 0856
Fax: 44 20 7379 0609
Web site: http://www.eurospanbookstore.com

Library of Congress Cataloging-in-Publication Data

Shah, Mahmood, 1971-

E-banking management : issues, solutions, and strategies / by Mahmood Shah and Steve Clarke.
    p. cm.

Includes bibliographical references and index.
Summary: "This book focuses on human, operational, managerial, and strategic organizational issues in e-banking"--Provided by publisher.

ISBN 978-1-60566-252-7 (hardcover) -- ISBN 978-1-60566-253-4 (ebook) 1. Internet banking. 2. Banks and banking--Automation. 3. Bank management. I. Clarke, Steve, 1950- II. Title.

HG1708.7.S53 2009
  332.10285'4678--dc22

                                         2009000081

British Cataloguing in Publication Data
A Cataloguing in Publication record for this book is available from the British Library.

All work contributed to this book is new, previously-unpublished material. The views expressed in this book are those of the authors, but not necessarily of the publisher.

Table of Contents

Preface

This book will explore issues critical for success in providing e-banking. The aim is to assist organizations in utilising the opportunities offered by this relatively new set of technologies. This book largely restricts itself to the organizational view of the problem, and is therefore primarily focused on organizational internal factors. External factors, such as the political or economical environment in which an organization operates, are well covered in other publications and will not be repeated in detail here.

It is not intended that the book should replace texts on existing management practices in its focused field, but rather that it be used as a complement to them. The main target audiences include undergraduate as well as postgraduate students of business administration, general management and technology management as well as practitioners of e-banking. The expected contributions to the academic community include development of a deeper understanding of the issues involved in e-banking as well as practical suggestions on how to tackle these issues. Apart from the introductory chapter, all other chapters are written as independent pieces so readers of this book can choose to consult the part of the book which is most relevant to the problem in hand.

E-banking forces most financial institutions to re-examine their systems and practices and to look for new ways to deliver their services over the Web. To do that effectively they seek to improve work flow, reduce paper work, provide online document imaging for users and create industry wide standards in order to improve cost efficiencies and profitability. This leads to many technical, managerial and strategic issues. Chapters I, II, and III present an overview of these issues, which will be covered in greater depth in subsequent chapters.

E-banking related technical issues may include developing an infrastructure to ensure 24-hour availability, integrating backend, front end and other supporting tools to create a seamless experience for the customer, and collection/analysis of data which enables the provision of timely information to the management for effective decision making. These issues are covered in chapters IV, VII and VIII.

Managerial issues include maximizing the generation of Internet revenue and differentiating a bank's services and products from other banks. Banks may fail if they are thinking only of providing low cost transactions. Re-organizing teams, departments or even the whole organization may also come into management's remit. Managing e-commerce projects, employing new ways of product development, marketing and selling to satisfy the needs of increasingly sophisticated customers are some of the key management challenges as well as complying with national, regional (such as European Union) and international regulations. These issues are covered in Chapters V, VI, VII, VIII, IX X and XI.

Strategic issues include determining the overall direction of the business, dealing with changes in the market, developing industry wide alliances for products/services development, and re-structuring organizations to cope with new business models. These issues are covered in Chapter VII, VIII, X and XI. Chapter XII is summary of issues and solutions covered in this book

Problems such as security, dealing with cyber-crimes, threats from new entrants to markets such as Internet only banks or supermarkets are also covered in relevant sections of the text.

Acknowledgment

Our gratitude is owed to colleagues past and present for their help and support in producing this book including professor Ray Paul, professor John Ward and David Walters. We also thank IGI Global for the support they provided during development of this book and reviews whom valuable comments helped improve this book. An finally our thanks will have to go to our partners and families for their patience and support during writing of this book.

Mahmood Shah & Steve Clarke

Chapter I
E-Banking Management:
An Introduction

INTRODUCTION

The fast advancing global information infrastructure (including information technology and computer networks such as the Internet and telecommunications systems) enable the development of electronic commerce at a global level. The nearly
universal connectivity which the Internet offers has made it an invaluable business
tool. These developments have created a new type of economy, which many call the
'digital economy'. This fast emerging economy is bringing with it rapidly changing
technologies, increasing knowledge intensity in all areas of business, and creating
virtual supply chains and new forms of businesses and service delivery channels
such as e-banking.

As a direct consequence of the emergence of the 'digital economy', the balance of
power seems to be shifting to the customers. Customers are increasingly demanding
more value, with goods customised to their exact needs, at less cost, and as quickly
as possible. To meet these demands, businesses need to develop innovative ways of
creating value which often require different enterprise architectures, different IT
infrastructures and different way of thinking about doing business. This transformation of business from an old company to a new agile electronic corporation is
not easy and requires a lot of innovative thinking, planning and investment. This
book will cover many of these issues in e-banking context.

This chapter is an introduction to the themes covered in the book. It sets the
background, defines the context and provides a basis for the material covered in
the subsequent chapters.

WHAT IS E-BANKING?

In its very basic form, e-banking can mean the provision of information about a bank and its services via a home page on the World Wide Web (WWW). More sophisticated e-banking services provide customer access to accounts, the ability to move their money between different accounts, and making payments or applying for loans via e-Channels. The term e-banking will be used in this book to describe the latter type of provision of services by an organization to its customers. Such customers may be either an individual or another business.

To understand the electronic distribution of goods and services, the work of Rayport and Sviokla (1994; 1995) is a good starting point. They highlight the differences between the physical market place and the virtual market place, which they describe as an information-defined arena. In the context of e-banking, electronic delivery of services means a customer conducting transactions using online electronic channels such as the Internet.

Many banks and other organizations are eager to use this channel to deliver their services because of its relatively lower delivery cost, higher sales and potential for offering greater convenience for customers. But this medium offers many more benefits, which will be discussed in the next section. A large number of organizations from within and outside the financial sector are currently offering e-banking which include delivering services using Wireless Application Protocol (WAP) phones and Interactive Television (iTV).

Many people see the development of e-Banking as a revolutionary development, but, broadly speaking, e-banking could be seen as another step in banking evolution. Just like ATMs, it gives consumers another medium for conducting their banking. The fears that this channel will completely replace existing channels may not be realistic, and experience so far shows that the future is a mixture of "clicks (e-banking) and mortar (branches)". Although start up costs for an internet banking channel can be high, it can quickly become profitable once a critical mass is achieved.

EVOLUTION OF E-BANKING

There have been significant developments in the e-financial services sector in the past 30 years. According to Devlin (1995), until the early 1970s functional demarcation was predominant with many regulatory restrictions imposed. One main consequence of this was limited competition both domestically and internationally. As a result there was heavy reliance on traditional branch based delivery of financial services and little pressure for change. This changed gradually with deregulation of the industry during 1980s and 1990s, whilst during this time, the increasingly important role of information and communication technologies brought stiffer competition and pressure for a faster pace of change.

The Internet is a relatively new channel for delivering banking services. Its early form 'online banking services', requiring a PC, modem and software provided by the financial services vendors, were first introduced in the early 1980s. However, it failed to get widespread acceptance and most initiatives of this kind were discontinued. With the rapid growth of other types of electronic services since mid 1990s, banks renewed their interest in electronic modes of delivery using the Internet. The bursting of the Internet bubble in early 2001 caused speculation that the opportunities for Internet services firms had vanished. The "dot.com" companies and Internet players struggled for survival during that time but e-commerce recovered from that shock quickly and most of its branches including e-banking have been steadily, and in some cases dramatically, growing in most parts of the world. One survey conducted by the TechWeb News in 2005 (TechWeb News, 2005) found e-banking to be the fastest growing commercial activity on the Internet. In its survey of Internet users, it found that 13 million Americans carry out some banking activity online on a typical day, a 58 percent jump from late 2002.

The spread of online banking has coincided with the spread of high-speed broadband connections and the increasing maturation of the Internet user population. Another factor in e-banking growth is that banks have discovered the benefits of e-banking and have become keener to offer it as an option to customers.

WHY IS E-BANKING IMPORTANT?

Understanding e-banking is important for several stakeholders, not least of which is management of banking related organizations, since it helps them to derive benefits from it. The Internet as a channel for services delivery is fundamentally different from other channels such as branch networks, telephone banking or Automated Teller Machines (ATMs). Therefore, it brings up unique types of challenges and requires innovative solutions.

Many banks and other organizations have already implemented or are planning to implement e-banking because of the numerous potential benefits associated with it. Some of these major benefits are briefly described below.

Choice and Convenience for Customers

In the fierce battle over customers, providing a unique experience is the compelling element that will retain customers. A 'customer first' approach is critical for success in e-banking. Customers hold the key to success and companies must find out what different customers want and provide it using the best available technology, ensuring that they are acting on the latest, most up-to-date information.

In modern business environments, customers want greater choice. They want the traditional range of banking services, augmented by the convenience of online capabilities and a stronger focus by banks on developing personal relationships with customers. Avkiran (1999) stressed the importance of the human touch in the customer services. Politeness and neatness, recognition in terms of greeting, willingness to provide prompt service, ability to apologise and express concern for a mistake are all important for bank customer. Most of these aspects of customer service cannot be automated. The adequacy of staff members serving customers can be expected to directly influence the customers' satisfaction. However, e-banking backed up by data mining technologies can help in better understanding customers' needs and customizing products/services according to those needs.

Offering extra service delivery channels means wider choice and convenience for customers, which itself is an improvement in customer service. E-banking can be made available 24 hours a day throughout the year, and a widespread availability of the Internet, even on mobile phones, means that customers can conduct many of their financial tasks virtually anywhere and anytime. This is especially true of developed countries, but increasingly in developing countries, the spread of wireless communications means that services such as e-banking are becoming accessible.

Attracting High Value Customers

E-banking often attracts high profit customers with higher than average income and education levels, which helps to increase the size of revenue streams. For a retail bank, e-banking customers are therefore of particular interest, and such customers are likely to have a higher demand for banking products. Most of them are using online channels regularly for a variety of purposes, and for some there is no need for regular personal contacts with the bank's branch network, which is an expensive channel for banks to run (Berger & Gensler, 2007).

Some research suggests that adding the Internet delivery channel to an existing portfolio of service delivery channels results in nontrivial increases in bank profitability (Young, 2007). These extra revenues mainly come from increases in non-interest income from service charges on deposit/current accounts. These customers also tend to be of high income earners with greater profit potential.

Enhanced Image

E-banking helps to enhance the image of the organization as a customer focused innovative organization. This was especially true in early days when only the most innovative organizations were implementing this channel. Despite its common availability today, an attractive banking website with a large portfolio of innovative products still enhances a bank's image. This image also helps in becoming effective at e-marketing and attracting young/professional customer base.

Increased Revenues

Increased revenues as a result of offering e-channels are often reported, because of possible increases in the number of customers, retention of existing customers, and cross selling opportunities. Whether these revenues are enough for reasonable return on investment (ROI) from these channels is an ongoing debate. It has also allowed banks to diversify their value creation activities. E-banking has changed the traditional retail banking business model in many ways, for example by making it possible for banks to allow the production and delivery of financial services to be separated into different businesses. This means that banks can sell and manage services offered by other banks (often foreign banks) to increase their revenues. This is an especially attractive possibility for smaller banks with a limited product range.

E-banking has also resulted in increased credit card lending as it is a sort of transactional loan that is most easily deliverable over the Internet. Electronic bill payment is also on rapid rise (Young, 2007) which suggests that electronic bill payment and other related capabilities of e-banking have a real impact on retail banking practices and rapidly expanded revenue streams.

Easier Expansion

Traditionally, when a bank wanted to expand geographically it had to open new branches, thereby incurring high start up and maintenance costs. E-channels, such as the Internet, have made this unnecessary in many circumstances. Now banks with a traditional customer base in one part of the country or world can attract customers from other parts, as most of the financial transaction do not require a physical presence near customers living/working place. In one case study presented in Chapter VIII, a bank based in the southern part of the UK was attracting customers from northern England, where it had no branches. In many countries banks share their resources such as ATMs or use post offices as their main interaction points, with customers for services such as cash and cheques deposits.

Load Reduction on Other Channels

E-Channels are largely automatic, and most of the routine activity such as account checking or bill payment may be carried out using these channels. This usually results in load reduction on other delivery channels, such as branches or call centres. This trend is likely to continue as more sophisticated services such as mortgages or asset finance are offered using e-Banking channels. In some countries, routine branch transactions such as cash/cheque deposit related activities are also being automated, further reducing the workload of branch staff, and enabling the time to be used for providing better quality customer services.

Cost Reduction

The main economic argument of e-banking so far has been reduction of overhead costs of other channels such as branches, which require expensive buildings and a staff presence. It also seems that the cost per transaction of e-banking often falls more rapidly than that of traditional banks once a critical mass of customers is achieved. The research in this area is still inconclusive, and often contradicting reports appear in different parts the world. The general consensus is that fixed costs of e-banking are much greater than variable costs, so the larger the customer base of a bank, the lower the cost per transaction would be. Whilst this implies that cost per transaction for smaller banks would in most cases be greater than those of larger banks, even in small banks it is seen as likely that the cost per transaction will be below that of other banking channels.

Having said that some sources of research in this area suggest that banks so far have made little savings from introducing e-banking (Young, 2007). It implies that, any efficiency related savings are offset by above average wages and benefits per worker due to the need for a more skilled labor force to run the more sophisticated delivery system. Other costs such as systems integration and extra security measures also take their toll.

Organizational Efficiency

To implement e-banking, organizations often have to re-engineer their business processes, integrate systems and promote agile working practices. These steps, which are often pushed to the top of the agenda by the desire to achieve e-banking, often result in greater efficiency and agility in organizations. However, radical organizational changes are also often linked to risks such as low employee morale, or the collapse of traditional services or the customer base.

E-MARKETING

E-marketing in the financial services sector (which is covered later) was made possible by the arrival of e-banking. E-marketing builds on the e-channel's ability to provide detailed data about customers' financial profiles and purchasing behaviour. Detailed understanding of customers enables customised advertising, customised products and enrichment of the relationship with customers through such activities as cross selling.

Other potential benefits of e-banking to organizations may include: improved use of IT resources and business processes; better relationships with suppliers/ customers; quick delivery of products and services; and a reduction in data entry and customer services related errors.

It is important to note that e-channels do not automatically bring these benefits, as other organizational issues also have been dealt with. There are only a few examples reported in the literature where e-banking is realising its promised potential. One such example is the Royal Bank of Canada, where its number of online relationships was 340,000 and was growing at a rate of almost 700 new enrolments a day during year 2002-2003. Another example of realisation of the above benefits is the Woolwich Building Society in the UK, which is described in Chapter VIII. The number of its online customer was growing so fast that it was cited as one of the main reason for its takeover by a much bigger bank, Barclays. Not only did the number of its online customer grow very quickly, but the new customer base was also very profitable. According to Woolwich's own figures, its online customers bought four financial products each - much higher than its 'branch banking only' customers.

CHAPTER SUMMARY

This chapter introduced the main theme, e-banking, covered in the book. It has set the background, defined e-banking, and briefly discussed its evolution and importance to the banking industry and customers worldwide.

E-banking is fast becoming a norm in the developed world, and is being implemented by many banks in developing economies around the globe. The main reason behind this success is the numerous benefits it can provide, both to the banks and to customers of financial services. For banks, it can provide a cost effective way of conducting business and enriching relationship with customers by offering superior services, and innovative products which may be customized to individual needs. For customers it can provide a greater choice in terms of the channels they can use to conduct their business, and convenience in terms of when and where they can use e-banking.

REFERENCES

Avkiran, N. K. (1999). Quality Customer Service Demands Human Contacts. *International Journal of Bank Marketing, 17*(2), 61-71.

Berger, S. C., & Gensler, S. (2007, April). Online Banking Customers: Insights from Germany. *Journal of Internet Banking and Commerce, 12*(1). *http://www.arraydev. com/commerce/jibc/2007-04/SvenBergerFinal_PDFVersion.pdf.*

Devlin, J. F. (1995). Technology and Innovation in Retail Banking Distribution. *International Journal of Bank Marketing, 13*(4), 19-25.

Rayport, J. F., & Sviokla, J. J. (1995, November-December). Exploiting the Virtual Value Chain. *Harvard Business Review, 73*(1), 75-85.

Rayport, J. F., & Sviokla, J. J. (1994). Managing the Market-space. *Harvard Business Review*, November-December, (pp. 141-50).

Young, R. D., Lang, W. W., & Nolle, D. L. (2007). How the Internet affects output and performance at community banks. *Journal of Banking & Finance, 31*, 1033–1060.

Chapter II
Delivery of Retail Banking Services

INTRODUCTION

The purpose of this chapter is to outline the online revolution which occurred in the banking sector, mainly in the developed world. It will briefly cover the history of banking and how it evolved through the centuries into a service which touches many aspects of our life on a daily basis.

Financial services is one of the largest and most important industries in developed economies. Within this, banking is the largest sector. There are several types of banks, such as retail banks, commercial banks, investment banks and credit unions. Increasingly other types of businesses such as supermarkets are also offering financial services.

Banks exist in a wide range of sizes and differ in the type and number of services they provide. Commercial banks dominate this industry, offering a full range of services for individuals and businesses, from safeguarding money and valuables to the provision of loans, credit, and bill payment services. This book largely covers the issues related to retail commercial banks which offer services such as current accounts, saving products and various types of loans to individuals as well as businesses. Issues related to private banking or investment banking are similar in many ways but are outside the scope of this book.

HISTORY OF RETAIL BANKING

Basic banking services such as deposits for safe keeping, saving, or borrowing for personal or business use is as old as human civilisation. Organised banking services started in 15th and 16 century Europe, when banks began opening branches in commercial areas of large cities. By the last quarter of the 19th century, banks were consolidating their branch networks so that they could operate in a more integrated manner (Consoli, 2003). Mergers and acquisitions allowed banks to grow quickly but, in the absence initially of information and communication technologies, their services remained largely local.

The policy of opening new branches continued throughout the twentieth century as a means of business expansion, but services were limited to the provision of routine operations such as deposits, withdrawals and basic loan services. To cope with the increasing volume of work, and to achieve consistency across branch networks, banks started to standardise their record keeping and accounting practices. This also helped them to effectively connect branches. Standard record keeping also resulted in the appearance of new professions such as bank clerks. The arrival of the typewriter in the late nineteenth century helped to standardise internal/external communications, and other tools such as the telegraph made communications between branches and headquarters a daily routine.

After the end of the Second World War, early forms of computers began to find their way into the banking industry, initially to automate routine data processing operations. This later gave way to more organized data processing to make data more accurate and easier to access. More advance database tools enabled the automation of clearing systems and retail money transfer which cleared the way for banks to widen their reach and improve and increase the delivery of financial services. At this stage, these technological developments were often confined to the banks headquarters, while branches continued to operate paper based systems.

In the mid 1960s IBM developed a magnetic strip on which data could be stored to be used through plastic cards for electronic reading (Consoli, 2003). Banks were again one of the first users of this technology, beginning with the development of cash machines. Later these became known as Automated Teller Machines (ATMs). ATMs not only provided cash but also showed balances, mini statements and requests for banking stationary such as cheque books.

During the 1980s the automation of data processing spread rapidly to branches, and most internal operations were fully automated, making considerable savings for banks. Their benefits to customers however remained very limited. In the late 80s and early 90s the use of computers started spreading to all areas of banking, and intra-bank networks further enhanced and enabled standardization of products and service delivery. This meant that technology itself was ceasing to be a source of competitive advantage, and banks had to differentiate their products and services in order to grow.

The standardization of products, processes and technologies, as well as liberalization of banking regulations, allowed the entry of new financial agents who operated in a diversified manner by offering, at lower prices, services traditionally available exclusively from banks. The use of IT, which drastically reduced entry costs (Consoli, 2003), further accelerated this trend. ATM use grew significantly as functionality improved, and this growth continues to the present day. The arrival of early forms of online banking further revolutionized the banking sector. This aspect of banking is covered in the next chapter.

STRUCTURE OF RETAIL BANKING

As mentioned in the previous section, the traditional banking business model is based on physical decentralization, with branches scattered around populated areas, providing a range of services. The rationale behind such branch investment is the need to distribute banking services, encourage usage, and maintain contact with customers. Such a structure allows these institutions to provide a large range of products and services, but all at the high costs associated with premises and staff. In the past, a large branch network was source of competitive advantage, as it gave customers easier geographic access and the reassurance that the bank has substantial resources and hence offers security for their savings (Jayawardhena & Foley, 2000) Banks needed large investments to develop and maintain such network, so it worked as an entry barrier for new entrants and retail banking remained mostly the preserve of a few large banks, especially in Europe. One notable exception is the US, where there are more than 8000 community banks and nearly 9000 member-owned banking institutions regulated by the National Credit Union Administration (Fraering & Minor, 2006).

During the last decade or so, new players such Internet only banks as well as other organizations such as supermarkets have also started to offer retail financial services. While large banks still hold the major market share, these other organizations are making significant inroads. The importance of services distribution channels is also changing at a rapid pace. In the past the main source of retail banking services distribution was 'brick and mortar' branches. With the arrival of other channels such as telephone banking and e-banking, the number of branches is steadily declining, a trend also fuelled by mergers and takeovers. Now, most banks choose to deliver their products and services through multiple channels, including the internet and telephone.

The density of a bank's ATM network, and hence the average proximity of an ATM for the customer, is important for the convenience of cash management. In the U.K., for example, during the last decade almost all banks have maintained or significantly increased the number of ATMs in their network. Recently this trend has started to change as the number of fee charging ATMs (mainly operated by small business) has grown, together with signs that the number of free ATMs may be starting to decline (Donze & Dubec, 2008).

Whilst the number of financial products available in the market is growing, current accounts still play an important role in the relationship between a bank and its customers. Current accounts offer access to deposit-holding services, payment services through payment books/cards, and direct debit facilities, and potentially act as a vehicle for instant credit through overdrafts. As such, they are key vehicles for building relationships between a bank and its customers and often serve as a gateway through which suppliers can cross-sell other banking products (Fraering & Minor, 2006).

However, the traditional structure of banking industry may be changing as the Internet-only banking model offers a potential alternative. The main idea of this model is the reduction in operational costs of traditional branch networks and telephone call centers. There is a potential competitive advantage to Internet only banks, as lower operational costs could mean they are able to offer higher value to customers. So far, however, this has not been the case, and the main beneficiaries of e-banking so far have been traditional banks, offering e-banking as just another service delivery channel.

ROLE OF ICT IN BANKING

Information and communication technologies are playing a very important role in the advancements in banking. In fact information and communication technologies (ICT) are enabling banks to make radical changes to the way they operate. According to Consoli (2003), the historical paradigm of IT provides useful insights into the 'learning opportunities' that opened the way to radical changes in the banking industry such as the reconfiguration of its organizational structure and the diversification of the product line.

Banks are essentially intermediaries which create added value by storing, manipulating and transferring purchasing power between different parties. To achieve this, banks rely on ICT to perform most functions, from book keeping to information storage and from enabling cash withdrawals to communicating with customers (see Table 2.1 for an overview of ICT enabled changes). In developed countries at least, this high degree of reliance on ICT means that banks spend a

Table 2.1. The Role of ICT in Banking (Adapted from Consoli, 2003)

Technological Events	Service Provision	Operational Function
Phases	**External Dimension**	**Internal Dimension**
• **Processors to Database (1945-1968)** • Magnetic Stripe (1965) • First Credit Card in U.K. offered by Barclays Bank (1966) • Facsimile machine (1966) • Database Management Systems (1967)	• The Cheque Guarantee Card is introduced and use of cheques become widespread • The first Automated Bank Statements are printed • Money Transfer is automated: more transactions available in branches.	• The cost of labor-intensive activities such as processing is reduced and the capacity to handle administrative tasks is enhanced; • Use of computers is mostly in the back-office of head-quarters; • Lack of specific software encourages the emergence of new professional skills of software development;
• **Automated Machines to Local Networks (1968-1980)** • Operating System with multi-tasking (1969) • Arrival of Microprocessor (1971) • Microchip is integrated in a plastic cards (1973) • Personal Computer (1975) • "Switching" technology in telecommunication (1979)	• Automatic Teller Machine arrive • Branches become automated and services are now more easily accessible; • Real time operations at branches becomes a reality • Customers can sort transac-tions in any branch of their own bank;	• More branches are opened as a complement to retail branch distribution; • Financial resources are sought and new skills are de-veloped to support the ATM; • Information systems provide quick and useful information for decision making;
• **Standardization vs Customiza-tion (1980-2007)** • Networking Software (1980) • Microchip is used in a telephone card (1982) • File Transfer Protocol (1985) • ITS implemented as major tech-nology for network connection (1988) • Wide use of Internet an wireless technologies in banking (1990s and 2000s)	• Gold Credit Cards are offered to selected customers; • Banks introduce telephone banking • Introduction of Debit Cards • Non payment services are introduced (i.e. mortgages, pensions); • Internet Banking is introduced and becoming prominent	• Number of branches is reduced: the personnel is re-qualified and is given a more prominent role; • CRM systems (described in Chapter IV) developed to help marketing; • LINK Interchange Network Ltd (LINK) formed as a company jointly owned by banks to expand distribution channels; • New issues such as privacy, security and reliability of in-formation processing become more prominant;

large chunk of their budget on acquiring as well as maintaining these technologies. Internal as well as external pressures often result in questions being asked about the return on ICT investments.

A focus on ROI reveals that ICTs provide a very limited return unless accompanied by changes in organizational structures and business processes. These changes also need to be followed by a diversification of service offerings, with many banks introducing new product lines such as credit cards, stock brokerage and investment management services. Thus ICT has mostly enhanced productivity as well as increased the choice for customers both in terms of variety of services available and the ways in which they are able to conduct their financial activities.

OTHER IMPORTANT FACTORS DRIVING CHANGES IN THE BANKING INDUSTRY

Although ICT played a key part in transforming financial industries, there are other important factors. These include:

Social Changes

Human beings have always changed and evolved, but perhaps the speed of change has increased over last two decades or so. This is mainly due to the communications revolution brought about by advancements in transport infrastructure (more travelling), print media and digital media. Customer awareness of financial products is increasing and they are demanding more for less.

Another significant change is that the number of young people entering the labor force continues to decline in most of the developed world, while an ageing population continues to dominate. The finance industries are responding to this change by offering a number of pension related products.

Political Changes

The political environment is also changing rapidly. Over the last three decades, the formation and expansion of The European Union has had significant effects on worldwide financial product offerings. Environmental issues are becoming more prominent, with businesses under pressure to "go green". Terrorism and political unrest in some parts of the world is a looming risk, as are the uncertainties related to the rise of new economic/military powers such as China & India.

Deregulation

There has also been a noticeable trend towards deregulation (or re-regulation as some in the industry call it) over recent years in many western countries resulting from political and economical changes. In some ways this has made it easier to grow the business, but it has also opened a flood gate of new entrants into the market. New sets of regulations from outside national boundaries such as EU, and international regulations, are making it difficult for some organizations to ensure compliance.

Changes in Economic Climate

There have been a significant shifts in the significance of different sectors of the economy. In most western countries, primary (such as mining, agricultural) and secondary (manufacturing) has been steadily declining, whilst the service (i.e. financial services) sector is growing in importance. This has increased the prominence of service sector organizations, resulting in more pressure on them to diversify their offerings and look beyond their immediate markets to create value.

More Demanding Customers

With an increased choice and easier access and switching, consumers are more demanding than ever. This has also resulted in increased legal rights as well as the willingness of customers to challenge banks if something goes wrong. A huge number of complaints and court cases concerning bank fees (or "charges") against banks in the U.K. during 2007 is a good example of this. Banks are under increasing pressure to deal with these issue in systematic ways rather than on an ad hoc basis. With the arrival of e-banking came phishing (it is a type of deception designed to steal customers' valuable personal data, such as credit card numbers, passwords, account data, or other information for fraudulent use) and other security threats such as electronic theft of cash, as well as consumer privacy issues which require large resources to deal with them properly.

Internal Pressures

With the above pressures, banks are faced with the challenge of achieving the right balance between staffing levels and customer service, right training for staff, investment in technology and what to do with branch networks. As banks seek new ways to create value, different skills and aptitudes are demanded from their management and employees. Increased pressure from new and often well resourced entrants such as supermarkets is driving down the profit margins from retail banking products.

The above developments and internal/external pressures have significant implications for the type of products and services that banks provide and how they are delivered. New organizational structures and management practices are emerging, whilst working patterns are changing and flexible working is growing. New technologies will only speed up these changes and it seems that only most agile organizations will survive.

CHAPTER SUMMARY

This chapter was an overview of how banking evolved over centuries, the factors which contributed to its current shape, and how it operates. Rapid advances in technology seem to have more impact on changes in the banking industry than any other single factor. Other factors do however play a part in these changes, factors which include changes in the social fabric of society (such as growth in one person households), political changes (formation and expansion of the European Union), economic changes (move from manufacturing to service led economies in western countries), and growing financial sophistication amongst customers.

REFERENCES

Consoli, D. (2003, September). *The evolution of retail banking services in United Kingdom: a retrospective analysis*. CRIC Working Paper No 13. ISBN: 1 84052 011 6. Available at http://129.3.20.41/eps/io/papers/0310/0310002.pdf/

Donze, J., & Dubec, I. (2008). *The effects of regulating interchange fees at cost on the ATM market*. Universit'e des Sciences Sociales de Toulouse, TSE (GREMAQ). http://mpra.ub.uni-muenchen.de/10893/1/MPRA_paper_10893.pdf.

Fraering, M., & Minor, M. S. (2006). Sense of community: An exploratory study of US consumers of financial services. *International Journal of Bank Marketing, 24*(5). http://www.emeraldinsight.com/Insight/viewContentItem.do;jsessionid=8F B4CF550BC6068EFFBC7BCC7E94816D?contentType=Article&hdAction=lnkp df&contentId=1567029&history=true.

Jayawardhena, C., & Foley, P. (2000). Changes in the Banking Sector – the Case of Internet Banking in the UK. *Internet Research: Electronic Networking Applications and Policy, 10*(1), 19-30.

Southard P. B., & Keng S (2004). A survey of online e-banking retail initiatives. *Communications of the ACM, 47*(10), 99-102. http://www.informatik.uni-trier.de/~ley/db/indices/a-tree/s/Southard:Peter_B=.html.

Chapter III
An Overview of E–Banking

INTRODUCTION

Chapter II provided an overview of the banking sector in general and its evolution over centuries. The purpose of this chapter is to discuss various aspects of e-banking including the sequence of evolution of e-banking as well as other issues which this has brought with it. The chapter starts with the general model of e-commerce to set the scene for subsequent sections, including a brief overview of how e-banking evolved and where it is heading in near future.

MODELS FOR ELECTRONIC SERVICES DELIVERY

E-commerce is about buying and selling information, products and services via computer networks such as the Internet and Electronic Data Interchange (EDI). E-banking is one form of e-commerce. The term commerce is viewed rather narrowly by some as transactions conducted between business partners. However, for the purpose of this book, a broad scope definition by Kalakota and Whinston (1997) will be used. They define e-commerce from the following perspectives:

- **Communications:** e-commerce is the delivery of information, products/services, or payments over telephone lines, computer networks, or any other electronic means.
- **Business process:** e-commerce is the application of technology towards the automation of business transactions and workflow.
- **Service:** e-commerce is a tool that addresses the desire of firms, consumers, and management to cut service costs while improving the quality of goods and increasing the speed of service delivery.
- **Online:** e-commerce provides the capability of buying and selling products and information on the Internet and other electronic channels such as EDI.

For firms e-commerce brings:

- Different and arguably lower barriers to entry;
- Opportunities for significant cost reduction;
- The capacity to rapidly re-engineer business processes;
- Greater opportunities to sell across borders.

Each and all of these potential benefits provides for increased competition and the ability to wrest market leadership from established players.

For consumers the potential benefits are:

- More choice;
- Better value for money obtained through greater competition;
- More information;
- Better tools to manage and compare information;
- Faster service.

The revolutionary growth of network technologies and especially the Internet has enabled us to conduct business electronically at a global level. For this reason, most of the literature in this field refers to technological issues and is mostly application driven. There is a significant stress on the technical infrastructure that supports e-commerce applications such as networks, multimedia contents, messaging and payments. E-commerce allows new products to be created and/or for existing products to be customised in innovative ways. In the long term, competitive advantage may only be achieved by providing innovative services, or services that are uniquely bundled using web capabilities. Banks should look beyond their own industry in benchmarking other facets of operations and examine other technologically advanced industries for innovative ideas. Successful Web-based companies, such as eBay and Priceline.com, have established profitable business models that may include features that banks could adapt, such as mortgage applications and transactional processes (Southerd, 2004).

Such changes may redefine organizations' missions and the manners in which they operate.

E-commerce also allows suppliers to gather personalised data on customers. Building customers profiles, as well as data collection on certain groups of people can be used as a source of information for customising existing products or designing new ones (Wind, 2001).

Mass customisation enables manufacturers to create a specific product for each customer, based on his or her exact needs. For example, Motorola gathers customer needs for a pager or cellular phone, transmits them electronically to the manufacturing plant where they are manufactured, according to the customers' specification, i.e. colours, features, and then sends the product to the customer within a day (Turban et al., 2000). Similarly, Dell Computers and Levi use this approach. Using online tools, customers can design or configure products for themselves. For example, customers can configure a PC to their exact needs (in case of Dell) or design their T-shirts, furniture, cars and even a Swatch watch.

In the service sector, e-commerce is playing a major role and has changed organizations as varied as the travel industry and the banking industry. This covers some of the sectors, which have considerably changed as a result of the emergence of e-commerce, and helps our understanding of e-banking from these different perspectives.

Travel and Tourism Sector

The Internet is an ideal place to plan, explore and arrange almost any trip. People can make potential savings by buying on the Internet, eliminating travel agents and buying directly from the providers. Websites like CheapFlights.com and lastminute.com allow customers to buy flexible fares on the Internet, where they can also make use of last minute deals. E-services are provided by all major airlines: American Airlines, Air Portugal and others conduct online auctions in which passengers can bid for tickets.

Broker Based Services

Brokers usually work for a commission, acting as intermediaries between buyers and sellers of services. The buyers can be an individual or a company. Some of the most notable services are travel agencies, insurance agencies, and stock market brokerages. The agents role in an e-commerce environment is changing, and increasingly they will need to put more emphasis on providing value added services, such as:

- Assisting in comparison shopping from multiple sources;
- Providing total quality solutions by combining services from several vendors; and
- Providing certifications and third party control and evaluation systems.

The Job Market

Thousands of employment agencies operate on the Internet, with companies advertising on their home pages. There are sites where one can assess market wages rate by entering skills sets. Similarly, it is possible to seek employment anywhere in the world as jobs are advertised on the Internet. Many recruitment agencies such as www.hays.com use the Internet as their main communication channel, both with employers and job-seekers.

The Property Market

One of the booming uses of the Internet is that of buying or renting property, through websites such as Yahoo, loot.com or Yourmove.com. Properties can be viewed on screen, sorted and organised according to customer criteria, and previewed.

In short, e-commerce is creating fundamental changes in the ways business operate, their functions, and the way they compete. Engaging in e-commerce requires rethinking the very nature of the buyer/seller relationship. It requires the fundamental transformation of business, because all or most human interactions and paper-based processes within the value chain will need to be changed.

FROM E-COMMERCE TO E-BANKING

In its very basic form, e-banking can mean the provision of information about a bank and its services via a home page on the World Wide Web (WWW). A more sophisticated Internet based service provides the customer with access to their accounts, the ability to move money between different accounts, make payment or apply for loans and other financial products. The term e-banking will be used in this book to describe the all types of provision of financial services by an organization to its customers. Such customers may be an individual or another business.

To understand the electronic distribution of goods and services, the work of Rayport and Sviokla (1994, 1995) is a good starting point. They highlight the differences between the physical market place and the virtual market place, which they describe as an information-defined arena. In the context of e-banking, electronic delivery of services means a customer conducting his transactions from a remote location (e.g. home) rather that visiting a local branch.

Automated teller machines (ATMs) were the first means of providing electronic access to retail customers, made possible through the introduction of computer networks. Telephone banking arrived next, which was a revolutionary concept since it made banking possible from anywhere as long as telephones were available.

In the mid eighties, online banking arrived. In its early form 'online banking services' requiring a computer, modem and software provided by the financial services vendors. Generally, these services failed to get widespread acceptance due to high call costs and unfriendly system interfaces, and were discontinued by most providers.

With the arrival and widespread adoption of The World Wide Web, banks renewed their interest in this area and started developing a web presence. The goal was for a bank's website to provide many, if not all, of the services offered at a branch. This may include transactions as well as information, advice, administration, and even cross-selling. However, the interactive nature of the Web not only allows banks to enhance these core services, but also enables banks to communicate more effectively and expand customer relationships. When combined with the improving analytical capabilities of data mining and related technologies, the potential for enriching the relationship with customers is unlimited. The most common services in current e-banking offerings are described in Table 3.1.

Most banks and other financial institutions in the developed world have established an Internet presence with various objectives. Some banks are there because their competitors have done it. Others prefer a 'wait and see' practice. Some are using it as a banking channel being part of their distribution /delivery management.

E-banking largely came into being as a result of technological developments in the field of computing and communications but there have been a number of other factors or challenges which played an important part in its development. According to Jayawardhena and Foley (2000) the challenges for banks are fourfold. First, they need to satisfy customer requirements that are complex and ever changing. Second, they need to deal with increased competition from old as well as new entrants coming into the market. Third, they need to address the pressures on the supply chain to deliver their services quickly. Finally, they must continually develop new and innovative services to differentiate themselves from the competition, as having a large branch network is no longer seen as a main source of competitive advantage. E-banking is seen by many banks as a key tool to address these challenges.

Other reasons for the adoption of e-banking by banks may include achieving competitive advantage (at least in short term), creating new distribution channels, improving image, and reducing costs. These issues are discussed in the previous chapter.

Table 3.1. Different types of e-banking services

Types of e-banking	Description
Account Access	Access online to all of one's account information (usually checking, savings, and money market), which is either updated in real time or on a daily bath basis.
Balance Transfer	Transfer funds between accounts.
Bill Payment	Pay any designated bill based on instructions one proves including whether to pay automatically or manually each month.
Bill Presentment	View billing statements as presented electronically, which allows inter- active capabilities such as sorting, drill-down details, or advertising, in addition to on-click payments.
Mortgage/Credit Card/ Misc. Lending	Search, apply, and receive approval online for various types of loans and then review your statements using online bill presentment.
Business Banking Services	In addition to all of the basic payment and account access services, merchant can manage their electronic lock box for received payment, accounts receivable posing, as well as initiative payment via networks.
Customer Service & Administration	While the Web will eventually enable live communication, it is most optimally designed to facilitate interaction with information so that customers can more easily service themselves. In the process, custom- ers receive as good, if not better, service while the bank saves money with each additional transaction as it realises the scale economies of its largely fixed online investment. Advanced e-Mail systems with automated replies and intelligent routing are also helping to improve the online customer service experience.
Cross-selling	Just as visitors to a branch are being offered new products by tellers and simple signage, so can Web bank customers. In most cases today, banks perform this function online with standard, broadly targeted text offers or by just making their product literature available online. In the future, banks will be able to harness the true power of the Internet by provid- ing targeted offers to Web customers based on a combination of their indicated interests and financial situation. Not only will banks be able to sell banks products, but non-financial products as well.
Personalised Content and Tools	As one visits the Web branch, one is instantly recognised and content displayed is oriented toward one's interests including weather, invest- ment, and hobbies. More importantly, by using the Web, bank customers could use online financial planning tools to better manage their finances.
Accounts Aggregation	Accounts aggregation enables a consumer to be presented with all his or her account details (current account, saving account, mortgage account etc.) on a single page. For access to external (to their first choice bank) financial data consum- ers to provide their account passwords to the aggregator (usually a bank). The aggregator uses the passwords to access automatically the consumer's accounts. The information is then provided to the consumer on a consolidated basis on a single page so the customer has a full view of his/her financial portfolio. In most cases funds can be transferred from one account to another.
Electronic Funds Transfer	Electronic Funds Transfer (EFT) is a system of transferring money from one bank account directly to another without any paper money changing hands. One of the most widely-used EFT programs is Direct Deposit, in which payroll is deposited straight into an employee's bank account. This system may also be used for debit transfers, such as mortgage payments.

The widespread adoption of the internet during late 1990s and early 2000s promised a revolution in the way consumers worldwide accessed and managed their finances. Many analysts predicted that e-banks, having the advantage of a low cost base, would win deposits and loans by offering superior rates. and that many existing providers of those products would be driven out of the market. In the US, large banks targeted affluent customers using this medium. For example, in 2000, HSBC and Merrill Lynch committed to spend $1bn on a joint venture that would combine online premium banking and share dealing. Within a few months, several other banks had followed suit (Larsen, 2004). But the response was generally disappointing. Banks found customers reluctant to give up their bricks and mortar branches, and the take up was much lower than expected.

Low ROI from e-banking initially meant that some traditional retail banks which used e-banking as just another channel rather than replacing branches or call centres benefited most. That early experience showed that even the most keen e-banking customers also wanted the convenience of branches and phone banking. This led to an argument that e-banking just adds another layer of complexity and unjustifiable costs. The growth of phishing', where fraudsters use spam e-mails and bogus websites to encourage people to reveal their account details, together with other security concerns, were also used to argue against the very existence of e-banking.

Nevertheless, in spite of some scepticism, given the real and promised benefits of the e-banking it continues to grow rapidly in most parts of the developed world. In developing countries the picture has been less clear. In China, for example, lower use of credit cards and a less sophisticated financial infrastructure has resulted in e-banking being adopted by only a small portion of the population. In other countries such as Pakistan most of rural bank branches still operate using paper filing system which means that e-banking is only available in large cities.

Emerging economies may consider adopting the Western e-banking models as e-banking is maturing in advanced countries. Continued economic and banking reform is a key requirement so that adapted e-banking models can easily be implemented in developing countries. This will involve a continuous reforms of legal, commercial, banking and bureaucratic infrastructures so that the development of new information and communication technologies, thus e-banking infrastructures can take place. Banks would find it difficult to properly implement e-banking without a strong ICT infrastructure. In addition, economic, political and banking reform is vital. Appropriate levels of regulatory supervision should be introduced to ensure adequate levels of capital adequacy. Attention must also be directed towards bank management training in the areas of electronic channels. If efficient e-banking is generally adopted by emerging markets, the path is likely to open for economic benefits to accrue both within each country and globally (Simpson & Evans 2003).

FUTURE OF E-BANKING

It is notoriously difficult to predict the future, but some educated guesses can be made using past and current experiences. In our view, the next developments in e-banking will involve new products and services that were not feasible in traditional banking models. This could involve enabling instant payments using mobile devices, or tools to help people manage their multi-bank financial portfolio, simultaneously. Internet only banking may also become more viable as the functionality of e-banking systems grows, and customers adapt to the new ways of conducting their financial activities. International banking might become a reality for ordinary consumers as banking payments systems are increasingly harmonised across borders. For example, in Europe, new measures are being introduced by the European Union to allow cross-border provision of e-commerce services by providing a single payment system. Similar initiatives are due to be implemented in other parts of the world.

E-banking has the potential to be a very rich and pleasant experience, and may provide more opportunities for banks to develop mutually satisfying, tailor made services to enrich relationship with customers. As technology evolves, the opportunities to extend the relationship beyond what is possible in the physical world continue to grow and will only be limited by a bank's ability to innovate or commitment to e-banking.

Some companies such as IBM have expressed their vision of the future of financial services, complete with biometrics, state-of-the-art branch offices, enterprise risk-management systems, and advanced customer interaction (Marlin, 2005). The use of financial decision-aid tools in e-banking is also set to grow. To date, the experiences of many e-banking users with these tools have proved unsatisfactory: with many firms do not even offering online advice tools, people often have little idea of the benefits such tools could bring. Banks need to promote the availability and use of these, and educate consumers about their benefits (Clarke, et al. 2008). One good example of a bank offering useful financial management tools is UBS which in addition to the usual e-banking functions, provides a number of such tools, for example (UBS, 2008):

- **UBS Pay:** This software allows entry and management of payments without connecting to the Internet. UBS Pay helps, for example, when entering payments abroad enabling selection of the most cost-efficient order type. Payment orders are then sent collectively to UBS via UBS e-banking in just a fraction of the time it takes to enter them directly online. With a user-friendly graphical interface, archiving and analysis functions, all of a user's executed payments and beneficiaries' details may be accessed at any time. A number of export options also simplify the transferring of data to MS Excel and MS Money.

- **UBS BESR e-list:** UBS BESR e-list is ideal for small and medium-sized enterprises or individuals who just need a simple accounts receivable system with integrated invoicing functions. It manages the collection of receivables, within Switzerland using banking payment slips with reference number (BESR). The new UBS BESR e-list software replaces the old paper accounts receivable list and makes a long process automatic and quick.
- **WebCalculator:**You can use the WebCalculator for stock exchange transactions to figure out quickly and easily the brokerage fees for transactions you are planning or you have already executed. Depending on the service package, it is available at a reduced price and includes the UBS investment advisory service, or may be purchased by professional investors at a price not including UBS advisory. In both cases your market orders can be given using UBS e-banking via the Internet or UBS e-banking using a mobile device.
- **PayPen:** Reads Swiss payment slips easily and quickly. With a quick brush of the hand payment slip may be imported into the e-banking system of the bank or payment software in seconds.
- **GIROMAT 130:** With GIROMAT 130 you can process all Swiss payment slips. It can read orange payment slips with the new or old dimensions. The special driver software means no tedious implementation of interfaces and protocols is necessary.

Smart cards are also beginning to make their mark in the e-banking field and are expected to play greater role in the future. A smart card is a credit card-sized plastic card with an embedded chip that provides power for multiple uses (I.D card, SIM cards for mobile phones, credit/debit cards, benefit claim, health cards, etc.). A smart cards is enhanced by PIN verification and cryptography, and the size and power of the chip determine its storage and processing capacities (M'Chirgui & Channel, 2007).

It is clear that, some of the hardware and software associated with such a vision are already in use but their feasibility of industry-wide use is still questionable. Schneider (2005) predicted that in fifty years customers will carry a translucent plastic bank card displaying a talking head with artificial intelligence. Cash and checks will have been eliminated in favour of the new electronic currency of "credits," which will be much easier to transfer, maybe using mobile phones. The early signs are that it is already started to happen. For example, mobile technology, such as the Bluetooth proximity-based data transmission standard, may work with banking systems to enable touch points to react intelligently when a customer approaches. In this case, when a customer carrying a Bluetooth-enabled mobile device approaches a service desk, the bank employee should be able to have the customer information ready at hand and in order to suggest other relevant financial services

(Schneider, 2005). Developments in biometric technologies may help to deal with the most persistent security issues as well as dealing with customers' difficulties in remembering many different login keys.

Finally, Schneider (2005) suggest that all of the infrastructure in the world cannot succeed without innovation and the willingness to take risks. The ATM is an example of technologies that consumers would never have requested, but nonetheless have been keen to embrace.

CHAPTER SUMMARY

This chapter was an overview of e-banking evolution, the main drivers behind its growth, main threats it has faced, and what future holds for this newest channel for financial services delivery. E-banking came into being mainly due to advances in information and communication technologies, but other factors such as globalisation, increasingly demanding customers, and de-regulation of the industry also played an important part.

Slower than expected adoption, and its failure to meet most of our early hopes has been the main source of threats, but the benefits it offers mean that this channel is growing in prominence every day and it is here to stay. Whether this growing prominence could mean the end of traditional banking channels such as branches remains to be seen. At present, it is helping to re-define the role of branch banking and moving branches away from transactional banking to become customer service centres.

The future of e-banking seems secure due the ever increasing adoption and arrival of new technologies to address existing limitations. Major innovations are expected in the area of e-banking using mobile phones, in security provision and customer services. Technologies such as biometrics would, if they make expected progress, help resolve many existing problems.

E-banking raises many complicated issues for banks and regulators alike. Much more work is need at both national and international level, to identify and remove any unnecessary barriers to e-banking. To benefit most from e-banking and related innovations, banks should (guidelines adopted from Sergeant, 2000):

- Develop a clear strategy and communicate it throughout the organization. It must be driven by the top management and should take into account the effects of e-banking
- Have an effective process for measuring performance of e-banking against the pre-determined criteria given in the strategic plans.

- Take into account the risks that e-banking will bring with it and manage these accordingly.
- Undertake market research, develop systems with adequate capacity and scalability and ensure that they have adequate resources to meet their commitments and a suitable business continuity plan in case of disasters.
- Ensure they have adequate management information architecture to help effective and timely decision making.
- Develop security plans and implement them to ensure information security. This requires acquiring relevant staff expertise, building in best practice controls and testing and updating these on frequent basis.

Overall, e-banking seems to serve as a complementary means of interacting with customers rather than a substitute for other channels such as physical branches. Despite the large investment in the Internet as a distribution channel, the branch network remains an important channel for retail banking products (Hernando & Neito, 2007). The profitability gains associated with the adoption of a e-banking are generally explained by a significant reduction in overhead expenses but this effect is slow in becoming noticeable.

REFERENCES

Clarke, A., Ensor, B., & Camus, L. (2008, April 15) *Investors Don't Understand The Importance Of Online Advice Tools*. Retrieved on November, 12, 2008 from www.forester.com

Hernando, I., & Nieto, M. (2007). Is the Internet delivery channel changing banks' performance? The case of Spanish banks. *Journal of Banking & Finance, 31*, 1083–1099.

Jayawardhena, C., & Foley, P. (2000). Changes in the banking sector: The case of Internet banking in the UK. *Internet Research: Electronic Networking Applications and Policy, 10*(1), 19-30.

Kalakota, R., & Whinston, A. B. (1997). *Electronic Commerce: a Manager's Guide*. Reading, PA: Addison-Wesley.

Larsen, L. B. (2004, November). The automatic pool trainer - a platform for experiments with multi modal user interaction. *Proceedings of the Fourth Danish HCI Research Symposium,* Denmark.

Marlin, S. (2005, August 17). IBM showcases tech innovations for financial services. *Information Week*.

M'Chirgui, Z., & Channel, O. (2007). The adoption and use of smart card technology in banking: An empirical evidence from the moneo electronic purse in france. In V. Ravi (Ed.), *Advances in Banking Technology and Management: Impact of ICT and CRM.* IGI Global Inc. USA

Rayport, J. F., & Sviokla, J. J. (1994, November-December). Managing the marketspace. *Harvard Business Review,* (pp. 141-50).

Rayport, J. F., & Sviokla, J. J. (1995, November-December). Exploiting the virtual value chain, *Harvard Business Review,* (pp. 75-85).

Schneider, I. (2005, May 26). Citibank, daring to dream of the year 2054, warns of lessons of history. *Bank Systems & Technology.*

Sergeant, C. (2000, March 29). E-banking: risks & responses. *UK Financial Services Authority.* http://www.fsa.gov.uk/pubs

Simpson, J.L., & Evans, J.P. (2003). *Benchmarking of economic and regulatory capital for international banking systems: A theoretical discussion.* University of Wollongong in Dubai Working Paper No. 1-2003. http://papers.ssrn.com/sol3/papers.cfm?abstract_id=443242

Turban, E., Lee, J., King, D., & Shung, H. M. (2000). *Electronic commerce, a managerial perspective.* London: Prentice Hall.

UBS (2008, November 12). *UBS e-banking: software and tools.* Retrieved on from https://www2.ubs.com/1/ssl/e/ebanking/software_tools.html?NavLB_Www=1226918854

Wind, Y. J. (2001, June). The challenge of "customisation" in financial services. *Communications of the ACM, 44*(6), 39-44.

Chapter IV
E–Banking Technologies

INTRODUCTION

E-banking relies heavily on information and communication technologies (ICT) to achieve its promise of 24 hours availability, low error rates, and quicker delivery of financial services. When considering e-banking, bank websites usually come to mind first, but e-banking requires much more than just a good website. It needs back end applications such as account systems, support applications such as Customer Relationship Management (CRM systems), communication technologies to link e-banking to the payment systems such as LINK, and middleware to integrate all these often different type of systems. This chapter is an overview of most common technologies in use to support e-banking.

E-banking may be viewed as one branch of e-commerce, so it is useful to briefly cover the interlink between the two. E-commerce is much more than just the use of the Internet, or having a website and enabling customers to move their money around. The Internet may be the most common and well known medium for e-commerce, but it is not the only one. Electronic Data Interchange (EDI) and similar systems have been in use since the mid-sixties. In a banking context, ATMs and credit cards are also classified as e-commerce. These other type of e-commerce application also need the support of technologies discussed in this chapter.

THE INTERNET

The emergence of the Internet has posed a host of new organizational opportunities and challenges. Given the Internet's potential to revolutionise business operations, it is important to understand the implications of it on businesses in general. Although other e-channels such as Interactive Television (iTV) and Wireless Application Protocol (WAP) technologies are available for services delivery, their use is still limited in the provision of financial services. Issues related to these technologies are also very similar to those of the Internet.

The Internet is a massive global network of interconnected packet-switched computer networks. Hoffman (2002) offers three (mutually consistent) definitions of the Internet: a network of networks based on the TCP/IP protocols; a community of people who use and develop those networks; and a collection of resources that can be reached from those networks.

The Internet has evolved over several decades with it's growth accelerating exponentially during the 1990s. The most exciting commercial developments however, are occurring on that portion of the Internet known as the World Wide Web (WWW). The WWW is a distributed hypermedia environment within the Internet, which was originally developed by the European Particle Physics Laboratory (CERN). Global hypermedia allows multimedia information to be located on a network of servers around the world, which are interconnected, allowing navigation through the information by clicking on hyperlinks. Any hyperlink (text, icon or image in a document) can point to any document anywhere on the Internet.

The homepages of the WWW utilise the system of hyperlinks to simplify the task of navigating among the offerings on the Internet. These attributes enable the Web to be an efficient channel for advertising, marketing, and even direct distribution of certain goods and information services. A more recent development is web 2.0 which may be described as a newer version of web-based applications (such as wikis, social-networking sites, and blogs) which aim to enhance creativity, collaboration, and interaction between Internet users. These developments on the Internet are expanding beyond the utilisation of the Internet as a communication medium to an important view of the Internet as a new market place.

The Internet influences the future services/products distribution channel structure in two ways. First, the costs of using it are different from those of other available distribution channels, and the service output it provides is often different from the service output provided by traditional distribution channels. Second, the Internet influences consumers. Many of them invest time and resources into becoming computer-literate and in getting to know the Internet. Other consumers do not become computer-literate and do not gain familiarity with the Internet. These two customer segments are likely to have similar needs. Therefore, the existing distribution channel also influences changes in overall distribution channel structure. The old distribution channels gradually give way to the new ones, but do not necessarily become redundant.

Consumers have benefited from the Internet a great deal. They have access to greater amounts of dynamic information to support queries for consumer decision-making. The interactive nature of the Web and the hypertext environment allow for deep, non-linear searches initiated and controlled by customers. There is also the potential of wider availability of products and services, which were previously difficult to find. Increased competition between suppliers is also likely to result in lower prices for consumers.

Internet technology can make a significant contribution to a company's value chain. It can improve a company's relationship with vendors and suppliers, its internal operations and its customer relations, and offers the prospect of reaching an expanding customer base. The Internet also promises to dramatically lower communications costs by eliminating obstacles created by geography, time zones, and locations (Tan & Teo, 2000).

The Internet provides a powerful platform for corporations with home pages to market and advertise their products and services. It has proved an efficient and cost-effective way of distributing information almost instantaneously to millions of potential clients in global markets. Many companies use the Internet to conduct market and scientific research, as well as to source business-related information to improve their products and services.

The rise of the Internet has resulted in the formation of virtual organizations, which have virtually no physical presence in terms of retail outlets but enjoy access to national and international markets. One well known example of such virtual organizations is www.amazon.com which is a virtual bookstore supplying books and other similar products such as music CDs and electronics to customers in many countries in the world. Some examples of virtual organizations in the financial services industry are Smile.co.uk, Cahoot.co.uk and Egg.

There is a scope for physical organizations to become virtual, as they can leverage their core competencies in primary activities. Physical companies often have a great deal more experience/knowledge of their products and how to sell them than new Internet traders and they usually also have established brands and a large customer base. However, Owens and Robertson (2000) contend that it takes longer for physical organizations to develop an integrated e-commerce structure than it does for virtual traders to commence trading. This is due to the reduced, simple physical structure of the virtual organizations. They argue that a structure of similar efficiency must be adopted by physical organizations for the provision of Internet services.

Having mentioned some practical benefits of the Internet as a business medium, it is important to mention some of the problems with this medium. Most common of them are information overload, security & privacy problems, rapid technological change, high initial cost and uncertainly about information reliability. These issues are discussed in detail within Chapter VII.

MOBILE BANKING TECHNOLOGIES

Some banks are making significant investments in mobile systems to deliver a range of types of business value, from increased efficiency and cost reduction, to improved operational effectiveness and customer service to provide a competitive advantage. A factor that has contributed to this development has been the extended availability and capacity of mobile communications infrastructure around the world. The number of types of mobile devices has been increasing rapidly and the functionality available has also improved. The shrinking costs of data transmission and, due to the intense competition from suppliers, the reduced costs of devices have catalysed the distribution of mobile technologies and amplified the growth of the worldwide mobile market. In those countries where traditional telecommunication infrastructure is not well developed, mobile technologies is transforming accessibility to the Internet based services.

Mobile banking may be described as the newest channel in electronic banking to provide a convenient way of performing banking transaction using mobile phones or other mobile devices. The potential for mobile banking may be far greater than typical desk-top access, as there are several times more mobile phone users than online PC users. Increasingly "mobile life styles" may also fuel the growth of anywhere, anytime applications.

There are two main types of technologies available for use in mobile Banking: Wireless Application Protocol (WAP) and Wireless Internet Gateway (WIG).

WAP is an application environment and set of communication protocols for wireless devices designed to enable manufacturer, vendor, and platform independent access to the Internet and advanced telephony services. WIG is a Short Message Service (SMS)-based service, in which a menu of available banking options is initially downloaded from the bank to the phone device (Brown et al. 2003). This enables users to browse bank accounts and conduct other banking related tasks.

Mobile banking was offered in the UK by the banks such as The Woolwich during early 2000s, but it failed to achieve a critical mass of users. The same story has been repeated in many other counties with mixed results. The main hurdle in development of mobile banking is low consumer adoption due to a number of factors discussed below:

- **Internet connectivity costs:** Although connection costs from mobile phones is steadily declining it is still high enough in many countries to deter customers from using their mobiles for applications such as e-banking.
- **Difficult user interface:** Human Computer Interface (HCI) issues are a key factor in mobile technology acceptance. HCI includes the use and context of computers, human characteristics, computer systems and interface architecture, and the development process (Perry, et al, 2001). A general rule is that the easier and more adoptable the interface, the greater is the user acceptance. HCI issues in mobile working are different in the mobile working context than in the traditional office environment. Kristoffersen (1999) identifies three key elements that define mobile work contexts and explain how they differ from the office setting:
  1. Users' hands are often used to manipulate physical objects, as opposed to users in the traditional office setting, whose hands are safely and ergonomically placed on the keyboard.
  2. Users may be involved in tasks ("outside the computer") that demand a high level of visual attention (to avoid danger as well as monitor progress), as opposed to the traditional office setting where a large degree of visual attention is usually directed at the computer.
  3. Attention span of a mobile device user is much shorter than a desktop computer user so design of mobile systems interfaces need to be much simpler with very limited amounts of text. Systems navigation needs to be very easy too.
  4. Methods to ease the burden of input and spread the requirements of processing output over all the human senses, while still maintaining data integrity are of importance (York & Pendharkar, 2004)
  5. Speech and handwriting recognition are two growing forms of input. The benefits of speech recognition include minimal user attention input, direct system entry, remote microphone capabilities, and faster speed of operation compared to other competing input methods (York & Pendharkar, 2004). These technologies need to be incorporated into mobile devices to improve the user's interface.
- **Lack of awareness amongst customers:** Many banking customers are not even aware of availability of mobile banking or associated benefits. As with other technologies, awareness increases with time and needs considerable promotional efforts.
- **Limitations in functionality of mobile devices:** Mobile technologies are still dogged by limitations such as limited battery life, unreliable network connections, volatile access points, risk of data loss, portability, and location discovery. Even in the developed world, until recently, wireless communica-

tions were very limited with regards to functionality of devices and speed of communications. Constraints such as screen size, memory, and storage capabilities as well as data transfer rates averaging 14.4 Kilo Bytes Per Second (KBPS), limited the amount of data that could be both displayed and accessed. These limitations are still one of the biggest barriers to the adoption of mobile working in many countries.

- **Accessibility issues:** High speed public Internet access is offering opportunities to get and stay connected in more locations. Today, hotels that cater to business travellers frequently offer in-room high speed Internet access. As these high speed access networks ramp up, mobile applications are growing in popularity (Phifer, 2004). It may take several years to reach that 'always connected' goal, and connectivity in less populous areas will lag behind high tech corridors.

- **Security concerns:** Mobile technology still suffers from questionable security. So it may not be suitable for transfer of highly confidential financial information. Mobile devices are increasingly becoming a target for virus writers, hackers, and short message service (SMS) spammers. According to Tower Group's research, over 200 mobile phone viruses have been identified since phones have been able to support PC-like applications such as email, instant messaging and Web browsing, and the number is doubling every six months (Blau, 2007). The resulting disruption of service and data theft can cause many problems for consumers, including lost revenues and customer dissatisfaction for mobile operators. However, the greatest loss may be absorbed by banks providing mobile access, as in almost all cases of fraud banks suffers from the losses. This factor may be making many banks hesitant in providing mobile banking. To be successful in mobile banking the industry must develop an ability to effectively contain the malware problems to a level that is at least on part with that of the existing Internet channels.

- **Organisational changes:** To offer mobile banking many organizations will need to change their business processes, ways in which information is provided and accessed, working practices and work relationships, working styles and most important of all, changes in roles, responsibilities and management structures. It may be a manageable task in some organizations but a very difficult one in others'.

- **Small number of choices (only a few banks offer mobile banking):** There are a bewildering number of options when it comes to providing mobile banking. It is possible to spend anything from a few thousand to several millions of pounds on any combination of mobile hardware, software and networks without realising many real benefits. With falling prices of mobile technology one may perceive that mobile working is cheap to implement. However, it is important to remember that technology costs are only a small proportion of the likely total costs. As a rule of thumb, these costs account for 30% of a typical mobile project, with the remaining 70% including items such as training, maintenance, security, management and integration (Flood date?). This implies that the real cost of mobile working could be much greater than promised savings (York & Pendharkar, 2004).

- **Technology overload:** The proliferation of personal information devices such as home computers, mobile phones and digital organizers, coupled with the rise of new media such as e-mail and the World Wide Web, have forever altered the way in which information consumers work and play. These fragmented information channels often result in inefficient working patterns as users switch from device to device and between different media (Evans, 2004) which may result in mobile savvy customers unable to use their devices for day to day tasks such as e-banking.

To promote adoption, customers need to be made aware of the advantages mobile banking offers over other channels. Customers should be provided with opportunities to try out mobile banking or see demonstrations, maybe at branches or through electronic media, of how this channel operates. This would raise awareness, and give people a better understanding of mobile banking options. In addition, services being offered should be widely advertised to the target market, such as young people who tend to be early adopters of innovative services. Perceptions of risk, as with many innovations need to be addressed by limiting customers' liability and implementation of latest security technologies. New versions of WAP use encrypted digital signature to enhance security. The functionality and user interface of mobile devices is improving all the time whereas the cost of Internet connectivity in the developed world is decreasing. These developments mean that the prospects of widespread mobile banking adoption now looks brighter than ever.

An example of a mobile phone banking system is reported by Geach (2007). Named M-pessa, the system is developed by mobile phone operator Safaricom in Kenya. It was launched to improve the efficiency of Microfinance by using mobile technology to make financial transactions cheaper, quicker and accessible to much wider population than currently was the case. M-Pessa is a fully operational service available to phone users in Kenya. The ideas and systems were adopted from South Korea and proved to be especially useful for people with no access to banking or Internet through their computers. Basically, M-pessa is a financial services application installed on a mobile phone. A new generation SIM card is needed with M-pessa software embedded. Upgrades to older SIM cards are available free of charge and works on most mobile phone sets so users don't have to buy a new handset to access it. Financial services available at present include:

1. Person to person (P2P) transfers
2. Individual to business transfers
3. Cash withdrawals at the registered outlets
4. Receipt or payment of loans
5. Balances in real time and ordering of statements.

All of which are executed by SMS text message. The transfer facility works in a similar way to PayPal. An area where M-pessa differs from PayPal is that PayPal requires users to have a bank account or credit card to transfer funds to their PayPal account and to obtain the funds on withdrawal from the PayPal account. Arguably, M-pessa could therefore, be better in terms of increased commercial transactions as people without any account or card such as under 18s could use it to make purchases.

In the case of M-pessa, a customer must have an account with Safaricom in which to pay cash into initially. The customer then selects the option he/she wants, for example 'Send Cash' and enters the phone number for the individual or business that they wish to transfer the funds to. The amount is then entered followed by the user's PIN. A message appears asking for confirmation; by selecting 'OK' an SMS will be sent to M-pessa. Soon after that the customer will then receive an SMS from M-pessa confirming that the funds have been sent, and a code for the recipient to use. The recipient will also receive an SMS stating they have been sent funds from the names person/business. To withdraw cash the recipient needs to go to the nearest registered outlet with the code that the funds sender sends directly to the individual, and identification. The transfer process would take just a few hours in most cases.

This or a similar system can easily be implemented in advanced countries such as the UK, US or Australia. The registered outlet could be a post office, a bank, a mobile phone retailer or a local grocery shop. The main advantage is that no access to a bank is needed by either party; all that is needed is traditional cash to pay into the service provider's (such as Safaricom) account. by the person wishing to send the funds. This means that service would be especially useful for people without a local bank or without a bank account at all. The Mpessa technology is therefore, a viable alternative to the traditional financial system.

M-pessa provides fairly low cost service in Kenya (18p to $1.24). Benefits for businesses are that the potential customer base is increased by providing another means of payment and an easy access to funds that for some people currently do not exist. This has the potential, therefore, to help maintain and increase trade in local shops - a much needed respite for them from increasing competitive pressures from supermarkets. Security of such a system could be a problem. The mobile phone itself could be stolen, potentially allowing the thief to transfer or withdraw funds.

The phone could be hacked into, akin to what is done in desktop environments. In the case of a stolen phone the built in PIN and authentication provisions of M-pessa should mean that provided these security details are not held with the phone the thief should not have the chance to use the phone for fraudulent purposes. Extra security could come from CCTV at the registered outlets or phone can be blocked by the network providers. Anti-virus software could also be provided to financial service users at low cost to counter the threat of hacking and viruses.

Recent trends suggest that, with the arrival of more functionality and user friendliness in mobile technologies, these technologies might be ready for the delivery of financial services. Riivari's (2005) research on mobile banking found that mobile banking is accelerating around Europe and beyond. Laforet and Li's (2005) research on mobile and Internet banking claimed that younger consumers were more interested in online and mobile banking than older consumers, and use of mobile banking amongst this segment is growing fast. To cash in on improved prospects, at least in the developed world, some banks such as Citibank in the US have re-introduced the mobile (or wireless device as they call it) banking. This new service will allow mobile phone or other wireless devices such as BlackBerry users to enter a six digit pin to access a wide range of financial services.

Experiments are also underway, mainly in Japan, Norway and US, to turn these mobile devices into payment tools. Often called 'Contactless Payments' it involves swiping an enabled mobile phone near a point-of-sale terminal to make payments which could be a bill or purchase of goods. These efforts to develop such systems often have support from credit card vendors who are looking for new ways to make payment processes more convenient.

BACKEND SYSTEMS

Banking is a complex business and the ICT systems supporting it are becoming increasingly complex. These backend or so called core systems can be divided in several sub-categories and this section will cover some of the most common banking related systems.

Product Applications

Most banks have several different computer applications for their products. In most cases these systems were developed decades ago so they are often labelled 'Legacy Systems'. There are many problems associated with such systems such as difficulties in integrating them with each other and with newer systems, inflexibility in terms of expansion or scaling down, and rising costs of maintenance. These problems often prevent even strategic level decision making such as forming partnerships with other banks or mergers, as integrating the legacy systems of two or more banks only multiplies the problem.

Legacy systems often fall short in provision of business intelligence for compliance, sales and management needs, or management decision making. This is mainly due to fact that the data formats used are often incompatible with modern data mining tools, and without data from these core systems the resulting business intelligence would often be incomplete or misleading. New product development can also be a problem, as the systems would have to be "hard-coded" even just to make simple product or fee changes, which can be very time-consuming and costly. Good customer service for e-banking customers is also difficult to achieve because the systems do not offer a consistent look and feel to the customer.

To improve customer service, the provision of information on timely bases, prevention of fraud, and to support new agile business models, banks need to deal with all the problematic issues associated with these legacy systems. One solution is, of course, replacement, but often high costs and unacceptable risks make this option unattractive. Another alternative is to reengineer these systems first and then wrap them with new technology, which can provide functionality as a service to other systems and allow changes to the core systems without the need to redevelop all systems. Later systems can be divided and replaced/redeveloped on a piecemeal basis (Kendler, 2005). This approach, if executed well, can help link a bank's infrastructure with modern business process driven applications. However, to implement it organizations may have at least to partially implement the Service Oriented Architecture (described later in this chapter). In addition, very good project management and support from top management in terms of provision of required resources would be crucial.

Another solution is outsourcing, as there are standard software packages available to manage most banking products. This option is often more risky and usually small or medium sized organizations take it up because they may not have enough resources to build these systems themselves. To mitigate the risks, software packages and more importantly vendors have to be chosen carefully to ensure best fit with the existing organization. Future changes in the organization and systems architecture in particular must also be taken into account.

Whichever strategy is chosen, banks need to ensure that new systems are process and customer oriented rather than the transaction orientation more common with legacy systems. Integration with other systems which support different service delivery channels such as branches or the internet is also key to ensuring efficient enterprise-wide work flow information and to giving the bank a uniform look and feel. Security should always be a major priority when any changes in core systems is implemented. To this end, core systems may have to work with new biometric technologies, whether that takes the form of retinal scans, fingerprints or voice recognition.

Business continuity, that is implementation of disaster recovery systems, is another fast developing area and receiving much more attention now due to ever increasing risks from natural disasters and terrorism. In the US, for example, many financial institutions were directly affected by the destruction wrought by Hurricane Katrina in 2005,. They learned the hard way how unprepared they really were. The damage was so severe in certain regions that some banks couldn't bring up applications until six months after the hurricane. Likelihood of this kind of event means that many banks have renewed their focus on preparedness as they rethink their risk management strategies and bolster their business continuity plans (Amato-McCoy, 2006). Costs of unplanned or even planned downtime is spiralling as 24 hours banking channels need to be available all the time.

Continuity plans need to be revisited and updated every three months as a minimum, as one or more components of the continuity systems may not work when needed. Regular testing and simulation of disasters and mock recovery exercises are often needed to uncover any weak links. Every scenario and every possibility needs to be accounted for and drills need to be exercised and recovery plans need to be put into action. This will ensure that banks can get back to business quickly in the event of a disaster.

Data Warehousing

Information has always been a cornerstone of good business decision making. Its importance however is growing all the time as the amount of data which can be collected from customer interaction is increasing at a faster pace than ever. It is important for businesses to seek ways to access, store, maintain, and utilize the enormous data efficiently. This data, if collected and processed in the right way, can provide a meaningful insight into the purchasing behaviour and needs of individual customers. To do this organizations need modern technological tools such as data warehousing systems.

Data warehouse technology can be described as collecting data from several dispersed sources to build a central data storage, so that users can use appropriate data-analyzing tools to analyze it and convert this data into meaningful aids for decision making. Banking activities highly information intensive, therefore the need for data warehousing is greater in this industry than most others. Data warehouse tools can collect daily transaction data both internally and externally, and then accumulate, categorize, and store data for further analysis.

From an implementation point of view, it is important to carefully evaluate and plan ahead before implementing data warehouse technology, owing to the large amount of investment and organizational effort required. The implementation process needs skilled personal, proper project management, and involvement of most stakeholders. Information consultants may be used to provide fresh ideas about the most suitable technologies and sources of information. Outsourcing may be an attractive option if an organization doesn't have the necessary knowledge and skills in-house.

Knowledge Management Systems

A detailed review of knowledge management systems (KMS) is beyond the scope of this chapter (Chapter X). Given the importance of this topic we have dedicated a whole chapter to discussing various aspects of KM. However, a few KMS issues are included in this chapter.

The key to understanding KMS is that not all knowledge can be codified and maintained in data or information management systems. Much of the knowledge we use on a daily basis is part of what we do as social beings – in KM terms, it is implicit rather than explicit. As banks seek to move more toward e-banking solutions, the computerised information systems will perhaps be able to cope with explicit knowledge, but the incorporation of implicit knowledge requires systems which combine technology with human expertise. Throughout this book, whilst technical systems have been presented as perhaps the catalyst for much of e-banking development, it has been made clear that this cannot be successfully implemented without recognition of the organizational and human change which will of necessity accompany this.

There are many sources to assist with this problem, and the reader might find initially referring to Lehaney et al. (2004) a good starting point.

Customer Relationship Management Systems (CRM)

CRM systems are technology enabled management tools which help manage an organization's relationship with its customers. CRM systems help gather/store customer data, analyze this data to enable customised marketing, and are often used to semi-automate customer services. The main purpose of CRM is often stated as 'enriching relationships' with customers to gain greater loyalty, but at times they are used to cut the costs of customer services processes. In an e-banking context, CRM software can help move customers from expensive branch or phone-based services to self-help services over the internet.

There have been numerous CRM successes and failures reported in the literature. As with other new technology and other type of change, success depends on how an organization manages the change process and implements the required processes.

One example of successful implementation of CRM is TotalJobs Group (Thomas 2007). For the Totaljobs Group, a recruitment company, the decision to implement CRM throughout its workforce proved beneficial. The company originally introduced a hosted CRM system from Salesforce.com to its own sales force during 2001-2002. Two years later, it rolled the system out to the rest of the organization, and it is now used by 268 of its 285 employees. The system gives each employee a single view of the customer, so that before a call he/she is able to appraise customer information. Whereas it is impossible to pinpoint the role that CRM has played in the rapid growth of Totaljobs, one useful indicator is the customer satisfaction survey, which regularly shows a continuing increase in customer satisfaction. The ability of CRM systems to segment customers also enables businesses to identify most profitable customers so that marketing efforts can be efficiently targeted at that segment.

Failures in CRM can often be traced to rigid corporate structures and cultures rather than technology itself. Vendors can also over promise, so organizations planning to implement CRM systems need to evaluate their own needs first and then conduct a detailed evaluation of how these systems can meet those needs rather than relying on the sales pitch of the vendors. A major reason why CRM systems may disappoint is that they do not overcome integration problems, as they often have to interface with problematic legacy systems.

One example of CRM related failures is DELL (Lester, 2007). Dell is well known for its "direct" business model that bypassed computer retailers and enables customers to customise the products they purchase using online tools. It has recently lost market share and damaged its stock market reputation, in part because its much-lauded technology enabled processes had a flaw. When a delivery goes wrong or a product is found to be faulty, customers will be left struggling as the human element in the customer-facing function has been cut to a minimum. The computer problems can often only be solved by humans with the necessary knowledge and authority. In Dell's case, customer frustration with the attention they received eventually found expression through a blog for the whole world to read. This case shows that technology itself cannot meet customer expectations. Only well motivated and trained staff, backed by the right business processes and technologies can do that (giving more support for the need to attend to knowledge management, as outlined in the previous section).

Another problem is that CRM can cost millions of dollars, and many of its benefits can be hard to quantify and justify in terms of return on investment. These figures are often calculated on a cost saving basis, with the possible enrichment of customer relationships, which is invisible, being easily ignored. It does not mean that CRM investment should not be evaluated at all, instead the evaluation should be done taking multiple dimensions into account. These dimensions may include customer retention rates, acquisition of new customers, effectiveness of marketing campaigns and so on. These success dimensions should be defined before the start of CRM implementation. This will provide a focus to the implementation effort as well as preventing CRM being labelled a failure if it fails to live up to one success criterion (such as cost savings).

MIDDLEWARE

Lack of integration with other systems is one of the most common reason for the failures of the above discussed technologies. There are many ways of tackling the problem of integration, such as re-coding parts of existing systems or replacing them altogether, but one method, the use of middleware technologies, has attracted a lot of attention and widespread implementation. These technologies enable different types of systems to interact with each other, and make it easier to integrate new systems which a company may implement in the future to into the existing infrastructure. There are many types of middleware technologies (some examples are described in case studies included in the Chapter VIII) but one which is becoming increasing dominant is Services Oriented Architecture (SOA). Potential benefits, such as reduced IT costs, systems integration and greater business agility have persuaded many organizations to adopt SOA (Knorr & Rist, 2005).

SOA is different from other computer applications development paradigms such as object oriented software development. According to O'Donnel (2007) the advantages of SOA over other software development technologies is that by externalizing functionality into reusable components and organising them into a logical framework, it minimizes two of the greatest causes of delay - the need for exhaustive communication between the business and IT, and the need for IT to write code. In addition, unlike other IT paradigms, organizations can also re-use their legacy systems as SOA enables legacy systems to communicate with other systems.

In the context of SOA, services are self describing, platform-independent computer programs that enable rapid and often low-cost composition of distributed IT solutions. Services perform functions, which can be anything from simple requests to complicated business processes (Papazoglou, 2003). As illustrated in Figure 4.1, services are offered by service providers or brokers – organizations that procure the service implementations, supply service descriptions, and provide related technical and business support. When an organization needs a service they look for it themselves using Internet based directories and contact a relevant provider/broker to purchase it. To use these services, organizations need to build an architecture based on universal standards so that new services can be added in a very quickly. That architecture is called 'Service Oriented Architecture'.

Figure 4.1. A Simple model of service oriented architecture

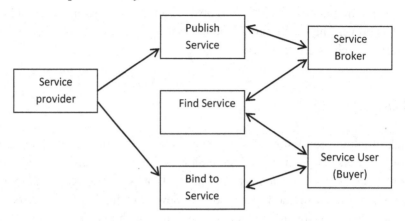

Knorr and Rist (2005) define SOA as a broad, standards-based framework, in which services are built, deployed, managed, and orchestrated in pursuit of new and much more agile IT infrastructure that responds swiftly to shifting business demands. As shown in Figure 4.3, SOA builds on the stacks of protocols such as Extensible Markup Language (XML), Simple Object Access Protocol (SOAP), Web Services Description Language (WSDL), and on the concept of Business Process Re-engineering (BPR). Typically a company would re-engineer its processes and use SOA to support those processes.

Often viewed as a methodology, the SOA can be implemented across multiple projects, both internally and externally, eliminating the need to rebuild similar services for each project. Many vendors now offer SOA related products such as messaging solutions or business process management tools (BPM) that help implement SOA. However it remains a complex task, which requires considerable upfront investment, a high level of technical expertise and very careful change management. Despite this, many organizations are adopting SOA because of the following benefits:

- **Integrating legacy systems:** SOA makes it easier to integrate new systems with old legacy systems under a single architecture. According to King (2005), integrating legacy into an SOA is relatively easy, as the IT department has only to build an interface to make the legacy application's data available in a standardised format that other SOA compliant systems can understand. Many retail banks are now focusing on understanding their customers and deepening the relationship with them. To do this they must achieve a single view of the customer so they can understand customer's needs. The SOA has potential to provide them by enabling end-to-end integration (Narter, 2007).
- **Service reuse:** Most components of SOA can be re-used several times. To fully benefit from this feature, organizations have to train, encourage and

reward programmers to reuse existing services (Kobielus, 2005). This is the key reason given for claims that SOA is cheaper than its alternatives. In the banking industry, services are usually coupled within a particular process. Generally speaking, banks are unable to decouple the process, and the services held within each process need to be rebuilt to get the same services in another channel. SOA, however, allows banks to decouple services and make them modular so they can be reused across channels (Feig, 2007).

- **Shorter development cycle:** Greater service reuse often translates into accelerated development cycles (Kobielus, 2005) which means that IT departments have greater ability to quickly respond to dynamic business needs. The development cycle is also shortened by the reduction in need for coding.
- **Long term cost savings:** Reusability of SOA components could also result in significant cost savings. According to Kobielus (2005), the marginal cost of building new applications will continue to drop as the reuse rate climbs. When an application component is reused, SOA becomes more than 30 % cheaper than traditional development approaches. Kobielus (2005) also points out that many of the SOA related savings come from its ability to consolidate silos of redundant application functionality and data throughout organizations.
- **Flexibility:** SOA offers considerably more flexibility than other architectures. Once an organization has built its systems using SOA, it becomes easier to add or replace one part without disturbing the other parts (King, 2005). This means than many business processes can be re-engineered or amended within a very short period of time.

A survey carried out by Information Week revealed that companies are getting or hoping to get many benefits from SOA adoption. These benefits include (Babcock, 2005): IT platform standardisation, business processes automation, business flexibility, operational savings, systems integration and so on.

Whilst these benefits will persuade many businesses to implement SOA, there are barriers to its adoption.

- **Large upfront investment:** In the previous section we discussed long-term cost savings. However, initially SOA will require significant investment, which some organizations may not be able to afford. Kobielus (2005) reports that Standard Life Group, an insurance company, maintains three SOA implementing development groups with about 500 people, about half of whom are delivering SOA services and applications. The company also has a staff of seven which just manages their SOA-enabling distributed application infrastructure. This type of operation is expensive, and the Return on Investment (ROI) can take long time to materialise. This issue is less of a problem for large organizations with large IT budgets, but for small and medium sized organizations it may be more problematic, and can be exacerbated by service reuse opportunities which are likely to be fewer than for large organizations.

- **Complexity:** Implementing SOA is not easy. Erlanger (2005) claims that SOA implementation is one of the most daunting projects that organizations can undertake because it represents a whole new of way of thinking which will change the way developers operate and interact with the business. This could mean that many organizations will not have enough or right kind of human resources to succeed in adopting SOA.

- **Lack of mature development tools:** Many SOA development tools are still in their early stages and it will be some time before the standards bodies develop universal standards for describing services and service platforms, along with delivering the management tools they will need. This could be a particular problem where an organization implements a multi-vendor solution.

These limitations create many problems for organizations in implementing SOA. According to an InformationWeek research survey, nearly a third of companies using SOA consider that they are falling short of expectations, a quarter have seen growing complexity in their IT systems, a third have been hit with higher-than-expected costs, and half report difficulties in integrating legacy systems into new software-development processes in a cost effective manner (Babcock, 2005). These findings suggest that we may be far from the SOA benefits claimed by SOA technologies vendors.

Implementing SOA is as much of management issue as a technological one. The main management issues include:

- **Choosing a vendor:** Just like other IT systems, this is also a key question in the SOA context. Should an organization buy SOA related technologies from a single vendor or implement a best-of-breed solution? Knorr and Rist (2005) recommend best of breed (multi vendor) solutions to fully benefit from the flexible nature of SOA and to avoid lock-in with one vendor. However, lack of standards in services description could mean that organizations have to use considerable financial and human resources just to evaluate the various services on offer.

- **Governance:** As SOA is a new IT paradigm, any governance issues and ways to manage them are still in their earlier stages of development. Knorr and Rist (2005) define governance in an SOA context as a combination of workflow rules: who is responsible for what service, what happens when quality assurance uncovers problems, the management of service interface definitions, and so on.

- **Adoption:** Like many other technology implementations, SOA may also suffer employee resistance. Erlanger (2005) reports that Verizon's efforts only took off after it developed incentives for business units to adopt SOA. In addition to incentives, SOA education and getting people to understand new roles and responsibilities may also help.
- **Security:** SOA is based on open standards, making reusability and security critical issues. The industry has, however, agreed on a simple framework for securing XML messages, called WS-Security which is the most often used Web service specification after SOAP and WSDL (Knorr & Rist, 2005).
- **Service management:** SOA should be managed like any other network resource. According to Knorr and Rist, (2005) several vendors offer dashboard-like solutions that monitor the health of services, maintain service levels, scale performance, set up failovers, handle exceptions and so on. Which of these solutions should be used depends on size of the SOA implementation budget.

In summary, SOA is a relatively new area, and many of the issues discussed above need further research. These may include an objective evaluation of benefits and drawback of SOA, or studying best practice in adoption or implementation of SOA in order to recommend an easy to follow practical model. Impacts of SOA on organizational structures, culture and business processes also form an interesting research direction. In-depth research and evaluation is needed to avoid pitfalls and to maximise benefits from SOA.

WEBSITE DEVELOPMENT ISSUES

In e-banking, a bank's website acts as a bank branch or front end. The main difference is that when customers login they do most of the work themselves without any assistance. Therefore creating a positive customer experience is more critical in the e-banking environment. There are many different types of website and a general classification is presented in Table 4.1.

E-banking websites and other related systems, without the benefit of human guidance, are expected to communicate effectively and enhance knowledge and understanding of the sometimes voluminous, and often technical, information involved in financial transactions (Tan & Teo, 2000). To create a positive experience, a great deal of planning, resources and expertise needs to be invested in the development and ongoing maintenance of websites.

To start with, a website must manage all the aspects that customers would expect from the buying process in a non-web environment. This requires a shift from website usability alone to interactivity and the ability to positively engage a customer (Coughlan et al, 2006). The focus should be on how the communication with customers can be improved by using the rich variety of available media. Giving more attention to the customer in the buying process could help in understanding the communication between customers and the bank, and subsequently lead to design and evaluation of websites that can stimulate the real-life buying experience more closely (Coughlan et al, 2006).

Table 4.1 suggests that in addition to the customer experience, e-marketing best practices and reliability/responsiveness of the website also play a major part in website success. Provision of decision aid tools such as interest rate calculators also helps create a positive impression. The ability of a website to provide a bank with useful feedback about customer behaviour for marketing purpose is also becoming a must for bank websites.

Some banks have also had positive experiences selling additional services. For example, Bank B bank in the U.K. provided new and used cars to customers looking for finance to buy a car. UBS sells Roman coins, United Overseas Bank offers

Table 4.1. Web site design strategy (adapted from Goi, 2007)

Web site design	Definition/ characteristic	Promotion measures/ways	Merits
Informational/ communicational design	This approach is for companies to use the Web as a supplement to traditional marketing, delivering additional benefits to customers and building relationships with them.	• Putting banking services on-line. • Building broad awareness and image. • Using the Web as a cost-effective way to augment their core products with related information and service function. • Obtaining cost savings from automating routine customer services.	• Providing large quantities of information to customers. • Giving a company an instant global presence and attracting people to one's ad, some of them are not the company's target market, but potentially will be. • Opening a new communication channel enabling enrichment of relationships with customers. • All at a reasonable cost.
On-line/ transactional design	This approach is for companies to use the Web to construct "virtual Business" - independent, profitable ventures that exist only on the Internet	• Creating a retail presence larger than any physical presence could. • Creating a virtual business providing extra information in a form competitors cannot imitate. • Creating a virtual business that takes a specialty product or collectible and sells it worldwide • Creating a virtual business that uses the Internet to produce superior economic benefits to customers that competitors cannot imitate • Creating a virtual business providing convenience to customers that competitors cannot match	• Providing a larger or more specialized selection of products than competitors can offer. • Providing higher quality and higher quantity information, more economic benefits, and more convenience than competitors can offer • Providing a sense of community for customers

discounts on restaurants, and Wells Fargo displays wanted posters. Many banks use their websites to market products, serve investors, inform the media, attract recruits, build the brand and much more.

Website development also suffers from problems encountered by traditional information systems. A view of website development as a purely technological domain is an inadequate one. Such a perspective reduces the complexity of the issues involved, and attempts to define it in terms of rules and procedures by which given inputs can be turned into predictable outputs. A human-centred approach is quite different. Human issues are 'complex' and 'adaptive', and cannot be fully described in terms of rules and procedures. To understand such issues we may consult social theory.

In the last two decades, information systems have become more fragmented and distributed, so the social issues have grown in importance. Arguably, the World Wide Web represents currently the most distributed form of technology-enabled system, in which a wide range of user types needs to be taken into account. It could be argued that the social issues are becoming much more important than technology related issues. Understanding this mixture of technological/social issues from a social theoretical perspective is covered in more detail within Chapter VI. Suffice it to say here that the web, for example, could be understood as a social, communicative, subjective phenomenon, in which the views and opinions of participants become fundamental to our approach to website development.

Further, from a radical humanist, or critical perspective, the dominant, technological view of IS as functionalist, 'hard', problem solving, is seen to be an impoverished, over-focused on the use of technology. 'Soft' or human-centred methodologies are employed as a solution to this problem. But some question the ability of either 'hard' and 'soft' approaches to achieve much by themselves, and suggest the need to combine approaches under the umbrella of social theory. One theory, radical humanism offers the potential to achieve this.

This reconceptualisation of the system as a social system is an important part of any intervention, focusing debate not on a clearly defined technical or organizational problem to which a solution is to be developed as well as on the complex interaction of all the issues involved. The aim would be to change the focus from technology or organizational functions to the views and ideals of the stakeholder groups involved. The task becomes not one of how to engineer a solution to a known and agreed problem, but how to study and improve a problem situation made up of complex interacting issues. From the issues raised by boundary debate, it becomes possible to consider balanced strategies.

E-BANKING SYSTEMS AS A WHOLE

The banking sector occupies an important position in the global economy. The sector has been subject to many external and internal forces. Of the external forces, technological change is likely to have the most far-reaching impact on the sector. Technology, in particular the Internet, is a key driver of these changes. In this sector computer systems in general, both backend and front end systems have largely remained centralised owing to the nature of the business and high security requirements. This to some extent helped banks to automate key business processes by integrating their systems (Ayadi, 2006). Systems integration, as discussed above is essential to delivering the same information across all distribution channels such as e-banking, phone banking and branch banking.

Despite some successes in e-banking implementation, many technological problems remain, as some banks still lag behind others mainly due to their inability to deal with their legacy systems problems. Diniz (1998) present two different classifications of e-banking systems. These two classifications are based on the level of interactivity of the site (weak, average, strong) and on the type of opportunities pursued by the bank (informational, transactional, client relationship). They found that that the type of technology to be used evolves with the interactivity and functionality of the Web site of the bank. For example, an informational site is primarily based on a brochureware model, while an e-banking web site which is oriented toward the management of client relationships requires more sophisticated technologies like Customer Relationship Management (CRM). Mizrahi (2000) proposed another model of e-banking systems evolution in which IS integration depends on two variables: adequacy of the customer-channel relationship and capacity of managing information across channels.

Availability of systems and security of data has always been an important issue, but is arguably even more critical in e-commerce, with 24 hours a day, seven days a week availability. Any unauthorized access to data or unplanned 'downtime' of systems can result in a public relations disaster. At the same time, threats from computer viruses, frauds and terrorism are increasing. This all means that a considerable IT budget is spent on fraud prevention and disaster recovery systems, which may include investment in encryption technologies, other security measures and maintaining two parallel sets of systems to ensure all time availability. The following are becoming an integral part of e-commerce related systems implementation.

1. Capacity and 'stress' testing should be done regularly, as prediction of demand for e-commerce systems can be more difficult than for traditional systems;
2. In the area of security, online systems opens up systems to the outside world. Investments in security related software/hardware will be a major expense;

3. Identity theft and fraud in online environments are one of the major threats to the existence of e-commerce. Firms need to keep up with new and evolving sources of threat.

Although many of these risks are unique to e-commerce, the principles of general good IT risk management apply in most cases.

CHAPTER SUMMARY

This chapter has covered some of the most common technologies used in e-banking. These technologies include product related back end systems, Data Warehousing, Customer Relationship Management (CRM) systems and Service Oriented Architecture (SOA). Product specific systems are often the oldest systems in banks, and pose the most challenging functionality and integration problems. These systems are also called back-end or legacy systems and require considerable upgrading to support e-banking. Data Warehousing systems help banks to gather, organise, store and analyze data for various operational and marketing uses. CRM systems are mainly used to enrich relationships with customers and to employ carefully targeted marketing strategies.

These systems become most useful when they work together. Integration is still a major technical challenge, and the arrival of integration technologies such as SOA is helping to resolve some of the problems. It is important to stress that technology is one dimension of e-banking and success in e-banking also requires careful management of social, managerial and strategic issues.

Website development related issues are also growing in complexity giving rise the debate about technical versus social approaches to the development. As usual in any type of technology, technical views take higher priority in the beginning and related social issues gain a slower acceptance. The main challenge here is *not* to see web development and management as a problem to be solved by an expert group of developers. A framework (for example, of user groups) needs to be developed, from which the contribution from representatives of all stakeholders should be sought. Membership of participating groups or committees should not be fixed, and, of course, should not be limited to managers or those in authority.

E-banking also brings a new set of risks and organizations have to put in place structures to manage these risk. This structure may include e-banking risk management framework that enables controls to address the security, availability and adequacy of systems. The nature of those controls will depend on several factors, such as the extent of the technological dependency, sources of threat, extent of cross industry collaboration to combat these threats. Organizations need to have a policy statement setting out the e-banking risk management framework; and an organizational structure with clear responsibilities for the implementation of the framework and relevant controls. Adherence to the principles of ISO Standard 17799, the international standard for information security management is helpful in developing organizational structures to manage e-banking related risks.

REFERENCES

Amato-McCoy, D.M. (2006, February 27). Planning for continuity. *Bank Systems & Technology.*

Ayadi A. (2006, April). Technological and organizational preconditions to Internet banking implementation: Case of a Tunisian bank. *Journal of Internet Banking and Commerce, 11*(1). Retrieved May 12, 2007 from http://www.arraydev.com/commerce/JIBC/2006-04/Ayadi.asp

Babcock, C. (2005, Oct 31). SOA: Work in progress. *InformationWeek, 1062*, 40-45. Manhasset, NY.

Blau, J. (2007, January 23). Hackers will target mobile banking, study warns. *TechWorld.* Available at http://www.techworld.com/security/news/index.cfm?newsID=7828&pagtype=all

Brown, I., Cajee, Z., Davies, D., & Stroebel, S. (2003). Cell phone banking: predictors of adoption on South Africa. An exploratory study. *International Journal of Information Management, 23*(5), 381-394.

Burrell, G., & Morgan, G. (1979). *Sociological Paradigms and Organizational Analysis.* London: Heinemann.

Chaffey, D., & Wood, S. (2004). *Business information management: improving performance using information systems.* Toronto, Canada: Prentice Hall Financial Times.

Clarke, S. (2002). Web Management and Usage: A Critical Social Perspective. In M. Anandarajan, & C. Simmers (Eds.), *Managing Web Usage in the Workplace: A Social, Ethical and Legal Perspective* (pp. 319-337). Hershey, PA: Idea Group Publishing.

Clarke, S. A. (2000). From socio-technical to critical complementarist: A new direction for information systems development. In E. Coakes, R. Lloyd-Jones & D. Willis (Eds.), *The New SocioTech: Graffiti on the Long Wall,* (pp. 61-72). London: Springer.

Coughlan, J., Macredie, R., & Patel, N. (2006). Moving face-to-face communication to Web-based systems. Moving face-to-face communication to Web-based systems. *Interacting with Computers, 19*(1), 1-6.

Diniz, E. (1998). Web banking in the USA. *Journal of Internet Banking and Commerce.* Retrieved May 1, 2007, from http://www.arraydev.com/commerce/JIBC/9806-06.htm,

Erlanger, L. (2005, November 7). Making SOA work. *InforWorld, 27*(45), 45-52.

Evans, D. (2004). An introduction to unified communications: challenges and opportunities. In *Aslib Proceedings: New Information Perspectives, 56,* 17-20.

Feig, N. (2007, March 30). A new foundation: SOA implementation and bank transformation. *Bank Systems & Technology.*

Gaech, N. (2007, April 16-17). *The digital divide, financial exclusion and mobile phone technology: Two problems, one solution?* BILETA 2007 Annual Conference, Hertfordshire, UK.

Goi, C.L. (2007, April 2007). A review of existing web site models for e-commerce. *Journal of Internet Banking and Commerce, 12*(1). (*http://www.arraydev.com/commerce/jibc/*)

Hoffman, K. E. (2002, May 14). Online banking aligns practices. *Bank Technology News.* http://www.eletronicbanker.com/btn/articles/btnmar02-03.shtml

Kendler, P.B. (2005, August 3,). Core systems to improve. *Bank Systems & Technology.*

King, B. (2005, August 3). Optimise your legacy. *Financial Times, 9.*

Knorr, E., & Rist, O. (2005, Nov 7). 10 Steps SOA. *InfoWorld, 27*(45), 23-35. San Mateo, CA. http://proquest.umi.com/pqdweb?did=930819081&sid=7&Fmt=3&clientId=3224&RQT=309&VName=PQD

Kobielus, J. (2005, October 10). Three steps to SOA nirvana. *Network World, 22*(40), 58-59.

Kristoffersen, S., & Ljungberg, F. (1999). Making place to make IT Work: empirical explorations of HCI for mobile CSCW. In *Proceedings of the International Conference on Supporting Group Work (GROUP'99),* (pp. 276-285).

Laforet, S., & Li, X. (2005). Consumers attitudes towards online and mobile banking in China, *International Journal of Bank Marketing, 23*(5), 362-380.

Lehaney, B., Clarke, S., Coakes, E. G., & Jack, M. (2004). *Beyond Knowledge Management.* Hershey, PA: Idea Group Publishing.

Lester, T. (2007, April 9). *More Than a Technology.* www.FT.com. Accessed May 9, 2007.

Midgley, G. (1992). The sacred and profane in critical systems thinking. *Systems Practice, 5*(1), 5-16.

Mizrahi, S. (2000, February). Approche multi-canaux : réinventer la banque. *Banque Magazine, 611,* 38-41.

Narter, B. (2007, February 1). The role of SOA in 2007: Channel forecast. *Bank Systems & Technology.*

O, Donnell, T. (2007, March). Addressing SOA's vulnerability. *Visual Studio Magazine.* Retrieved June 22, 2008, from http://visualstudiomagazine.com/features/article. aspx?editorialsid=2311

Oliga, J. C. (1991). Methodological Foundations of Systems Methodologies. In R. L. Flood &, M. C. R. L., Jackson (Eds.),, M. C. *Critical Systems Thinking: Directed Readings* (pp. 159-184). Chichester, UK: Wiley.

Owens, I., & Robertson, D. (2000, April 26-28). Aligning e-Commerce with Business Strategy: The Case of the Bank of Scotland. In *Proceedings of the 5th UKAIS Conference,(pp.* 67-75). University of Wales Institute, Cardiff, UK.

Papazoglou, M. P., & Georgakapoulos, G. (2003, October). *Service-Oriented Computing, CACM, 46*(10).

Perry, M., O'Hara, K., Sellen, A., Brown, & Harper, R. (2001). Dealing with mobility: Understanding access anytime, anywhere. *ACM Transactions on Computer-Human Interaction, 8,* 323-347.

Phifer, L. (2004). Roaming far and wide with mobile vpns. *Business Communications Review, 34,* 42-47.

Riivari, J. (2005). Mobile banking: A powerful new marketing and CRM tool for financial services companies all over Europe. *Journal of Financial Services Marketing, 10*(1), 11-20.

Tan, M., & Teo, T. S. H. (2000, July). Factors Influencing the Adoption of Internet Banking, *Journal of the Association for Information Systems, 1.* http://jais.aisnet. org/articles/1-5/default.asp?view=pdf

Thomas, K. (200,7 March 17). The business case. *FT.com.* Accessed May 09, 2007. http://www.ft.com/cms/s/18093c7a-d3e0-11db-8889-000b5df10621.html

Ulrich, W. (1996). *A Primer to Critical Systems Heuristics for Action Researchers.* Forum One: Action Research and Critical Systems Thinking, Centre for Systems Studies, , University of Hull, Hull, UK.

York, J., & Pendharkar, P. C. (2004). Human-computer interaction issues for mobile computing in a variable work context. *International Journal of Human-Computer Studies, 60,* 771-797.

Chapter V
A Managerial View of E-Banking

INTRODUCTION

As discussed in the Chapter IV, e-banking is different from other forms of technological projects. It brings a different set of challenges for managers which are
discussed in Section one of this chapter. It is widely acknowledged that complexity in the managerial environment has increased because e-services often require
decisions that focus on integration of internal/external systems, adoption of new
business models and frequent restructuring of existing business processes and
structures. This chapter discusses some of those challenges and ways in which
they can be met.

MANAGEMENT CHALLENGES

Many authors have outlined the impact of new technologies on organizations. For
example, CRM systems can force a general realignment of business processes,
which in turn can cause major changes in a firm's activities. Similarly it is widely
recognised that new technologies like the Internet may have a deep influence on a
firm's organization structure (Ayadi, 2006).

Implementation of e-banking often results in significant changes in the organization, giving rise to new and complex challenges for managers. The Internet also impacts market structure, and affects competitive advantage in the banking sector. Some organizations implement changes required to respond to the above challenges before they implement e-banking technologies, some do so while implementing them, and others respond to the need as and when it is forced upon them. Which of these managerial strategies should be adopted is another managerial challenge.

Increased Customers Expectations

Arrival of online services has increased customer expectations, leading them to expect better value products delivered more quickly. E-banking has the potential to be a rich experience for customers, with the foremost goal being to increase the depth of the relationship between the customer and the bank. As technology evolves, the opportunities to extend and enrich the relationship with customers also grow.

The goal of e-banking should be to provide many, if not all, of the services offered at a branch. This may include transactions as well as information, advice, administration, and even cross-selling. However, the interactive nature of the Web not only allows banks to enhance these core services, but also enables them to communicate more effectively and expand customer relationships. When combined with the improving analytical capabilities of data mining and related technologies, the potential for innovative product and services development can go well beyond our current limits.

Security Problems

Internet security is still one of the major issues hindering the growth of Internet related trade. Owing to the structure and intention of the Internet to be an open network, financial transactions may involve high security risks. Internet frauds are common, and related stories get immediate media attention, making people hesitant to bank online. Different security methods (for both hardware and software) are being tested and employed continuously but there is still some way to go to win the trust of many customers. E-banking managers need to be aware of new security threats as well as new methods of combating those threats to stay on top of this challenge.

Managing information security is a very complex issue. Clarke (2007) argues that the domain is dominated by a set of practical controls which are seen as rigid, unclear and largely irrelevant to the business needs of most organizations. Even within some recent developments that have sought to provide a more accessible model for managing information security, most current practice is based around the needs of the technology and of information rather than the needs of people in general and users in particular. Where human issues are considered, it is to confer responsibilities and education on people to conform to the needs of the system with an aim to regulate their behaviour.

Figure 5.1 summarises the position reached so far, and gives some idea of the complexity of the issues. This model would be useful in planning for a comprehensive security provision.

The above figure does help in understanding the various dimensions in managing information security. Actual implementation requires more practical guidelines. Clarke (2007) suggests the procedure (outlined in Table 5.1) which is a helpful approach to implementing a security practice.

Figure 5.2 provides some structure to these steps, suggesting that the path through these steps should be continuous. Getting the basic controls in place is highest priority because failure to do this would most likely undermine the whole security practice irrespective of its social/technical biases. Next priority is to make sure that the practice is continually reviewed to check whether it is meeting the needs of its users and the business. Thirdly, use the evaluative model to identify opportunities to improve the practice towards a more socially aware approach. Underpinning all of this is the need to identify and deal with neutral, counter-productive and other-responsibility biased controls. One way to deal with this is to remove neutral and counter-productive controls altogether and to reassign other-responsibility to the appropriate department within the organization but clearly maintain such controls as dependencies for the information security practice.

Figure 5.1. The complexity of information security (Clarke, 2007)

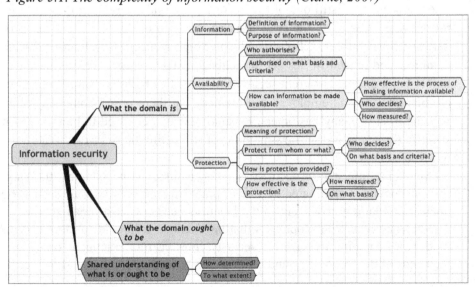

Table 5.1. Adapted approach to information security

Number	Step	Comments
1	Assess presence of essential controls. If there are gaps they should be addressed unless there is a good reason not to.	Absence of essential controls puts the organization at risk of loss of information and access in a way that cannot be addressed through application of sociologically-biased controls.
2	Assess security practice of organization against Evaluative Model and create security profile map. Compare this profile with other organization of similar size, industry sector, complexity etc.	As more organizations are assessed the baseline of organizations' security profiles will grow and provide this additional dimension of analysis
3	Determine whether any implemented system-biased controls can be easily converted to lifeworld-biased by changing context, environment, people involved, means of capturing feedback etc.	This represents the easiest step to moving the very common goal-attainment focused security practice to a lifeworld focused one
4	Determine whether any of the lifeworld-biased controls identified above have not been implemented but could be deployed reasonably easily.	If an organization has built its practice around audit requirements and/or functional concerns it is quite likely that not all lifeworld-biased controls have been implemented.
5	Reassess security profile and compare with the previous practice of target organization along with other organizations of similar size, industry sector, complexity etc	This gives a new baseline from which to measure improvements towards a lifeworld-biased approach. There are few measurements available as the practice changes but deployment of lifeworld controls is a useful indicator of progress. Other specific measures such as user satisfaction, number of security incidents etc should be formulated on a case by case basis. Have regard for the outcomes that are sought by the organization.
6	Identify Neutral (N), Counter-productive (C) and Other-responsibility (O) controls and eliminate or reassign.	It is critically important that N and C controls are not just dropped and ignored. Careful thought should be given to determine whether they are correctly classified and consideration of whether they are important to some other organizational function (in which case, presumably, they would be reassigned as O. If O controls remain a dependency after they have been reassigned the dependency must be surfaced and appropriate service levels agreed and documented.
7	Use the action loop through public and private spheres to drive the security practice towards a lifeworld focus	This action step is key to maintaining a focus on both technical and human centred issues throughout the life of an information security system.
8	Reassess security profile and compare with last baseline. Redo action loop at action step 6.	This becomes a long-term (perhaps continual) process to achieve desired outcomes and sustain the required focus.

Technological Challenges

There are numerous technological issues with regard to e-banking. Lack of unified messaging standards is one of them. While internet messaging standards are fast evolving towards unification, the problem of legacy systems still remains one of the main obstacles to e-banking. Many banks still operate on large mainframe-based legacy systems for their core processing functions. While for some isolated functions this is fine, e-banking will require capabilities such as the ability to integrate with other systems, that legacy systems are ill equipped to provide. Being at the forefront of technology adoption for many years, the financial services industry faces cutting-edge technological issues before other industries (Dewan & Seidmann, 2001). E-banking systems are complex, large-scale systems with demanding requirements for performance, scalability, and availability, and even the most technologically sophisticated organizations are struggling to manage them.

Success in e-banking requires far more than a Web server, a storefront and transaction processor or a database. It requires a comprehensive approach to address

Figure 5.2. Framework for applying security practice (Clarke, 2007)

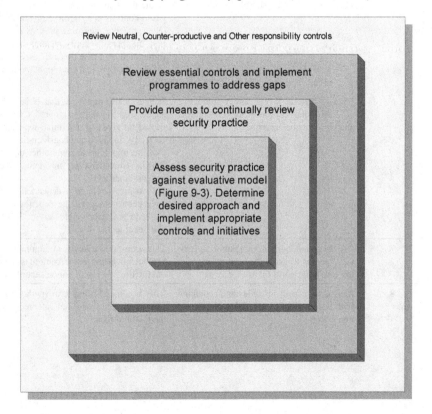

integration and scaleablity, and dynamic responses to changes in requirements and technologies. E-banking, like other electronic business systems is complex, large-scale, and mission-critical. Organizations should start with new Web technologies and e-commerce functionality and combine them with the design, development and implementation of management practices that have been proven successful for other types of large-scale, complex, mission-critical systems.

E-commerce is about how an organization has to re-shape itself to enable commerce online. An organization needs to have process oriented and fully integrated systems to achieve the desired benefits from e-commerce. Even in cases of disparate applications, or where the company does not abandon existing applications (e.g. legacy systems), there are solutions to the problem. Several alternatives are available for increasing the level of systems integration. Data warehousing, a bundle of technologies that integrate data from multiple source systems for query and analysis, provide a cheap alternative for data integration. Other technologies, such as Enterprise Applications Integration (EAI) or Service Oriented Architecture (SOA), may turn legacy systems (as well as other business applications) into strategic assets at a relatively low cost. EAI is a new class of software that aims to provide an integration infrastructure for all business applications. A similar approach is the development of middleware software for systems integration. This approach is used by banks like Bank A and the Bank B (see Chapter VIII).

One key technology management challenge is that systems must scale to accommodate business growth. Maintaining excellent performance across growing workloads is imperative. There is no greater customer inconvenience than a poor, unpredictable response, and in e-banking competitors are only a few clicks away. The requirement for scalability goes beyond the ability to use more powerful servers, to distribute workload across a few server platforms, or to balance communications traffic across multiple Web servers. Approaches to system architecture, software structure, and workload distribution are needed to ensure scalability.

E-Channels Specific Marketing

Electronic distribution channels such as the Internet are shifting the balance of power from financial services providers to customers. This is largely due to the increasing number of choices available to customers and to declining switching barriers (Mols, 2000). For these reasons, the enrichment of relationships with customers has become an important issue. Greenland (1994) was one of the earliest to suggest this in his work about rationalisation and restructuring in the U.K. Financial Sector. He argued that personal relationship building is highly desirable for financial services institutions, as relationships can be actively cultivated to promote the company's image and stimulate cross selling. Greenland's (1994) work was focused on using branch banking for this purpose. Modern data mining and customer relationship management software has added another dimension to this proposition, which may now also change the e-channels to personalise financial services at an individual or a segment level. Some organizations such as the Bank B are already making progress in this area (see Chapter VIII).

As the Internet is a relatively new delivery channel, customers need a lot of persuasion to switch to it. Offering incentives, such as higher interest rates or low cost services (for example insurance) is often used for this purpose. This can be costly and success may be uncertain. Any decision regarding this must be backed up by concrete marketing information. Promotion of e-banking to employees is also important. Change resulting from e-commerce implementation affects many people in organizations. Uncertainties resulting from changes are usually addressed by getting as many employees involved as possible at all stages of a project life cycle. This may lengthen the project duration but the benefit can be immense. It is also important to keep communication going and keep all stakeholders, including users, informed of the progress for the entire duration of the project. Some organizations such as the Woolwich also use incentives such as free WAP phones and bonuses for e-banking promotion within the organization.

Change Management

When considering the implementation of e-banking, a question to think about is the structure as well as the organizational culture (Jayawardhena & Foley, 2000). This requires focusing on an organization's business structure and business processes with the existing IT systems, as well as examining new processes designed specifically for e-commerce. Existing processes often have to be re-engineered in order to align them with the new processes. Therefore, companies should be ready to face this challenge (Kalakota & Robinson, 1999) and strategic planning is required to manage ongoing changes. Change management is the process of planning, controlling, co-ordinating, executing and monitoring changes that affect the business (IBM Global Services, 2001). It requires considerable emphasis on management of change skills and responsibilities (Morton & Chester, 1997). Morton and Chester proposed three main steps in managing change:

- Use of the initial, vision-creating phase to unfreeze the organization and to make employees 'change prone'. At the same time, attention should be paid to the potential causes of resistance and dissent, and to ensure that these are eliminated or minimised.
- Placing a duty on all staff for appropriate aspects of change.
- Placing specific responsibility on one or more senior executives to facilitate the process of change.

Core to successful change management is commitment from the work force. It is important to maintain communications and to consult on the meaning of change.

The importance of change management when implementing e-banking cannot be over emphasised and it may dramatically influence the outcome of the project.

Project Management

Project management is a vital part of an e-commerce implementation strategy. Such projects must be carefully planned and executed. Appleton (1997) recognises that the key skills needed for a systems implementation are team building and communication skills, which she refers to as 'soft skills'. Projects need to be business driven with a cross-functional project team, and rapid decision making processes have to be in place to help ensure that the project delivers desired outcomes. E-banking projects pose similar challenges as other new technology implementation projects and have to be managed accordingly. This topic is covered in greater detail in Chapter IX.

Most of the factors discussed in this section require careful management of organizational issues, and the next section outlines some methods of managing change in organizations.

TREADING THE ORGANIZATIONAL MAZE

A considerable portion of an e-banking implementation project involves dealing with organizational change management related issues. The previous section outlined some of the most pressing issues faced by management. This section suggests and discusses some of the ways in which required changes can be implemented and managed.

The process of effective change management starts with quick recognition of a need for change in response to a new threat, changes in the market place, or simply the implementation of new business plans or technologies. For example, when a 'brick and mortar' bank decides to take part in online trade it is not just a matter of buying new hardware or software; this kind of initiative has a profound effect on organizations and needs a strategic managerial response. Adopting new technologies requires a degree of interaction between technical and managerial staff and both have to work together to manage the process of change effectively. The following issues will have to be managed throughout any new technology implementation project.

User Resistance to Change

An e-banking system will be used by a number of different types of people including customers, executives, management staff as well as other interested parties such as trade partners and even competitors. Many systems fail simply because one or more type of user refuses to use a system or uses stealth tactics to undermine the new system. This phenomenon is often referred to as user resistance. Resistance to change can be defined as implicit or explicit negative reactions against change, or restrictive forces opposed to any reorganization of work process and new competences acquisition (Bareil, 2002). To minimise user resistance it is important to understand what are the main causes of user's resistance. Generally speaking, user acceptance is often linked to two outcome variables: system quality and system acceptance. But underlying these are the more complex issues of cognitive and motivational factors which give rise to improved quality or improved acceptance.

The first step in dealing with user resistance is to ensure that users from all hier-archical levels are involved in consultations about the need for the new technologies. Consultations should include the choices an organization has, and should continue throughout the development stage, including training and incentives for adopting new technologies or working practices. Ayadi (2006) argues that implementation failures of new technologies in banks often occurs because the bank executives focus on financial and technical feasibility rather than organizational or social feasibility. An organizational or social feasibility study would have dealing with user issues at its core. It is also essential in e-banking to get customers (arguably most important user of the system) involved, but this is much more complex than the implementation of internal systems, and requires different strategies. Customer involvement in feasibility studies, systems testing and so on requires a higher level of incentives than is required where the users are employees. Paid focus groups is one way around this problem.

At implementation stage, internal users may fear job losses, or loss of power or status, which in the extreme may result in a demoralised workforce. In extreme cases, some employees may even try to sabotage the new system in order to avoid the perceived negative consequences. This issue can be addressed by implement-ing a comprehensive human resources management strategy covering changes in working practices, job appraisal and training programmes.

The size of the organization is one of the key factors affecting the adoption of new technologies. The larger the size of the organization, the more resources and capital need to be allocated to facilitate adoption. The existence of a new technol-ogy's champions also influences the adoption. Champions are need amongst top management as well as at middle and lower ranks of an organization. Perceived usefulness is also widely believed to be a key facilitator of adoption. If people in organization get convinced that a new initiative is good for organization as well as for themselves they become more motivated to adopt a new technology.

Many customers will also be reluctant to adopt e-banking. Understanding the rationale in resisting e-banking is of value to companies in enabling the development of plans to achieve widespread adoption. What motivates someone to use e-banking for their banking transactions? Consumers have access to ATMs, telebanking and the wide distribution of branches and the enhanced customer service in them, so there has to be an added value in using internet banking. Many would only use it if they perceive e-banking to be of higher value (Awamleh & Fernandes, 2006).

If lack of awareness, is causing people to hesitate or resist Internet based services, the bank can launch a properly planned communications campaign to give information tailored to help in this situation (Kuisma et al., 2007). Banks need to understand the nature of resistance in order to take this factor into account when developing a new channel or a new type of service. According to Kuisma et al. (2007) banks should identify causes of resistance and address them directly. The feelings of insecurity and learning issues which are common barriers to adoption could be avoided by proper marketing campaigns, communication with customers, customer training and user-friendly website design. To facilitate adoption, banks also need to pay systematic approach to customers' learning processes and adopt their tutorials and other training material according to the learning needs of their customers.

Channel Integration

Services distribution channels for banks have evolved over a long time driven primarily by need, changes in regulations, market environment and technological advances. Before the arrival of e-banking, the need for channel integration was rarely on top of the management agenda. But now that financial institutions are juggling numerous channels and ways in which they communicate with customers, banks need to integrate these channels in more pro-active ways. Furthermore, banks need to invest in a consistent and seamless customer experience across all channels, which requires integration of real-time cross-channel communications.

Usage of the major delivery channels is split and changes with time. Branches and ATMs remain the most heavily used channels but e-banking is also gaining ground, although many online customers still also use other channels. All channels are useful to customers for the specific purpose each serves. For example, e-banking may be good for checking balance or transferring funds between different accounts, ATMs for withdrawing cash and branches for discussing mortgages and so on. The demographic details of different channel users is also changing as more and more older customers also begin to use multiple channels, following the lead from younger counterparts.

In the electronic goods industry, some large retailers such as www.argos.co.uk, allow customers to buy products online and then pick them up at the nearest store location. Generally speaking, banks have not been able to deliver this level of service because different products are offered in different channels and with no real interface to unite the systems (Feig, 2006).

Banks need to build integrated channels that facilitate customer information and process flows which will enable them to achieve the operational efficiencies they expected from the implementation of e-banking. But most banks need to deal with the problem of legacy architectures which are not easy to integrate. Legacy systems are very inflexible so maintaining them is also time-consuming, prone to error, and expensive.

As discussed in the previous chapter, one of the best approaches to achieving multichannel integration is service-oriented architecture (SOA). SOA can be used as a platform for all IT operations/applications. This type of platform can provide many benefits including: customer responsiveness, operational efficiency, cost savings by reducing errors, easier future growth and quicker project life cycles as SOA enables to re-use services (computer programmes) that may have been developed for other parts of an organisations. SOA enabled channel integration can help banks to utilize data spread across many systems and turn it into comprehensive, meaningful and useful information available for use by staff who need it.

In addition, banking rules change constantly, due to regulatory and other pressures, and making these changes is usually very expensive from an IT point of view. An SOA based platform can help reduce these costs because these changes only need be done once and applied across all channels (Feig, 2006)

When implementing e-banking an acute feeling of competition between distribution channels can result. For example, staff at bank branches may fear branch closures, or staff at a telephone banking call centre may feel that their jobs will no longer exist in future if e-banking is implemented. These conceptions can easily intensify if special incentives are introduced to promote one channel (maybe at the expense of other). Again a comprehensive approach to managing these conceptions is required which, if carried out properly, can result in different channels actively promoting each other. For example, call centres can be used to support both e-banking and branch banking. This also helps in creating an integrated feel for customers, many of whom may like to interact with multiple channels rather than just one. One useful approach in this regard is to provide opportunities for managers to work (maybe on short term basis) in a different channel to facilitate mutual understanding. Rhee and Mehra (2006) argue that when managers proactively participate in each other's functional activities, it can create a harmonious environment thereby minimizing hostile actions detrimental to a banks' performance.

Creating Flexibility in Organizations

Organizational flexibility has long been considered, in the literature, as a precondition to enhanced productivity and profitability of ICT (Soh et al, 1997). For example, one of the reasons for the success of First Direct, the fully online British bank, is based on its flexible organization (Zollinger, 1999). Flexibility in this context may be defined as an organization's ability to rapidly re-organise itself when needed. Flexibility in an organization can be created by using a number of the change management tactics discussed above. In general, organizations with flatter structures show more flexibility than those with a large number of hierarchies. Similarly organizations with modern computer systems can respond to change faster than those organizations still using legacy systems.

Managing Internal Adoption

A number of factors contribute to success or failure of e-banking adoption within an organization. These factors include a company's commitment to e-banking leadership of this initiative and involvement of stakeholders in the full process, from planning to actual implementation. Executives need to have a good understanding of the fast changing capabilities for related technologies and adjust their e-banking functionalities according to the business need, and communicate the value of e-banking throughout the organization. E-banking also requires systematic attention to organizational learning processes, organizational structure/culture, and technology infrastructure. A summary of critical success factors in adoption of e-banking is given in Table 5.2. It presents a classification of success factors into three major categories: strategic, structural, and management-oriented factors.

These factors suggest that to realize the full benefits of e-banking, organizations need to develop a suitable vision for the firm, appoint an e-banking champion who owns the transformation process, create a collaborative organizational culture and implement a rigorous communication strategy to reduce resistance amongst employees and customers.

MANAGING RELATIONSHIPS WITH CUSTOMERS

Managers responsible for managing relationships with customers in an e-banking context often walk on an unchartered territory with little to guide them on how to manage relationships with a customer whom you may never see or speak to. This section discusses some of the ways this can be managed.

To start with, mangers need to know that it is not just the technologically sophisticated or affluent consumers who are using e-banking and there is link between the consumer's technological sophistication and their financial sophistication. Therefore managers need to understand and cater for a wide variety of customers' segments. Time and experience is needed for customers to adjust to new types of risks and word-of-mouth recommendations are still a powerful influence on people's behavior towards risks associated with e-banking. Some people need extra counseling before buying an online product due to their inability to understand complex financial products or technology. This should be available by in the form

Table 5.2. Summary of major success factors for e-banking (adapted from Dubelaar et al., 2005)

Strategic factors	Structural factors	Management-oriented factors
• Internet and related technologies used as a complement to the existing strategies • Basis of competition not shifted from traditional competitive advantages such as cost, profit, quality, service, and brand name • New competitors and market shares tracked • Web specific marketing strategy • Company's image and strategic position in the market strengthened • Buyer behavior intelligence gathering and services personalization • Good products and services offered • Innovation facilitated • Customer's and partner's expectations from the web well-managed	• Right technological infra-structure • Good e-banking education and training to employees, management, and customers • Current systems expanded to cover entire supply chain • Good cost control	• Organization-wide commitment to e-banking leadership (in terms of roles, responsibilities, budget matters, cross-functional interdependencies) • Support for e-banking from top management • Awareness and understanding of capabilities of technology by executives • Communication of the e-banking value throughout the organization by top management

of customer services over the phone. Banks also need to be aware that new users of e-banking are likely to be most exposed to technology related risks. Most common of these include (FSA, 2008):

- Ordering a product or service twice when only once was intended;
- Not knowing how to navigate a web-site and thereby missing important information;
- Not understanding how to minimize security risks on-line; and
- Not realizing that an agreement may be binding even though a written document has not been physically signed.

Mols (2000) suggests that the Internet changes the way a bank interacts with its customers in the way they initiate, develop and terminate relationship. One of the key success factors of e-banking is an organization's ability to successfully manage its internal relationships as well as those with customers and suppliers such as technology vendors. Management of internal factors is discussed above. This section discusses some of the ways in which a relationship with customers can be enhanced. One way of doing this is utilising banks' existing call centres to build rich relationships. If the call centre can respond to other forms of queries such as emails, they become a 'contact centre' rather than just a 'call centre' (Bruno-britz, 2006).

If these 'contact centres' are equipped with data mining and Customer Relationship Management (CRM) systems they can be used to track customer's preferences and enrich relationships with existing customers, therefore increasing the products per customer ratio, as well developing new products to acquire new customers. In practice it needs a database system which is able to hold data from external sources, and integrated with all banking applications. Various software tools are needed to collect this data, process it to turn it into usable information and delivering it to the point where it is needed such as the CRM system or sales force. Needs of modern customers are unstable and constantly changing so it is important that these systems are able to monitor individual customer preferences and update the database on a real-time basis. If this kind of integrated system can be implemented, and some banks have achieved it, it becomes possible to target individual customers with greater accuracy and to come close to niche marketing.

Integrated systems therefore make it possible to employ a number of marketing concepts like niche marketing, database marketing, micro marketing, interactive marketing, relationship marketing and mass customization. Srirojanant & Thirkell (1998) argue that these modern approaches to marketing are far reaching, and satisfy the needs of individual consumers more effectively and efficiently than traditional marketing approaches. If used properly these approaches can be used to fully utilize the opportunities offered by the Internet.

Another possible use of modern technologies to serve customers better is utilizing internet picture telephone/video conferencing to offer one-to-one discussion and advice. Dannenberg and Kellner (1998) argue that person-to-person counseling through the Internet can mimic face-to-face counseling at a branch office, except that the Internet is cheaper, faster and more convenient. Similarly Aladwani (2001) describes how the Internet combined with a customer database (described above) may be used for identifying and recommending new products to complement previous customer purchases, or to offer price discounts to customers who have shown an interest in a particular product but have not yet purchased it. In this way, Internet banking may be used for strengthening cross-selling and price differentiation. Rust and Oliver (1994) argue that the use of video-based interactions in the communication with customers will actually improve customer services, customer satisfaction monitoring and complaint handling. Therefore the banks offering these services may be able to forge a closer relationships with the customers.

Another method of enriching relationships with customers (Mols, 2000) is the development of virtual communities. A virtual community is an Internet based group of users, who share a common interest. The members of a virtual community usually contact each other by different communication platforms such as: newsgroups, web forums, web chat, online notice boards and blogs. Banks can use this to facilitate discussion between its customers and as a result improve its services.

The richness of the website content is important factor in attracting a sharply growing number of websites visitors and commercial users. Many banks usually feed their websites with contents such as corporate profile, product and pricing information, interest rates, and some applications forms. However they need to look beyond usual contents and make their websites far richer to attract larger numbers of visitors. For example, some financial services firms are already experimenting with offering community bulletin board and discount shopping services as an added 'community benefit'.

The development of integrated, customised financial services is becoming an active area of competition between financial sector organizations. Consumers do not want to navigate from website to website to keep track of their finances. Web based services have to be more convenient, easier to use, and less expensive than the alternative to win the loyalty of consumers. This type of real-time integration of distributed resources is, after all, one of the greatest potential advantages of e-banking. It is not that easy, for many of the key players in banking and finance today to provide the necessary links to the back-end systems because these so called legacy systems were not built with integration in mind. Importance of upgrading old technological infrastructure (which still depends on slow and fragmented legacy systems in some cases) to bring it up to the speed with e-Commerce. Technology failures lead to lost customers, often forever. Any bank hoping to make a success-ful future in online banking must test the technology thoroughly before releasing it for customers' access.

The internet makes it easier for customers to search and compare a wide variety of products and services. The banking sector was one of the first affected by this, as most of its products and services can be digitised. This has fuelled a healthy competition between different financial products suppliers, resulting in erosion of profits. The winner in this competitive environment will be those banks which make an effort to understand their customer needs and tailor their products/services to serve those needs. Another aspect of this new reality is that some organizations have invested too heavily in Internet technologies in anticipation of the benefits it may offer, and have failed to realised these benefits simply because the market wasn't ready. On the other hand some managers resisted the need for change and chose to ignore this phenomenon, and were left struggling when the technologies became competitive. Having a balanced view of these issues together with proper cost/benefit analysis can help in achieving a balanced approach.

To maintain relationship with different segments of customers banks should use the Internet as an additional channel of distribution and should keep their traditional channels such as branches and phone banking intact. This gives the banks the op-portunity for a gentle transition from a branch banking strategy to an e-banking strategy, and it provides good market coverage. It is also a way for bank managers to hedge their bets by making a number of smaller investments in the e-banking systems while simultaneously continuing a traditional branch banking strategy. However, this dual strategy may lead to conflicts between the e-banking channel and branch banking.

Winning Customer Trust

One of the biggest obstacle in the growth of e-commerce is the lack of trust many people feel when they conduct transactions online. Developing a trustworthy online brand is a strategic as well as a managerial challenge. This section will discuss what managers can do to win customer trust. Trust in e-banking is much more important than in some other areas of e-commerce simply because of the potential for greater damage if a customer is subject to an online fraud.

Traditionally, trust in an online environment generally meant a secure website, but according to Chankar et al (2002) perceptions of online trust have steadily evolved from being a construct involving security and privacy issues on the Internet, to a multidimensional, complex construct that includes reliability/credibility, emotional comfort and quality for multiple stakeholders such as employees, suppliers, distributors and regulators, in addition to customers.

Different stakeholders have different perspectives of online trust. From a customer viewpoint, a Web site may need to be trustworthy for doing business and getting a reliable product or service. According to Chankar et al. (2002) most customers would be primarily concerned with questions such as how trustworthy is the firm's Web site for doing business, making purchases, getting customer information, and getting service? How safe is the transaction and my personal/company information that I give on the Web site? How comfortable do I feel in my online experiences with the firm?

From a supplier perspective, the key requirements may be efficiency, preservation of confidentiality and the firms' "worthiness" for online collaboration. Employees may be concerned with accuracy of the information available to them. A distributor or an intermediary such as an independent financial advisor might be concerned about the timeliness and completeness of information about products. Financial regulators would like to know whether the website complies with relevant laws, privacy regulations and security regulations, and whether the bank website has reliable and fair mechanisms for addressing failures in the provision of accurate data, product delivery or any other violation of regulations. This means that trust online spans the end-to-end aspects of e-business rather than being just based on the electronic storefront or website.

The issue of online trust building can be addressed in a number of ways. To start with a professional customer advisor in a dedicated call centre can do a lot to inspire confidence. When a stakeholder knows that somebody will be there to speak to if anything goes wrong in an online environment, he/she will have confidence in conducting financial transactions online. Other factors such as keeping product/delivery promises, providing unbiased comparisons with competitor's products, giving detailed product information, and providing tools such as financial calculators to enable a customer to play what-if type scenarios also helps. Customers also need assurances that their liability in the event of things going wrong would be limited.

In an online environment, having visible (on website) endorsements from third parties, such as large companies or financial regulators, helps facilitate trust. Historical data is also important: if a company can truthfully claim that it has sold 20000 online mortgages during last three months, it strengthens the customer belief in company's Internet procedures. Other important issues, which will require different organizations such as retailers, regulators, and other intermediaries to work together, include having clear and fair refund policies, clear pricing (e.g. interest rate) policies, and so on.

Human Resources Management

Human resources management is a key factor of in the success in e-banking. E-banking HR requires special skills because HR functions such as (HR) planning, job analysis and job design, recruitment and selection, job progression, appraisal process, training, and compensation would be different than for other traditional business areas. Often, e-banking professionals need special skills and as a result they are still in short supply and nature of e-banking operations also changes much quicker than other business functions so e-banking brings special set of challenges for HR as well as other managers. To succeed in this, managers much recognize the inherent differences between e-business and traditional bricks-and-mortar business and adapt to these changes.

The most obvious changes for human resources may include the need to identify employees with skills different from those found in more traditional organizations. People working in e-banking often are doing jobs that did not exist before and are working in an organization or division that did not exist before. Therefore, basic human resource problems are exaggerated for e-banking environments. For a typical e-banking project, HR need to recruit employees with a wide range of skills, such as:

- Technical staff like Web architects and designers, infrastructure specialists, Web developers, Web site managers, Internet security experts, and a team administrator.
- Business-focused staff like content experts for marketing or sales and specialists like Web graphics designers.
- IT-related staff such as programmers and analysts.
- Managerial staff for strategic planning, relationship management, project management, content creation/management, and process integration.

In addition to above specific skills, knowledge, aptitudes, and other characteristics (KSAO's) are desirable and combined in a proper way so they can work together to accomplish the desired goals. Since e-banking staff are in short supply, skills that are in short supply must be used most efficiently (Mitchell, 2001). For example, Some non-IT tasks (such as report writing, routine coding, and systems administration) can be shifted to non-IT staff so that the IT staff can have more time to use their skills efficiently. A good understanding of these job roles, skills and issues would be required to recruit, retain, organize and develop an e-banking department or team.

Another reason for change in HR functions is that E-banking expertise is rare and employees with relevant skills are aware that they easily can find an attractive job in an active job market where their skills are highly valued. Problems in HR could mean that organizations loose these valuable employees. A related HR problem concerns organizational design. Some firms find that the changes resulting from e-banking can only be best managed by a new organizational design. Some choose to create a separate "online unit" division that handles the e-banking operations. This separate entity usually is expected to be integrated onto the rest of the operation after time. These separate entities often have a more entrepreneurial culture which is suitable for online business operations so they are better able than their parent companies to attract the type of talent needed (Mitchell, 2001).

According to Huselid and Becker et al (2000) HR managers can experience a gap between understanding an Internet-based economy and actually adapting their function to make the most of the new economy. Understanding the capability offered by the Internet and designing an HR system to deliver optimal HR services in a digital economy may not be as easy as it sounds. Just like other changes, this change will also needed to be carefully managed. For example, certain HR professionals (especially those who entered the field many years ago) traditionally are not as technology oriented as professionals in areas such as finance or operations and need considerable efforts in terms of training to adapt to the change.

Huselid and Becker (2000) suggest that to do well in the digital economy, HR needs to build new organizational capabilities, rather than focusing on existing structures or hierarchies. These new capabilities may include flexible corporate DNA and culture, shared mindset, firm equity or brand, key success factors, or processes. These capabilities are necessary whether e-banking is a small part of the business or constitute a whole business.

Greengard (2000) suggested seven guidelines for HR managers who want move at the speed necessary for managing human resources for online businesses:

1. Understand the fact that the online business is very different from other types of business. It requires learning new ways to communicate, creative thinking and less bureaucracy. The Internet creates new business opportunities but potential benefits can only be achieved if people are ready to move quickly and effectively utilize them.

2.   Obtain the support of senior management. To do it HR managers will have to justify the need for specific changes and clearly communicate the possible benefits of these changes.

3.   Successful e-banking is multi-disciplinary and relies on participation from different departments, so a multi-disciplinary HR team is also need to reflect the range of expertise and business knowledge. Team members must be able to communicate effectively and understand the differences in requirements of other team members. For example a marketing manager should have good idea of technical issues involved and vice versa to be able to contribute positively. Decisions must be made quickly, and put into actions swiftly.

4.   Use different Return-On-Investment (ROI) calculations than traditional ones. Many initiatives in e-banking are new so it is difficult to measure the ROI objectively. Potential long term benefits should be taken into account along with hard financial figures.

5.   Work with all departments within an organization to make good business decisions. Working closely with these departments will enable HR to collect information to see the effect of various decisions on the whole organization, not only HR or e-banking.

6.   Create an IT system that is flexible and scalable so that it supports the operations at a quicker pace.

7.   Do not let fear of mistakes or failure slow decisions and actions. The best systems may include mistakes (especially at early stages). Organisations should expect that the increased desire for speed will result in some mistakes and develop some tolerance to accommodate it. The fear of making these mistakes should not prevent action. HR functions should continuously analyze itself and organizational conditions and making any necessary changes whenever required.

For a service such as e-banking whose product involves personal interaction, strategies to achieve competitive advantage needs to take HR as a key function and implementing some of the relevant strategies suggested above to do well is a key cornerstone of success in e-banking.

MANAGING EXTERNAL RELATIONSHIPS MARKETING AND SALES

In addition to building trust in an online environment, managers have to tailor their marketing strategies to suit e-services. This section presents a number of issues related to marketing and sales of online banking services.

Traditionally, both direct and mass marketing, were aimed at a large number of customers, but the arrival of the interactive channels such as e-banking has changed the marketing dynamics. New marketing paradigms are about allowing customers to browse, explore and compare products before a marketing message is customised to suit their needs. Table 5.3 shows a comparison of different modes of marketing and shows an emphasis on customised/relationship marketing

Talha et al. 2004 argue that dramatic changes in marketing have resulted in an addition to the traditional "4 Ps" (Price, Product, Place, Promotion): 'Personalization' which means the process of customizing products according to a customer's needs, has become a cornerstone of marketing efforts. In addition the nature of traditional Ps has changed significantly.

New pricing strategies need to be much more sensitive to the market place as any unjustifiable price increase can damage a company's reputation, especially since price comparisons are much easier. At the same time subtle changes in pricing which are sensitive to the online market place can be made on a dynamic basis to suit different target markets (market segments). As illustrated in Table 5.4 below, the Internet enables banks greater precision in setting prices, more flexibility/adaptability in terms of responding to market changes, and the ability to gather richer information for effective market segmentation.

The second P of new marketing strategy is e-Products or e-services. Banking services can be modified or developed from scratch in matter of days to respond to the dynamic market place. This also has resulted in shortened life cycles of financial products, and many banks are offering new services or withdrawing weak products much more frequently than in the past. This means that the process of traditional product development needs to change considerably to accommodate this new requirement of dynamic flexibility.

Table 5.3. Comparison of different marketing approaches (adapted from Kalakota & Whinston, 1997)

	Mass Marketing	Direct Marketing	Interactive Marketing
Distribution Channel	Broadcast and print media (consumer is passive)	Postal service using mailing lists (consumer is passive)	The Internet (consumer is active and is the catalyst for what is shown on screen)
Market Strategy (and sample product)	High volume (food, beer, autos, personal and home-care products)	Targeted goods (credit cards, travel, subscriptions)	Targeted audience (services and all types of product information provided)
Enabling Technology	Storyboards and desktop publishing	Databases and statistical tools	Information servers, client browsers, bulletin boards, and software agents
Authors of Marketing Material	Advertising agencies	Advertising agencies and companies	Companies and consumers
Expected Outcome from Successful Implementation	Volume sales	Bounded sales, data for analysis	Date for analysis, customer relationships, new product ideas, volume sales

New types of services also enhance the ability of an organization to bundle related products on the basis of individual needs. With the Internet, bundling of information is easy because of hyperlink and other related capabilities. Bundling is a sales approach in which two or more complementary services are offered as a bundle at a discounted price (Talha et al., 2004). In e-banking context, an example of bundling could be offering discounted mortgage rates to existing current account holders.

Third P of marketing mix, Personalisation, has also changed due to the arrival of online services. The nature of financial products and the process of product/service development is changing rapidly due to the dynamic nature of online trade. Now it is possible to create so much flexibility in a product/service that customers can customise it, within pre-defined limits, to meet their exact needs. Advanced databases/data mining tools, internet cookies which provide detailed insights into a customer's behaviour when they conduct their financial activities, and new communication technologies make it easy and cost –efficient to mass market personalized services, because the whole process of personalization can be automated.

Mass customization is defined by Papathanassiou (2004) as the use of flexible processes and organizational structures to produce varied and often individually customized products and services at the low cost of a standardized, mass-production system. He further proposed a number of actions (See Table 5.5) to achieve mass customization in service sector.

A generic classification of Mass Customization approaches is given by Gilmore and Pine, (1997):

a. The collaborative customization approach suggests conducting an interactive dialogue with customers to help them specify their requirements, to identify the suitable offerings and customize the services to meet those requirements. This approach is useful when there is a wide range of products or services available to choose from.

Table 5.4. Internet pricing strategy sources (adapted from Baker et al., 2001)

	Source of value from the Internet	Conditions for Selection
Precision	• Greater precision in setting right price • Better understanding of zone of price indifference	• Testing needs to be run large number of transactions to be significant
Adaptability	• Speed of price change • Ease of response to external shocks to the system	• Inventory or capacity is perishable • Demand fluctuates over time
Segmentation	• Ability to choose creative and accurate segmentation dimensions • Ease in identifying which segment a buyer belongs • Ability to create barriers between segments	• Different customers value your products' benefits differently • Customer profitability varies widely

b.   The adaptive customization approach implies that an organization offers a standard but customizable product which is developed so that customers can modify it according to their needs. Dell's offering of customized PCs fall into this category. Many insurance companies are following this model.

c.   The cosmetic customization approach suggests that a standard product is presented differently to different customers. Scope for customization is limited in this model but product/service characteristics are advertised in different manners to appeal different audiences.

d.   The transparent customization approach implies that organization should provide individual customers with unique products and services. This approach is useful when customer requirements are clear or in case of high value services where each product can be modified before delivery.

The fourth P of the e-marketing mix, Promotion, has perhaps changed most. Traditional promotional campaigns used to rely on branch, newspaper and radio/TV advertising. However new advertising mediums such as Internet banners, mobile texting and interactive marketing have significantly changed promotion operations. Some banks such as the Woolwich in the U.K. has found Internet based interactive marketing much more effective than traditional advertising. The financial services industry is one of the biggest spenders on online ads (Gonsalves, 2006). Gonsalves points out that with consumers spending as much time online as watching TV (a median of 14 hours a week) the shift of advertising budgets to the Internet advertising is inevitable.

Internet marketing takes various forms. Firstly there is the mass broadcasting model, in which direct emails or interactive TV is used to broadcast an advertis-

Table 5.5. Recommended actions for the development of mass customization (adapted from Papathanassiou, 2004)

- adopt business models that reflect the interdependencies between services and resources such as IT infrastructure, employees' knowledge and customers' requirements as well as their purchasing behavior.
- Develop a modular IT applications architecture, such as Service Oriented Architecture (SOA), with each IT module supporting product and services' across an organization. This will increase the degree of reusability and flexibility of technological capabilities
- Re-engineer the business processes to support the integration of the varius channels of organizations with their customers taking into consideration issues such as flexibility and reusability which are needed for implementing mass customization.
- Utilize the potential of the Internet for mass customization. Innovation should be encouraged to find new ways of using the Internet as a marketing tool.
- Prepare customers to support mass customization, so that organizations will gain their support for collaboration
- Facilitate planning for mass customization that would also engage IS, business staff and key employees.
- Implement employees' training programs in various aspects of e-marketing and mass customization

ing message. The target audience depends on availability of email addresses or viewing numbers for a particular program on TV. This type of marketing can use multimedia contents, but the message has to be very brief as long messages will not get the desired results. One main drawback of direct emailing is increasing spam and junk mail which can turn customers away.

The fifth P of e-marketing, Place, is has had many of its key features changed over the last decade or so. Traditionally most services were delivered via bank branches. This system worked well for large banks as it was difficult for smaller banks to get full access to the market and for new players to enter into the financial market due to the high cost associated with developing or maintaining a branch network. The arrival of e-banking has changed this. Now it is relatively easy for smaller banks to offer their services countrywide or even worldwide. Entry barriers to financial market have diminished significantly, so that organizations with a much smaller base of resources/skills such as supermarkets have started offering their own financial services.

Changes in all the Ps discussed above has resulted in a greater emphasis on interactive marketing. Interactive marketing is not just about promotion of products to customers by the suppliers but also includes customer interaction with each other via email, chat room, electronic bulletin boards and virtual communities. According to Talha et al., (2004) these new types of interactions create innovative relationships between consumers, marketers and suppliers of products and services. These relationship can enable exchange of an unprecedented flow of information in all directions. Effective exploitation of this information and its flow might be the main source of competitive advantage in future. This could especially be true of financial services owing to fast changing customer needs, high diversification of products and leadership in technological innovations.

Many financial sector organizations now use the Internet to gather customer-specific information based on previous interactions and they are using this information to anticipate new product needs. In addition, there is a growing realisation among banks that the Internet has forever changed the traditional paradigm of marketing and remote customer contact. This made it possible to focus on building relationships with individual customers and to make direct and personalised contact with each customer.

Another aspect of successful e-marketing is brand management. Owing to security issues and perceived fraud threats many customers only deal with trusted brands in online environments. For this reason, well established banks often outperform new Internet only banks. For new entrants to the e-banking market, building a trusted brand may therefore require considerable effort and resources. To build a new e-brand, an appropriate logo & key message should be developed. Customers can be focused on a range of services related to the site. Usage can be made accessible and easy to operate. To build trust in a new brand, banks need to take a number of steps which are described in an earlier section. Building an e-brand is not just a management challenge, all levels of the organizations, its customers and intermediaries need to be involved in this process. Verma & Agarwal (2004) propose an outline, summarised in Table 5.6, of what each level of management should do to effectively contribute in e-brand development.

Understanding the customers of a virtual organization can be a major challenge, which is even more of a concern to start ups.

REGULATIONS MANAGEMENT

Financial services are regulated by various regulatory bodies around the world. Typically the main objectives of regulatory bodies may include:

a.   Maintaining market confidence;
b.   Promoting understanding of the financial system;
c.   Protecting consumers against frauds and privacy violations; and
d.   Reducing financial crime.

Regulators play a vital role in the delivery of financial services regardless of the channel used, and are taking a keen interest in e-banking related developments owing to the new opportunities this channel has brought for the financial sector and the new threats to organizations and customers. For this reason many regulatory bodies have set up consultation committees and are developing new regulations to address e-banking specifically. One problem is that e-banking is evolving very rapidly, and to keep pace with it new regulations are coming into force on almost monthly basis. This in turn has made the task of regulations management even more challenging.

Managers involved in e-banking, whether it is development of e-products or e-marketing or delivery, need to be aware of relevant regulations to ensure compliance. Many banks employ specialist staff to ensure compliance with regulations. Although financial regulators are generally 'technologically neutral' there are some exception such as Union's Electronic Commerce Directive (ECD). One consequence of this Directive is that the requirements which a service provider from one EU Member State has to meet in a non-face-to-face interaction with a United Kingdom client may depend on the technology used. This implies that if the telephone or post is used, the marketing and disclosure requirements will be those of the country where the recipient of the service is based. If the same service is made available via a web-site or by e-mail, the service will be governed by the ECD, and the requirements will, with certain exceptions, be those of the country where the provider of the service is based. Where a firm uses both on and off-line channels the Directive will apply to the on-line channels and not to the off-line ones (FSA Report on E-commerce,

Table 5.6. Showing roles of the three levels of management in developing e-brands (Verma & Agarwal, 2004).

Factor	Top Management	Middle Management	Lower Management
Downloading speed	Norms	Technical strategy	Implementation techniques
Logo and Punch line	Mission, vision and objective statements	Communication objectives	Advertising Campaign
Range of Services	Defining market orientation	Developing strategic gamut of the services	Synergizing the various services under a single umbrella
User Friendliness	Consumer orientation	Research input and strategy for prioritizing consumer concerns.	Technical support
Layout of the site	Organizational structure and strategic framework	Aligning technical support with marketing objectives	Technical layout, testing and implementation
Site? Positioning	Corporate strategy with hints of Marketing strategy	Marketing objectives and related positioning strategy	Communicating the positioning strategy
Image of the site	Corporate image	Brand image	Communicating image related facts
Security policy	Factors of Security considered	Technical aspects of security policy	Implementation and communication of the same to the consumers
Brand Personality	Corporate personality statement	Brand personality statement	Communication tactics related to brand personality
Name relevance	Branding strategy	Brand taxonomy	Creating awareness of brand name
Online promotion	Corporate promotion strategy	Brand promotion strategy	Creative communication tactics
Offline promotion	Corporate promotion strategy	Brand promotion strategy	Creative communication tactics

2001). These types of e-commerce-specific regulations exist in other parts of the world, and e-banking managers need to be aware of them.

When it comes to global e-banking, the regulatory situation is even more complicated. The internet is global medium, and in theory many banks should be able to offer their services to customers in other countries, but legal and regulatory obstacles means that this type of trade is difficult in practice. For example, in any cross-border provision of financial services, it is possible both for the country where the firm is based and for the country where a customer is based to assert regulatory jurisdiction. So both countries face the issue of whether they will both seek to regulate the firm, product or activity or whether they will divide responsibilities between them in some way. This requires global co-operation between governments and financial services authorities to harmonize core standards and to streamline supervision across the world. Co-operation takes place on a bilateral basis between regulators, and on a multi-lateral basis in forums such as the Basel Committee, International Organization of Securities Commissions (IOSCO), International Association of Insurance Supervisors (IAIS), and various EU committees.

The Basel Committee's importance to the banking sector makes it worthy of further explanation. It is a committee of the International Regulations Bank and the G10 Nations, responsible for guaranteeing the international stability of the banking system, the safety of depositors, banks, shareholders and the whole economy, and for setting univocal rules for all banks. The Basel Committee E-Banking Group identified some important issues such as: authorisation, prudential standards, transparency, privacy, money laundering, and cross border supervision. Details of these recommendations may be found at http://www.bis.org/publ/bcbs28c.htm and other related websites.

International co-operation often focuses on issues of policy, the supervision of individual firms, the investigation of potential wrongdoing and taking enforcement action. Despite these efforts the dream of international unified standards seems far away, and managers have to deal with multiple sets of regulations.

CHAPTER SUMMARY

This chapter covered a number of challenges and issues faced by managers when offering financial services online. We discussed consumer issues, employee management, some aspects of project management. E-marketing and how it helps in e-banking was covered in detail, as was the ways in which banks can win online customer trust.

Online trust is important to a firm's e-banking initiative. Although trust in e-banking shares many common elements with offline trust, it is different in that technology rather than just the organizational entity is an object of trust. The consequences of breach of trust include loss of stakeholder satisfaction, loyalty and ultimately loss of customers. We also discussed how management of financial regulations is a necessary but challenging task, especially in an e-banking environment, and have suggested some of the ways in which compliance issues can be managed.

Information Security management is a another area covered in this chapter. Information security in e-banking is very much dominated by technologically–biased, operationally–focused, pragmatic controls. Human considerations are largely ignored, so we have suggested an approach informed by social theory. The approach gains its credibility from an explicit basis in social theory, from which an evaluative model and method of implementation have been crafted.

REFERENCES

Aladwani, A. (2001). Online banking: a field study of drivers, development challenges and expectations." *International Journal of Information Management, 21*(3), 213-25.

Appleton, E. L. (1997, March). How to Survive ERP. *Datamation*, (pp. 50-53).

Awamleh, C., & Fernandes, C. (2006). Diffusion of Internet Banking amongst educated consumers in a high income non-OECD country. *Journal of Internet Banking and Commerce, 11*(3). http://www.doaj.org/doaj?func=abstract&id=207835

Ayadi, A. (2006, April). Technological and organizational preconditions to Internet Banking implementation: Case of a Tunisian bank. *Journal of Internet Banking and Commerce, 11*(1), Retrieved May 12, 2007, from http://www.arraydev.com/commerce/jibc/

Baker, W., Marn, M., & Zawada, C (2001, February). Price Smarter on the Net. *Harvard Business Review.*

Bareil, C. (2002). *Managing Resistance to Change or Readiness to Change?* http://web.hec.ca/sites/ceto/fichiers/04_02.pdf

Becher, B., Huselid, M., & Ulrich, D. (2001). *The HR Scorecard: Linking People, Strategy, and Performance.* Boston: Harvard Business School Press.

Blount, Y., Castleman, T., & Swatman, P. (2005 Spring). E-Commerce, Human Resource Strategies, and Competitive Advantage: Two Australian Banking Case Studies. *International Journal of Electronic Commerce, 9*(3) 74–89. Retrieved June 22, 2008, from http://mesharpe.metapress.com/app/home/contribution. asp?referrer=parent&backto= issue,6,8;journal,14,32;linkingpublicationresult s,1:106045,1

Bruno-Britz, M. (2006, January 3.). Opportunity Calling: Banks finally are realizing the contact center's potential as a relationship-building resource and profit center. *Bank Systems & Technology.*

Chesher, M., & Kaura, R. (1998). *Electronic Commerce and Business Communications.* London: Springer.

Clarke, S. A. (2007). *Information Systems Strategic Management: An Integrated Approach, Second Edition.* London: Routledge.

Dannenberg, M., & Kellner, D. (1998). The bank of tomorrow with today's technology, *International Journal of Bank Marketing, 16*(2) 90-7.

Dewan, R., & Seidmann, A. (2001). Current issues in e-banking, *Communications of the ACM*, June, *44*(5), 31-32.

Dubelaar, C. Sohal, A., & Savic, V. (2005). Benefits, impediments and critical success factors in B2C: E-business adoption. *Technovation, 25*, 1251–1262.

Feig, N. (2006, November 1). Integrating the Channels: Banks are turning to multichannel integration to deliver seamless customer service, boost speed to market and increase organic growth. *Bank Systems & Technology.*

FSA (2008). *E-commerce Regulations*. Retrieved June 22, 2008, from http://www.fsa.gov.uk

Gilmore, J. H., & Pine, B.J. (1997). The four faces of mass-customization: . *Harvard Business Review*, (January-February) (pp. 91-101).

Gonsalves, A. (2006, November 06). Financial services among top four industries to spend big on online ads. *InformationWeek.* http://www.informationweek.com/news/showArticle.jhtml?articleID=193600020. Accessed June 12, 2008.

Greengard, S. (2000). Net gains to HR technology. *Workforce, 79*(4), 44-48.

Greenland, S. J. (1994). Rationalization and Restructuring in the Financial Services Sector. *International Journal of Retail & Distribution Management, 22*(6), 21-28.

Huselid, M. A., & Becker, B. E. (2000). Comment on measurement error in research on human resources and firm performance: how much error is there and how does it influence effect size estimates? *Personnel Psychology, 53*(4), 835–854.

IBM Global Services (2001). E-business Strategies for Conventional Insurers. *IBM White Paper,* http://www-5.ibm.com/services/uk/pdf/e-bus-strat.pdf

Jayawardhena, C., & Foley, P. (2000). Changes in the banking. Sector: the case of Internet banking in the UK. *Internet Research: Electronic Networking Applications and Policy, 10*(1), 19-30.

Kalakota, R., & Robinson, M. (1999). *e-Business, Roadmap for Success,* Addison-Wesley, Reading, USA.

Kalakota, R., & Whinston, A. B. (1997). *Electronic Commerce: a Manager's Guide,* Reading, MA: Addison-Wesley.

Kuisma, T., Laukkanen, T., & Hiltunen, M. (2007). Mapping the reasons for resistance to Internet banking: A means-end approach. *International Journal of Information Management, 27*, 75–85.

Losey, M., Meisinger, S., & Ulrich, D. (2005). *The Future of Human Resource Management: 64 Thought Leaders.* http://books.google.co.uk/books?id=1m0i_YK PDNwC&pg=PA224&lpg=PA224&dq=ulrich+2001+Human+resource+issues+.& source=web&ots=yu6FUCcHk_&sig=EH4at69Ph7IvDJrye7pEkcMXJq8&hl=en& sa=X&oi=book_result&resnum=1&ct=result#PPP1,M

Mitchell, M.E. (2001). Human resource issues and challenges for e-business. *American International College Journal of Business.* http://www.encyclopedia. com/doc/1G1-82256136.html

Mols, N.P. (2000). The Internet and services marketing ± the case of Danish retail banking. *Internet Research: Electronic Networking Applications and Policy,* 10(1), 7-18.

Morton, R., & Chester, M. (1997) *Transforming the Business: the IT Contribution.* London: McGraw-Hill.

Papathanassiou, E.A. (2004). Mass customisation: management approaches and internet opportunities in the financial sector in the UK. *International Journal of Information Management, 24,* 387–399.

Rhee, M., & Mehra, S. (2006). A strategic review of operations and marketing functions in retail banks. *International Journal of Service Industry Management, 17*(4), 364-379.

Rust, R.T., & Oliver, R.L. (1994). Service Quality. Insights and Managerial Implications from the Frontier. In R.T. Rust & R.L. Oliver (Eds.), *Service Quality. New Directions in Theory and Practice,* (pp.1-20). London: Sage

Chankar, V., Urban, G.L., & Sultan, F. (2002, December). Online trust: a stakeholder perspective, concepts, implications, and future directions. *The Journal of Strategic Information Systems, 11*(3-4), 325-344.

Soh, C., Mah, Q. Y., Gan, F. J., Chew, D., & Reid, E. (1997). The Use of the Internet for Business. *Internet Research: Electronic Networking Applications and Policy, 7*(3), 217-228.

Srirojanant, S., & Thirkell, P. C. (1998, March). *Journal of Market-Focused Management, 3*(1), 23-46. http://www.springerlink.com/content/u3h74873r7n517nk.

Talha, M., Shrivastva, D., Kabra, P., & Salim, A. S. A. (2004). Problems and prospects of internet marketing. *Journal of Internet Banking and Commerce, 9*(1). http:// www.arraydev.com/commerce/jibc/0402-02.htm

Verma, S.Y., & Agarwal, N. (2004). Cyber branding: an exploratory study of virtual organizations. *Journal of Internet Banking and Commerce*, *9*(3). http://www.arraydev.com/commerce/jibc/2004-12/Nikhil.HTM

Zollinger, M. (1999). The influence of gender on attitudes towards money and banking. *Proceedings of Fordham University Conference on the Marketing of Financial Services.* http://www.fordham.edu/cba/pricecenter/Proceedings.2006.pdf#page=33

Chapter VI
Human Involvement and E-Banking

INTRODUCTION

The aim of this chapter is to offer the reader a means by which human involvement in e-banking may be evaluated and improved. At the heart of this problem lies a need to characterise human involvement, since, once the issues are clear, the specific e-banking factors can be related to them in the form of a model. In this chapter we therefore take as our task:

1. What do we mean by human involvement or participation, and how does this compare to the often overwhelmingly technology-based approaches to information systems developments?
2. Where might human involvement be grounded theoretically?
3. How is this theoretical grounding to be taken forward to a set of pragmatic approaches to be applied by practising managers?

Whilst e-banking is a relatively recent phenomenon, the issues outlined above have been the subject of considerable research and practical application over a number of years. Consequently, we will first look at participation from a recent historical perspective, and use this to develop an approach to human involvement which is applicable to the domain of e-banking. Finally, we will present action guidelines for human involvement in e-banking, and describe how these may be used to evaluate and implement e-banking solutions which are true to participative needs.

It is important here to emphasize that this chapter does not seek to cover ground already well trodden elsewhere. Specific approaches to such issues as consumer trust and technology adoption are well covered in other texts, and the technology acceptance model (see, for example, Davis, 1989) will be well known to many readers. Similarly, service quality forms the basis of many user-based studies, most frequently making use of the SERVQUAL framework (Parasuraman et al,1985, 1988, 1993). The aim of this chapter is specifically to look at the deeper social issues which underlie the human side of e-banking, and form a perspective from which any of these human issues may be viewed.

HUMAN INVOLVEMENT

As has been argued earlier in this book, e-banking owes its existence to a revolution in the enabling technologies. In this chapter, however, we are less concerned with the technologies in themselves, and more with how value and advantage may be leveraged from them. To understand the issues here we need to go back to their roots, which lie in the adoption and application of information technology. In the early days of IT, most approaches to its implementation and management focused on the technology (the so-called "technology-based" approach). The sections which follow therefore begin with this, before outlining the more recent human-centred methods which are of such value in e-banking.

The Technology-Based Approach

It has been argued that the design and development of information systems (IS) has been traditionally dominated by technical, problem solving approaches, leading to tensions when the system to be developed is more user based. The need for discovering the requirements of users seems not to be disputed by information systems developers, but is typically achieved by including a user analysis stage within an existing problem solving approach. This approach, inherited from computer systems development, relies primarily on the systems development life cycle (Figure 6.1).

The systems development life cycle is a stage wise or waterfall method, whereby each stage is undertaken in a linear sequence, and in principle requires the completion of one stage before the next is commenced. So, for example, work on system design would not be authorised until the system specification was written and approved. User requirements specification fits uncomfortably into this process, since such requirements are seldom fixed, but change over the life of a project. As can

Figure 6.1. The systems development life cycle

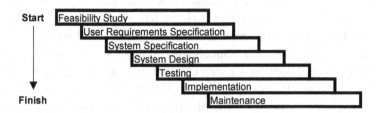

be seen from the following example, there are situations where such an approach is desirable, but care needs to be taken to ensure that the necessary conditions are in place for it to succeed – and e-banking simply does not fit this model.

CASE
EXAMPLE

Computer Systems Development at Litronix Europe

In the early 1980s, Litronix Europe, with a head office in Hitchin, England and a subsidiary north of Munich, Germany, was operating a manual order processing and invoicing system. With a turnover of some 20 million US Dollars, selling electronic components at often just a few pence each, the strain on the stock control system in particular was becoming unmanageable. What was needed was a computerised system, but one which could handle multiple currencies, and product pricing to four decimal places.

The solution was to specify a system, which, it turned out, was written as a bespoke solution. The problem could be clearly stated in terms of inputs (e.g. orders, stock items), constraints (e.g. credit limits, stock holdings), and outputs (e.g. reports, invoices, credit lists). The system to be designed was deterministic: if the inputs were known, the outputs could be predicted with certainty, given the constraints. A technological approach could be taken, and resulted in a successful working system which significantly enhanced the company's business capacity.

This was a classical functionalist solution to a standard business problem, was up and running within a year, and worked pretty well without a hitch: a prime example of the circumstances in which a 'hard' or technology-based approach is likely to prove successful.

A number of methodologies adhere to these principles, through which information systems development is perceived largely as a technology-based, problem solving, engineering task, geared to engineering the best solution to meet a given requirement specification within the known or anticipated constraints.

Technology-Based Approaches: The Problem

The argument for an alternative to these technology-based approaches is supported by the findings from a number of studies of systems failure. Examples range from simple failure to meet performance goals, to catastrophic failure of the type evidenced in the London Ambulance Service and Taurus, the London Stock Exchange System. The British Computer Society has a special interest group which looks at organisational aspects of information technology (OASIG). A study by this group (OASIG 1996) concluded that up to 90% of information technology (IT) investments do not meet the performance goals set for them, and listed the technology-led nature of the process, and the lack of attention to human and organisational factors as key issues in this lack of success.

Beath and Orlykowski (1994) support this view, and mount a convincing critique of the interaction between users and systems professionals in IS, concluding that the concentration on, and commitment to, user participation is revealed as ideological rather than actual, with users frequently shown to be passive rather than active participants in the process. They see the various systems development methodologies as containing 'incompatible assumptions about the role of users and IS personnel during systems development.'

Human-Centered Methods

The limitations of technological approaches to IS gave rise, from the 1960s on, to the so-called 'soft' or human-centered methods. It is argued that traditional 'engineering' approaches are 'hard' or technology-based, being premised on a view of the World which sees it as composed of determinable, rule-based systems. 'Soft' methods, by contrast, take a human-centered stance: issues are seen as determinable only from the viewpoints of human participants. Many examples are available for the use of human-centered approaches to IS, including, for example, soft systems methodology (Checkland & Haynes 1994) and interactive planning (Ackoff 1981), which rely on a more holistic view: to understand an information system, the technology, organisation, and human activity need to be addressed interdependently, not as separate, independent issues.

This recognition of the merits of both 'hard' and 'soft' approaches to IS has further given rise to a number of methods of IS development which may be categorised as mixed (for example: ETHICS (Mumford and Henshall 1978; Mumford 1994), multiview (Wood-Harper, Antill et al. 1985; Watson & Wood-Harper 1995), and client led design (Stowell 1991; Stowell & West 1994)).

The information systems failure example from London Ambulance, outlined below, is a clear example of the need for integration of technical and human issues in an intervention, and the outcomes to be expected when this is inadequately carried out.

CASE
EXAMPLE

**Information Systems Failure
The London Ambulance Service**

The London Ambulance Service (LAS) computer-aided dispatch system failed on October 26 1992, its first day in operation. From its inception, the system had been treated as a technical problem, to which a viable solution could be found. But LAS exhibited social and political dimensions which the technologically based approach proved ill-equipped to address.

A report on the failure (Hamlyn, 1993) makes it clear that implementation of any future system must be supported by a full process of consultation. Whilst the project management, and technical aspects of the implementation, were far short of that which would have been expected for this kind of project, there were in addition a number of 'human' aspects which had been inadequately considered, including poor training and incomplete 'ownership' of the system. The finding by consultants reviewing the failure that 'the computer system itself did not fail in a technical sense ... but ... did what it had been designed to do..', further suggested issues stretching beyond purely technical boundaries.

Following this initial failure, a new computer-aided dispatch system was successfully implemented, but only through an approach which paid heed to the whole system of concern, of which the technical system was just one interactive part.

A clear trend can be discerned here, toward approaches which have the potential to address both technical and human-centered issues within a single intervention. In the next section, a theoretically and practically informed grounding for such an approach is developed and discussed.

INFORMATION SYSTEMS AS SOCIAL SYSTEMS

The conclusion to be drawn is that a view of information systems as a purely technological domain is an inadequate one. Such a perspective reduces the complexity of the system of study, and attempts to define it in terms of rules and procedures by which given inputs can be turned into predictable outputs: a so-called deterministic system. A human-centered approach is quite different. Human activity systems are 'complex' and 'adaptive', and cannot be fully described in terms of rules and procedures: to understand such systems requires recourse to social theory.

Recent work with emergency services, outlined in the example below, serves to highlight some of the benefits to be derived from seeing IS as social systems.

  CASE EXAMPLE	**The Use of Metaphor with Emergency Services in The United Kingdom** The Fire, Police and Ambulance Services in the U.K. operate with a large degree of autonomy, to the extent that, in 2001, I was asked to look at how information is exchanged between the three services.

One of the tasks undertaken as part of this study was a set of brainstorming sessions with key participant groups, using metaphor as the main investigatory technique.

Participants were invited to form self-selected groups, each nominating its own chair and note-taker, with me acting as a facilitator and explicitly not taking on the role of expert. The central issues were stated as:

1. At all levels of the service, how is information exchanged between each of the organisations?'
2. 'At all levels of the service, how ought information to be exchanged between each of the organisations?'

A number of key issues emerged from this which helped guide the future of the study. One key example was that, in spite of massive investment in communication technologies, most operational-level communication used mobile telephones. This was surfaced by one group seeing their operation as 'isolated islands of information, linked by tenuous pieces of wire'; when they should have been 'complex, social, communicative structures with no perceivable barriers to communication.' The interesting fact was that the technology to support the later is already owned by each service, but is not used in the way that those involved in the day to day operation would see as most beneficial.

Furthermore, such a conclusion demonstrates the relevance of this debate to e-banking. In the last twenty years or so, information systems have become more fragmented and distributed, 'user' issues have grown in importance. E-banking represents a highly distributed form of technology-enabled information, in which a disparate user base needs to be catered for. In effect, the social system to be 'served' is gaining ascendancy over the technical system: the later has the task of facilitating or enabling – technology has finally ceased to be an end in itself!

The question to be answered, then, is how this system of concern might best be perceived from a social theoretical perspective.

Many information systems theorists have found the classification presented in Figure 6.2 to be the most applicable categorisation of social theory within the IS domain. This is drawn from original work by Burrell and Morgan (1979), according to whom all social theories can be categorised into one of four paradigms: functionalist, interpretivist, radical humanist and radical structuralist. A functionalist approach sees social action as the application of labour to advance humankind through instrumental means. The World is seen as a set of problems to be solved: objective problems which can be determined independently of any human viewpoint. In e-banking design (Figure 6.3), for example, this describes well a technological, expert-informed approach, where the views of users are seen to be secondary. Through interpretivism, the World becomes socially constructed through communicative action. Here, e-banking (Figure 6.3) would be understood as a social, communicative, subjective phenomenon, in which the views and opinions of participants become fundamental to its understanding.

From a radical humanist, or critical perspective, the early, technological, view of IS as functionalist, 'hard', problem solving, is seen to be an impoverished one, over-focused on the use of computer technology. 'Soft' or human-centered methodologies have been pursued as a solution to this problem, and have been to some extent successful. But recent thinking questions the ability of 'hard' and 'soft' approaches to

Figure 6.2. A classification of social theory (Clarke, 2000)

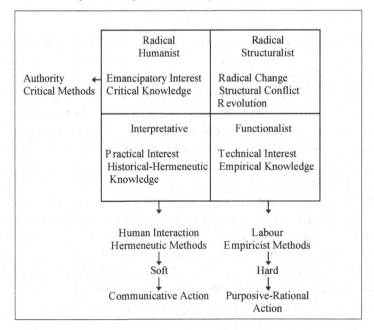

achieve the agenda they apparently set out for themselves, and points to a need to combine approaches under the umbrella of social theory. Radical humanism offers the potential to achieve this, and is therefore pursued in the next section, with focus on two issues of particular relevance in e-banking management:

1. Determination of the scope, or boundaries, of the system.
2. Given the boundaries, choice of development, implementation, and management methodologies.

To complete the picture from the perspective of social theory, radical structuralism looks to ways of changing the World in which we live by altering the material conditions that surround us. In terms of e-banking, this might be relevant where direct political action were required – for example, if a particular Political regime banned the use of relevant technologies. Our view is that this perspective has limited relevance in Western industrialised economies.

SCOPING E-BANKING MANAGEMENT: THE CRITICAL ASSESSMENT OF SYSTEM BOUNDARIES

In e-banking management, making a decision on the system boundary is therefore an issue to be settled before further progress can be made. Whilst the problem of

Figure 6.3. Social theory and e-banking

Radical Humanist	**Radical Structuralist**
E-banking as a social construction, but now introducing a need to ensure inclusion of those involved and affected to challenge authoritative views.	E-banking as a social form. Change society to match e-banking issues
Interpretative	**Functionalist**
E-banking management and usage seen to be a social construction. Technical (functionalist) issues serve only to enable the social interaction.	E-banking management and usage as a technical problem, to be solved by experts. Reference to underlying user issues poor.

system boundaries has exercised the minds of both academics and practitioners for many years (for a summary of early work see Jones 1982), it is from Ulrich (1983; 1988; 1996) and Midgley (1992) that the recommendation to critically challenge what should or should not be considered part of any system is drawn. Midgley's approach is to begin with a boundary definition which is accepted as arbitrary, and progress by " … looking for grey areas in which marginal elements lie that are neither fully included in, nor excluded from, the system definition." The critical choices made at the boundary are of truth and rightness: truth being represented by questions of what is, and rightness by questions of what ought to be. In respect of e-banking, we have to balance availability and security, whilst gaining the enabling benefits of new technologies. Taking such a stance gives a starting point for the critique of boundary judgements in an e-banking intervention as represented by Figure 6.4.

Here, a typical approach to e-banking design, implementation and management, is represented by the primary boundary. The information to be included is often corporate, but at best might be requested from an expert group (marketing, for example). Most of the activity takes place between designers and managers, with system users cast in a passive role.

By contrast, it is recommended that critical assessment of the system boundary be undertaken by a representative sample of participants in the system. The approach might work as detailed below.

1.   An arbitrary system definition is presented (Figure 6.4). The primary boundary represents the main area of concern, whilst the secondary boundary encom-

Figure 6.4. Critique of the system boundary (adapted from Midgley, 1992)

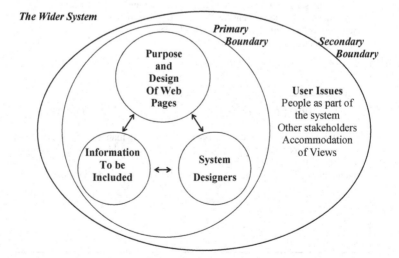

passes that which is seen to be marginal to that area. Beyond this, all other issues are represented by the 'wider system'.

2. A brainstorming session (de Bono 1977) is set up, attended by representatives of all the key participant areas. The purpose of the session is to enable participants in the system (those 'involved and affected') to conduct the critique on their own behalf.

3. The system is critiqued within the brainstorming session by a combination of Midgley's and Ulrich's approaches to boundary critique:

    a. Midgley's (1992) approach to examining what is in the margin for elements which support the secondary boundary or the primary boundary.

    b. Ulrich's (1996) approach to challenging system boundaries through twelve "critically heuristic boundary questions" which address issues of motivation, power, knowledge and legitimisation (see Table 6.1).

In this example, Ulrich's critical boundary questions are applied to the web design aspects of e-banking.

This reconceptualisation of the system is an important part of the intervention, focusing discussion not on a clearly defined technical or organisational problem to which a solution is to be found, but on the complex interaction of all the issues involved in maintaining a web presence. The effect will be to change the focus from technology or organisational functions to the views and ideals of the stakeholder groups involved in the system. The task becomes not one of how to engineer a solution to a known and agreed problem, but how to study and improve a problem situation made up of complex interacting issues. *People are not only part of the system, they are the primary focus of study.*

From the issues raised by boundary critique, it becomes possible to consider intervention strategies.

DISCUSSION: FUTURE TRENDS

The impetus for undertaking this study has been the failure of hard and soft systems development methodologies to address the needs of all participants in an e-banking system. Theoretically it has been demonstrated that this failure, at least in part, can be traced to the uncritical nature of both hard and soft methodologies, and a need, from a social systems viewpoint, to combine hard and soft approaches within a critical framework.

Critical boundary setting, focusing on the normative system definition, has further enhanced this study. Just as a structured approach tends to focus on technical issues, so a concentration on 'what is' tends to lead to a belief that there is only one accurate perception of the system of concern. A critical approach to boundary

Table 6.1. Critically heuristic boundary questions

Question	"Is" Mode	"Ought" Mode
1	Who is the client? Whose purposes are served by the system? *The web site manager.*	Who ought to be the client? *All who are involved in and affected by the system of concern.*
2	What is the purpose? *To present a corporate presence via the internet.*	What ought to be the purpose? *To meet the changing requirements of all involved and affected.*
3	What is the measure of success? *Up-to-date web presence.*	What ought to be the measure? *"User satisfaction".*
4	Who is the decision maker? *Senior management.*	Who ought to be the decision maker? *Decision rests with management, but should be informed by participant involvement.*
5	What conditions are actually controlled by the decision maker? *Resources, final approvals.*	What components of the systems ought to be controlled by the decision maker? *Should manage, not control.*
6	What conditions are not controlled by the decision maker? *External factors.*	What resources and conditions ought to be part of the system's environment? *All on which it potentially impacts.*
7	Who is the system's designer? *Web designers under the web site manager.*	Who ought to be the system's designer? *Web design should be professionally carried out, but informed by the changing requirements of participants.*
8	Who is involved as an expert, what is the nature of the expertise, and what role does the expert play? *Designers: control the whole development within guidelines laid down by management.*	What kind of expertise ought to be involved, who should exercise it, and what should his/her role be? *Mixture of technical and social issues to be considered.*
9	Where is the guarantee of success? With experts, political support etc? *Experts.*	Where ought the guarantee of success to be? *Full participation.*
10	Who represents the concerns of the affected (but not involved)? *Not represented.*	Who ought to represent these concerns? Who among the affected ought to become involved? *The views of all involved and affected should be taken into account.*
11	Are the affected given the opportunity to emancipate themselves? *Not involved.*	To what extent ought the affected to be given such an opportunity? *Participation only works where users are free and able to participate.*
12	What World view underlies the system of concern? *Command and control system.*	On what World view ought the design of the system to be based? *Inclusive, participative, informed.*

judgements has opened up a wider consideration of 'what ought to be' in e-banking, including those involved and affected as participants with whom expertise is seen to reside. The richness this has brought to 'user analysis' within the web systems analysis example contrasts with the simplicity with which this part of an e-banking intervention is normally undertaken.

Since the early stages of this study, theoretical and empirical work in this domain has progressed significantly, and this chapter would be incomplete without a consideration of these issues.

A useful general summary of thinking concerning mixing of methodologies, methods or techniques, can be found in Mingers and Gill (1997). In outline, the thrust of both theoretical and empirical analysis has focused on the perceived shortcomings of approaches which concentrate on a single methodology or paradigm, and alternative conceptions of how methodologies, methods or techniques drawn from different paradigms might contribute within a single intervention. So, for example, Mingers and Brocklesby (1997) see the main approaches to mixing "methods, methodologies and techniques within the broad field of management science" as the system of systems methodologies (Jackson & Keys 1984) and TSI. They criticize these approaches for effectively promoting the use of whole methodologies – a view which it could be contended is supported by the strong suggestion within TSI that there should be dominant and dependent methodologies within an intervention. A better approach, they suggest, would be to mix methodologies, or parts of methodologies, from different paradigms, promoting this approach as "multimethodology". They argue, for example, that TSI: "provides no structure for the ongoing process of the intervention – leaving that entirely up to the selected methodology", and offering in its place an: "appreciate, analyze, assess, act" framework.

Midgley (1997) argues that it is more helpful to think in terms of methodology design than just the choice of whole methodologies, or even, by implication, simple choice of parts of methodologies, and promotes the idea of the "creative design of methods" as an application of their oblique use (Flood & Romm, 1995), and as a way of enhancing TSI in practice.

Another stream that has informed intervention practice in recent years is action research (AR). AR explicitly relies on critical reflection as a means of validating the outcomes of a given investigation, and in this sense may be seen to have much in common with the critically informed intervention approached recommended in this chapter. Further information on the position of AR in relation to organisational intervention may be found initially in Flood and Romm (1996) and Clarke and Lehaney (1997).

Our position in relation to these approaches is still developing, and it offers many challenges which have not as yet been addressed by me or other practitioners. To progress this, I feel concentration now needs to be on a Kantian view of critique as promoted and developed, for example, by Ulrich (1983), and on creatively designing methods, having regard to the issues raised from the critiques of TSI and the system of systems methodologies, always within a critical framework. Finally, action research practice needs to be embedded into the intervention framework.

CONCLUSION

Arguments about whether to use a hard or soft methodology, and which hard or soft methodology to use, in web development, implementation and management, seem to offer only a limited perception of most e-business problem situations. A 'critical complementarist' view gives a richer image. The argument should not be about whether to use this or that methodology, but rather what critically, theoretically, and practically informed mix of methodologies best deals with the problem contexts encountered in a given intervention. From this perspective, the hard-soft debate seems to offer only a partial view of e-banking. Such systems are not *per se* computer systems, but are systems of human activity or micro social systems, consequently, functionalist science or interpretative sociology appear an inadequate basis on which to study them, a wider critical social context seeming more relevant.

The approach currently most widely tested in this respect is total systems intervention, underpinned by the theoretical endeavour of critical systems thinking, but emerging evidence suggests developing this into a richer critical systems practice, focusing on a Kantian view of critique within a broader action research framework.

From all of this can be drawn general findings, together with guidelines for future development, implementation and management of e-banking, which are presented in summary form below.

FINDINGS

From the discussions of this chapter, the following general findings can be distilled:

1.   The domain of information systems is dominated by technology-based methods, weakly mediated by human-centered ones.
2.   Human activity is more fundamental to the domain than such an approach acknowledges, and consequently the investigation of methods underpinned by theories of social interaction are indicated.
3.   From research in the social domain, a foundation in critical social theory emerges as a promising direction.

4. Within such an approach, the first issue to be addressed is that of *understand-ing* the problem context. For this, critical social theory points to the use of critical systems heuristics and critical boundary judgements to critique and determine the system boundary.
5. Boundary critique further informs intervention strategy. The methods required must embrace functionalist (technological), interpretivist (human-centered), and radical humanist (emancipatory, participatory, 'social inclusion') issues.
6. In any future work, the ongoing research in the application of critical theory to management issues must be considered, and a brief outline of this is pro-vided.

Given these findings, how might a manager seek to action them?

Guidelines: The Implications for Managers

*   Determine the initial scope of the system of concern.
*   Identify the social group(s) involved in and affected by that system.
*   Form representative samples from these groups.

In terms of management action, the challenge here is *not* to see e-banking development and management as a problem to be solved by an expert group of de-velopers. A framework (for example, of user groups) needs to be established, from which the contribution from those participating in web usage can be drawn. But a word of caution: the groups and membership of them should not be fixed, and, of course, should not be limited to managers or those in authority.

Actions

*   Conduct boundary critique to initially determine the system of concern. Con-tinue this throughout the project.
*   Use participative forums to discuss all issues of web design, development and implementation.
*   Choose and implement the relevant methodological approaches in a critical complementarist framework.

Initially, formal boundary setting sessions will be needed to set the scene. Quite quickly, groups will form their own clear views about the scope of e-banking de-velopments within a particular organisational context (it will become 'culturally' ingrained), and less time will be necessary in formal sessions to discuss this. The particular forums can then be used to surface the issues, the only primary require-ment in terms of expertise will be a facilitator who can assist with guidance on the process.

E-banking management is a task to be conducted within a social framework. A purely technical approach, or even a technical approach informed from participative analysis is insufficient to address the complexity of the problem contexts encountered. It is essential to recognise that what is being dealt with is a social system, albeit enabled by technology, and, this being so, it is difficult to envisage how such an undertaking could be informed from anywhere other than social theory.

What has been presented in this chapter is argued to be a thoroughly theoretically and pragmatically informed approach based on these principles.

Try it – it works!

REFERENCES

Ackoff, R. L. (1981). *Creating the Corporate Future.* New York: Wiley.

Beath, C. M. & Orlikowski, W. J. (1994). The Contradictory Structure of Systems Development Methodologies: Deconstructing the IS-User Relationship in Information Engineering. *Information Systems Research, 5*(4), 350-377.

Burrell, G. & Morgan, G. (1979). *Sociological Paradigms and Organisational Analysis.* London: Heinemann.

Checkland, P. B. & Haynes, M. G. (1994). Varieties of Systems Thinking: The Case of Soft Systems Methodology. *System Dynamics, 10*(2 3), 189 197.

Clarke, S. A. (2000). From Socio -Technical to Critical Complementarist: A New Direction for Information Systems Development. In E. Coakes, R. Lloyd-Jones and D. Willis (Eds.) *The New SocioTech: Graffiti on the Long Wall,* (pp. 61-72).. London: Springer.

Clarke, S. A. & Lehaney, B. (1997). Total Systems Intervention and Human Inquiry: The Search for a Common Ground. *Systems Practice, 10*(5), 611-634.

Clarke, S. A. & Lehaney, B. (1998). Intervention methodologies in coercive situations. *Analytical Approaches to Studying Power and Influence in Contemporary Political/ Military Affairs,* Defence Evaluation Research Agency, Farnborough, UK.

Davis, F.D. (1989). Perceived usefulness, perceived ease of use and user acceptance of information technology. *MIS Quarterly, 13*(3), 318-339.

de Bono, E. (1977). *Lateral Thinking.* Aylesbury, UK: Pelican Books, Hazell Watson & Viney Ltd.

Flood, R. L. & Romm, N. R. A. (1995). Enhancing the process of methodology choice in total systems intervention (tsi) and improving the chances of tackling coercion. *Systems Practice, 8*(4), 377-408.

Flood, R. L. & Romm, N. R. A. (Eds.) (1996). *Systems Practice 9/2*. London: Plenum.

Jackson, M. C. & Keys, P. (1984). Towards a System of Systems Methodologies. *Journal of the Operational Research Society, 35*(6). 473-486.

Jones, L. M. (1982). Defining systems boundaries in practice: some proposals and guidelines. *Journal of Applied Systems Analysis, 9,* 41-55.

Midgley, G. (1992). The sacred and profane in critical systems thinking. *Systems Practice, 5*(1), 5-16.

Midgley, G. (1997). Developing the methodology of tsi: from the oblique use of methods to their creative design. *Systems Practice, 10*(3), 305-319.

Mingers, J. & Brocklesby, J. (1997). Multimethodology: towards a framework for mixing methodologies. *Omega, 25*(5), 489-534.

Mingers, J. & Gill, A. (Eds.) (1997). *Multi Methodology.* Chichester UK: Wiley.

Mumford, E. (1994). Technology, communication and freedom: is there a relationship? *Transforming Organizations with Information Technology* A-49, 303-322.

Mumford, E. & Henshall, D. (1978). *A Participative Approach to Computer Systems Design.* London: Associated Business Press.

OASIG (1996). Why do IT Projects so often Fail? *OR Newsletter.* 309, 12-16.

Oliga, J. C. (1991). Methodological Foundations of Systems Methodologies. In R. L. Flood & M. C. Jackson, *Critical Systems Thinking: Directed Readings,* (pp. 159-184).. Chichester, UK: Wiley..

Parasuraman, A., Zeithaml, V.A., & Berry, L. (1985). A conceptual model of service quality and its implications for future research. *Journal of Marketing, 49*(4), 41-50.

Parasuraman, A., Zeithaml, V.A., & Berry, L. (1988). SERVQUAL: A multiple-item scale for measuring consumer perceptions of service quality. *Journal of Retailing, 64*(1), 12-40.

Parasuraman, A., Berry, L., & Zeithaml, V.A. (1993). More on improving service quality measurement. *Journal of Retailing, 69*(1), 140-147.

Stowell, F. A. (1991). Client participation in information systems design. In *Systems Thinking in Europe (Conference Proceedings)*, Huddersfield, UK. London: Plenum.

Stowell, F. A. & West, D. (1994). 'Soft' systems thinking and information systems: a framework for client-led design. *Information Systems Journal* 4(2), 117-127.

Ulrich, W. (1983). *Critical Heuristics of Social Planning: A New Approach to Practical Philosophy.* Berne, Switzerland: Haupt.

Ulrich, W. (1983). *The Itinerary of a Critical Approach.* Berne, Switzerland: , Haupt..

Ulrich, W. (1988). Systems Thinking, Systems Practice, and Practical Philosophy: A Program of Research. *Systems Practice, 1*(2), 137-163.

Ulrich, W. (1996). *A Primer to Critical Systems Heuristics for Action Researchers.* Forum One: Action Research and Critical Systems Thinking, Hull, UK, University of Hull, Centre for Systems Studies.

Watson, H. & Wood-Harper, T. (1995). Methodology as Metaphor: The Practical Basis for Multiview Methodology. *Information Systems,* 5, 225-231.

Wood-Harper, A. T., Antill, L. et al. (1985). *Information Systems Definition: The Multiview Approach.* London: Blackwell.

Chapter VII
Problematic Issues in E-Banking Management

INTRODUCTION

The implementation of a successful e-banking strategy is far from being straight forward, as there are numerous inherent difficulties/barriers. The Internet as a channel for services delivery is fundamentally different from other channels such as branch networks or telephone banking. Therefore, it brings up its own unique challenges that require innovative solutions. Thus, a logical step for the management of banking related organizations may be to fully understand the organizational barriers inherent in e-banking.

The Internet has not only created previously non-existent opportunities for cost effective, all time available financial services, it has also increased the significance of a number of risks which did not exist or were not significant in the past. Furthermore, a number of change management issues usually associated with any new technology implementation are compounded simply because some applications such as e-banking have a greater and more immediate impact on the organization.

Building on the previous chapters, this chapter will discuss some of the most common problematic issues in e-banking implementation and management. The main focus will be on those issues which pose considerable risks to e-banking projects and may prevent banks from achieving their desired e-banking related goals. These include: traditional structures which some banks still have and which are unable to respond to agility required for e-banking, resistance from employees, legacy systems which are an obstacle to the integration of systems, security issues, new and complex regulatory issues, and project management problems.

TECHNOLOGY RELATED PROBLEMS

IT and Telecommunication Infrastructure Issues

At present, the availability of e-banking is substantially greater in developed countries than in developing economies. Many developing countries do not have the necessary telecommunications, banking, commercial, bureaucratic and legal infrastructures to support the widespread introduction of e-banking (Simpson, 2002). Access to the Internet is a major problem in the developing world, and presents an obstacle to the growth of e-banking.

Capacity/Scalability Problems

It is difficult to predict the usage of e-banking on an hourly or daily basis. These 'scalability problems' can give rise to a slowing down of the website, or even a website crash (temporary unavailability). This can cause many reputation problems and financial damage. This was the case at Northern Rock Bank in UK. This bank ran into credit problem when news spread that this bank was in trouble, thousands of people rushed to the bank website to transfer their money elsewhere which resulted in numerous technical problems in their e-banking system for many days. Some of the ways of addressing this problem according to Seargeant (2000) are:

- Undertake market research to predict demand,
- Adopt systems with adequate capacity and scalability,
- Undertake proportionate advertising campaigns, and
- Ensure adequate staff coverage and develop a suitable business continuity plan which not only helps coping with scalability problems but with other causes of systems failure.

A number of other technical solutions are also available to address this problem but owing to the high cost associated with them, some banks do not implement them.

Availability and Systems Integration

One of the basic requirements of e-banking services is their 24-hour availability. This often requires e-banking applications' integration with legacy systems, which were designed to provide services during only specified periods, often with suspension of services at other times for various reasons such as data backups and end-of-day processing (Mohamed & Al-Jaroodi, 2003). Usual legacy systems are accounting, banking, payroll, customer information, product management (such as current accounts or savings accounts), and inventory systems. The new business applications are often not built from scratch and they normally rely on the functionality of the existing legacy applications.

Incompatibility between e-banking applications and legacy systems means that most banks require middleware to integrate these systems, which can be expensive and may bring its own set of problems. Systems integration has been and is still, to some extent, a key barrier in e-banking. As pointed out in (Shah et al, 2007; Shah & Siddiqui, 2006), shortcomings in technological infrastructure are often the biggest hurdle in the implementation of e-business channels and their integration with other parts of a business. This type of integration is essential for the success of e-banking, as an electronic request for a typical financial transaction passes through a number of different systems before an action is complete.

Web Site Design and Operational Functionality

There is considerable weight attached to the appropriate design of e-banking websites. Poor design of website has been estimated to result in the loss of up to 50 percent of potential repeat visits (Cunliffe, 2000). Poor design may include use of inappropriate colours, contrast, font or navigation functions. Lack of proper functionality, excessive use of graphics or other similar factors can also deter customers from coming back to that website. Web usage barriers can also be attributed to vision, cognition, and physical impairments associated with the normal aging process. Vision changes include a decline in visual acuity resulting in inability to see objects on a screen clearly, decreased capacity to focus at close range, or increased sensitivity to glare from light reflecting or shining into the eye. These physiological changes, and many others, impact the users ability to see Web objects and read online content (Becker, 2005). These factors need to be taken into account when designing a website as aging population in most industrialized counties means that this segment is increasing in size. These are the people who might need the online services most due to mobility issues. Several software tools, including Dottie and Usability Enforcer, are available for senior-friendly web sites. Numerous organisations, such as National Institute on Aging (http://www.nia.nih.gov) provide guidelines for making senior-friendly web sites.

Poor website design can also result in decreased trust in using online financial services as look and feel often creates a lasting impression. This issue is further covered in greater detail below in the section on trust issues.

MANAGEMENT PROBLEMS

Regulatory Issues

As the Internet is a global medium, it creates opportunities for trading on an international basis, but every country has its own laws and regulations concerning the provision of financial services. The issue of preventing money laundering, which is considered to be the main source of finance for terrorism and other related criminal activities, has further complicated the situation . This is one of the major problems in expansion of e-banking services on a global basis.

The Internet is also a major source of consumer intelligence (personal information, buying patterns and behaviour) which raises a number of privacy, security and data protection issues which regulators must address effectively. To do this new regulations must be put in place more quickly than in the past, leading to constant changes in laws and regulations, and complicating compliance; again a major obstacle to the growth of e-banking.

Information Management

Good information management enables organizations to become more effective in their operations as it provides the information employees need to analyze and conceptualize information, thereby adding to the firm's store of knowledge and making their jobs more meaningful and efficient. This gives employees an opportunity to add value to the organization's products and services (Blount et al. 2005). In online services operations, good information can be a vital difference between success and failure. However managing information has been a problem for organizations across many industries.

This problem is not unique to e-banking but information management requirements for e-banking are usually much greater. Therefore if a bank is not good at managing information, their participation in e-banking simply increases the scale of the problem. Effective e-banking requires that management has up-to-date and timely information in an understandable format. Any improvements in this area can lead to significant benefits in operations and the marketing of e-services.

Outsourcing Problems

Development or implementation of e-banking systems and other technical tasks such as upgrading and integrating existing legacy systems are very complex. They require very high levels of technical and project management competence to carry out without outside help. Even the best companies need to recognise the limitations of their expertise and when to outsource certain e-Commerce functions (Hirsh, 2002). Many banks outsource all or part of e-banking related operations owing to a lack of in-house expertise or simply to cut costs. Some aspects of outsourcing, for example the type and number of partners, can present particular management challenges. Outsourcing works in some cases but can create a risk of the bank losing control of its critical functions. For this reason, if a bank needs to outsource its e-banking operations, it should do so with due consideration to outsourcing risks. General good practice in planning, negotiating and actual outsourcing is applicable here.

Many banks such as Credit Suisse outsource their entire or part of e-banking for the reasons outlined above with mixed results. McDougall (2007) reported the case of Credit Suissie which is summarised here to demonstrate how things generally work when e-banking operations are outsourced:

Credit Suisse Outsources to BT in Deal Worth $1.1 Billion (McDogall, 2007)

Financial services giant Credit Suisse is outsourcing the operation of its critical information and communications networks to British telecom provider BT Group and Swiss telco Swisscom under a deal worth $1.1 billion. Deal is that Credit Suisse will outsource maintenance and operation of its global network to BT and Swisscom for a period of five years with an option for seven years. As part of the arrangement, 231 Credit Suisse technical staffers and 50 contractors will transfer to BT.

The deal will allow the bank to access state-of-the-art telecom technologies, such as wireless and mobile communications tools, faster and more cost effectively than it could through its in-house organization. The deal also includes a provision that calls for BT, Swisscom, and Credit Suisse to contribute to a multimillion dollar "innovation fund" to finance the development of new technologies for Credit Suisse.

Another example is reported by Schneider (2004) which demonstrates how an e-banking marketing operation was outsourced.

Italian Bank Taps Accenture and E.piphany for Marketing Muscle (Schneider (2004)

Cassa di Risparmio di Firenze Bank (CRF; Florence, Italy; $18.5 billion in assets) relies upon its central marketing department to design campaigns that reach over

600,000 customers across 270 regional branches, as well as the customers of five smaller banks within the CRF group.

In measuring the success of any particular marketing campaign, CRF looks at the "redemption rate," which it calculates as the percentage of customers targeted by a campaign who end up purchasing the product offered. But in mid-2002, the bank's internal analysis demonstrated that it was falling behind competitors on that metric, only reaching a redemption rate of 3 percent. That's when the bank called in Accenture, New York (a consultancy company) to help it craft a new strategy.

Over the following 18 months, Accenture introduced new tools for sales force management, customer segmentation and real-time modeling of propensity-to-buy and customer acquisition. The solution consists of software from E.piphany (San Mateo, Calif.) running on an Oracle (Redwood Shores, Calif.) database. With its new marketing system, the bank has been able to double the frequency of its campaigns, and most importantly, triple the redemption rate to 9 percent. Furthermore, the bank has adapted the capability to suggest a likely "next product" for any given customer, which it has successfully deployed at its branches to reach a redemption rate exceeding 30 percent for mass market customers, according to Stefano Puccioni, head of commercial planning for CRF.

These capabilities allow CRF to go head-to-head with its larger competitors. Italy's five largest banks "probably have a system that is similar" to that of CRF, notes Puccioni.

Nevertheless, the bank's smaller size can lead to greater agility, including the ability to conduct monthly meetings with all of the bank's branch managers. "You can communicate a change very quickly," says Puccioni. "We have extended the system and we have trained all the branches -- in just three to four months." As for CRF's smaller competitors, its latest technology push gives it a market advantage, relates Puccioni. "Our position is better than the banks that are of the same size," he says. "I don't think there are a lot of banks [in Italy] with 300 to 400 branches with this system."

Outsourcing is not a panacea and there are advantages and disadvantages (see Table 7.1) associated with both approaches, in house development/implementation and outsourcing.

When choosing a vendor a bank may analyze these aspects in great detail: the vendors' reputation, it's relationship with existing customers, experience of successful management (for example, number of successful cases and types of successes), the capability to plan and manage a project, the capability with latest technologies, and the ability to provide sufficient information about their capabilities. Instead of going for most well known, cheapest or personal contacts, banks need to analyze their own requirements and then analyze the capabilities of several vendors to meet

Table 7.1. Outsourcing vs. in-house e-commerce systems development

	Outsourcing	*In-house System Development*
Advantages	• An attractive option for replacing legacy systems (Hirsh, 2002) • Low risk (Gibson, 1999b) • Known costs (Loh & Venkatraman, 1994) • Expert support from vendors (Loh & Venkatraman, 1994) • Easier upgrades (Hirsh, 2002) • Ability to focus on core business issues (Hirsh, 2002)	• Development of in-house expertise • Flexibility (Loh & Venkatraman, 1994) • Own developers have better understanding of business • Less changes may be required in business processes (Loh & Venkatraman, 1994) • Unique processes may lead to competitive advantage
Disadvantages	• Possible inflexibility • High external consultancy costs • Difficult change management issues • High dependency on vendors	• High risk strategy (Hirsh, 2002) • High costs (Hirsh, 2002) • High training expenses • Difficult and costly upgrades.

these requirements as well as other factors mentioned above before making a choice of outsourcing vendor.

Security

Security related issues are a major source of concern for everyone both inside and outside the banking industry. E-banking increases security risks, potentially exposing traditionally isolated systems to the open and risky world of Internet. According to McDougall (2007) security problems can mainly be categorized as; hacking with criminal intent (e.g. fraud), hacking by 'casual hackers' (e.g. defacement of web sites or 'denial of service' - causing web sites to slow or crash), and flaws in systems providing opportunities for security breaches (e.g. a users is able to transact on other users' accounts). These threats have potentially serious financial, legal and reputational risks associated with them. Luckily actual financial losses from these breaches have been very low in comparison to (say) credit card frauds. Financial regulators also demand a very high standard of security from banks.

Information is a valuable asset and to fully utilise it needs wide availability at least within an organization. However security requirements might hinder wider information sharing. Therefore organizational objectives of security and of availability may be seen to pull against each other: the more confidential a set of information, the less available it would be. This has raised the question of 'available to whom?', and has led to a consideration of information as a human issue, as well as technological and managerial. Drake and Clarke (2001) suggested a human centered approach called critically normative approach to information security (Table 7.2). Their approach proposes a very different approach to information security to the one generally favoured.

The 'current view' may be seen as a set of guidelines or principles on which present approaches to information security are explicitly or implicitly based. The 'critically normative approach' provides the foundation for moving ahead to develop, pilot, and refine, an implementation framework for information security, based on human issues.

In an e-banking environment, security threats largely fall into the following categories:

- **Login detail disclosure:** This is most basic threat to the financial system. Using a number of means, criminals acquire login details, such as a customer number, pin, and use it to access the account and steal money from it. This threat could be mitigated through promotion of good practice amongst consumers to keep their login details safe.

Table 7.2. An alternative future for information security (adapted from Drake & Clarke, 2001)

General View	Critically Normative Approach
Confidentiality / Restriction	Availability / De-restriction / Sharing
Information Restriction	Information Sharing
Pragmatic	Theoretical / Empirical
Technological / Computer Systems	Human Activity Systems
Instrumental	'Practical' Critically Normative. Apply Critique to: Normative Content Norms Boundary Judgements 'System'
Pseudo-Scientific	Social
Rule-Based	Challenge the Rules
Truth	Normative Validity
Formal-Logical: Unreflective	Dialectical: Free to Think
'Is'	'Ought'
Functional	Radical
Accept the 'Material Conditions'	Critique of 'Material Conditions'
Rational equals Seeking the 'Truth'	Rational equals a dialectic between the 'involved and affected', all of whom are free to contribute

- **Computer spy viruses:** These are computer programs which are circulated through email or other means. Once a customer opens a malicious email a program is automatically installed in his/her computer. These programs collect login id or other financial information which is used to conduct a range of criminal activities such as credit card cloning or unauthorized funds transfer.
- **Dummy sites:** Here customers is lured to the dummy or look alike website. These website look very similar to a bank's website, and when login details are entered, these are recorded and used for criminal activities.

Most of these threats can be mitigated by promoting good password practice. Banks, regulators and professional association provide good practice guidelines to customers. For example, The British Bankers' Association (BBA) has published a leaflet entitled 'Your money and the Internet: a guide to home banking and Internet shopping'. This leaflet presents a ten point Internet guide advising customers on how to keep their login details safe and secure as well as providing information about keeping their computers free from spyware. Spyware are small programmes which discreetly install themselves on computers and send details of a user's activities to another computer.

Many technical as well as managerial types of solutions are available, and show various degrees of success. One of the main problem with implementing security solutions is customer resentment against several layers of security which might lead to loss of customers. Another problem is the high cost associated with them; most sophisticated systems can be implemented only for the highest value parts of e-banking systems. Hackers are not the only security threat, employees or contractors can do as much damage as a hacker can. Therefore security provisions are also necessary for internal threats.

In the face of multi faced, multi directional security threats, implementing ad hoc security systems may not be the best approach. McDougall (2007) suggests that banks need as a minimum to have:

- A strategic approach to security, building best practice security initiatives into systems and networks as they are developed;
- A proactive approach to security, involving active testing of security systems, controls (e.g. penetration testing), planning response to new threats and vulnerabilities and regular reviews of internal as well as external threats. Advice from financial regulators can be sought on how to do it;
- Sufficient staff with security expertise and responsibilities;
- Regular use of system based security and monitoring tools. This may include use of digital signatures (A security option that uses two keys, one public and

one private, which are used to encrypt messages before transmission and to decrypt them on receipt), or Public Key Infrastructure (policies, processes, and technologies used to verify, enroll and certify users of a security application. A PKI uses public key cryptography and key certification practices to secure communications.) etc.

- Continuity plans to deal with aftermaths of any security breaches.

The following article on the BBC (British Broadcasting Corporation) Website published on Wednesday, 13 December 2006 highlights the rise in security threats.

Phishing for Bank Customers has Boomed this Year

The UK has seen an 8,000% increase in fake internet banking scams in the past two years, the government's financial watchdog has warned. The Financial Services Authority (FSA) told peers (members of house of Lords, UK) it was "very concerned" about the growth in "phishing". Phishing involves using fake websites to lure people into revealing their bank account numbers. The amount stolen is still relatively small but it is set to go up by 90% for the second year running, peers (members of UK House of Lords) heard.

Between January and June 2005, the number of recorded phishing incidents was 312, the Lords science and technology committee was told. The figure for the same period this year was 5,059, according to banking trade body APACS figures.

The amount of cash stolen in the first half of 2006 was £23.2m, the committee was told, and was likely to be £22.5m in the second half of the year. The decrease was put down by APACS security chief Philip Whitaker to better detection. But Mr Whitaker told peers the criminals behind "phishing" scams were also becoming increasingly "industrialised" in their approach.

Lord Paul said the committee had been told one bank was being targeted far more than any other. But Apacs director of communication Sandra Quinn rejected the peer's call to name the bank concerned, saying it would breach commercial confidentiality. She said Apacs was there to represent the banking industry not the consumer, and had no plans to make public its list of banks being targeted by fraud. Mr Whitaker said just because a bank had been targeted, did not mean that their security systems were worse than its competitors. "There is no evidence that one bank is any worse or any better-off than another," he told the committee.

He also rejected a call for banks to routinely inform customers of security breaches involving their details, such as when a bank employee's laptop was stolen. He said banks did not want to cause undue alarm to customers, as had been in the case in some U.S. states, where customers were constantly given such information.

Rob Gruppetta, of the FSA's financial crime team, said "phishing" was growing rapidly in the UK. "We are very concerned about the rate of increase. It has gone up by 8,000% in the past two years. "But in the grand scheme of total fraud it is still quite small." Even so, he said the scams were becoming "more sophisticated," compared to the primitive early examples.

Philip Robinson, the FSA's head of financial crime, said he believed internet banking was generally "safe". But he raised concerns about the banks' apparent lack of transparency when it came to internet fraud. He said they were "wary" about making concerns public in case the information was "misrepresented".

They were also reluctant to report incidents to the police, he said, because "the likelihood of fraud being investigated is very low indeed". He said being "open and transparent" was important to "maintain confidence" in the banking system and he would be meeting the Information Commissioner next week to discuss ways of increasing transparency.

The above article highlights a number of security issues and demonstrates that security is no longer an internal issue for a bank, financial sector or regulator, it has become one of the major political/business issue in several counties and needs to be taken very seriously. It is also important to realise that response time to address any incident is very short, minutes or hours rather than days or weeks we had in the past. Response to security incidents is not a technical issue anymore, a significant public relations exercise is also required to minimise reputational damage. Organizations also need to be aware of "over-killing" security issues. Too many passwords, codes, can prevent many customers from using e-banking. New solutions, including biometrics, one-time password tokens and peripheral device recognition may provide a good balance between security and convenience.

A number of initiatives are under development around the world to adopt common standards to manage security issues in online environment. For example, an early and still considered influential work on information security is the United States Department of Defense Computer System Evaluation Criteria (the so called 'Orange Book': DoD, 1987). Although constructed around the security of computer systems to be procured for the US Department of Defense, the initiative established many of the basic information security principles in use today, and was followed by the European Information Technology Security Evaluation Criteria (EC, 1991). It is in this document that the ubiquitous Confidentiality, Integrity and Availability (CIA) principles of information security were first suggested in a formal way. CIA adopts the key principles of information security as practised by the industry, the implication of which is that there exists a primary need to restrict information to those entitled to have it, keep it accurate and up to date, and make sure that only authorised users have access when they need it.

In UK, in the early to mid 1990s, a group of representatives from some of the largest organizations decided to collaborate to formalise matters. They formed a committee under the stewardship of the United Kingdom Department of Trade and Industry and the British Standards Institute to create a British Standard (BSI 1999a; BSI 1999b). Each of these organizations (and others) had been working to establish frameworks to adequately secure the information systems within their organizations, and the British Standard had the simple aim of standardising these frameworks into a model that could be applied to any organization.

Fewer organizations than was expected have embraced the standard. Typically, the most keen to do so are those originally involved in developing and maintaining the standard (including major multi-nationals such as Shell Oil and Unilever, as well as public sector organizations like Cambridgeshire County Council in the U.K.); and those that have been the subject of adverse external audit reports due to potentially inaccurate information systems or information security incidents such as sabotage and malpractice.

Loss of Personal Relationship

Another key barrier in e-banking is a lack of personal contact between customers and banks. Harden (2002) suggests that e-channels erode a direct relationship with customers as compared with traditional over-the-counter banking: e-banking does not offer face-to-face contact in what is essentially a one-to-one service relationship. To compensate, e-banks must deliver higher quality services in order to compete with other service delivery channels (Liao & Cheung, 2005). Another factor in the loss of personal relationships is the convenience of Internet shopping: it is much easier now to compare products and switch between different providers. This creates the need for offering high value products and to cut operational costs to remain competitive, which in turn may further erode the avenues for building personal relationships with customers. The solution to these problems appears to be offering a multi channel experience which is better than direct competitors.

Organizational Structures and Resistance

The introduction of e-banking can generate conflicts and morale problems as changes required to succeed in e-banking may have profound effects on the way an organization is structured. Confusions resulting from fast paced changes can also have negative effects on customers and suppliers.

Black et al. (2001) points out that resistance to change from, for example, middle management is common in many significant change projects. He stated that this type of resistance to change constitutes a major barrier to the success of change projects in the banking industry. A major source of conflict is over the best ways in which to move into the future. Many people will have different views about future directions and may resist when their opinion is not valued.

Change management projects have very poor success rates. Organizational change is a dynamic process encompassing different but interrelated forms of diversity. This diversity might be related to several dimensions such as organizational structure and culture, or the interactions between different dimensions of an organization. Causes of failures can often be found in inefficient interactions of technical and human activities, the organization with its environment, or organizational design and management style. Lack of systematic change management methodologies or problems in their implementation is another commonly cited problem. Most of the change management methodologies focus on four common dimensions of an organization (process, design, culture and politics).

Process change may involve changing services development process (from market research to actual roll out) cash flow (from investments to profits), human resource input, and information flow. Structural change involves changes to organizational functions, their organization, co-ordination and control, such as changes in horizontal and vertical structures; in the decision systems or policy and resource allocation mechanisms; and in the processes used for recruitment, appraisal, compensation and career development. Culture encompasses such issues as values, beliefs and human behaviour in terms of mutual relationships and social norms. Politics may involve the power of change makers or those who resist it, which stakeholders will be effected and why etc.

The above categorisation is useful in understanding not only of the diversity in organizational change, but also of interaction between these dimensions. The four types of organizational change are interconnected through a dynamic process so a change in any one dimension will result in changes in others. Therefore an initiative to carry out changes to one or two area in isolation is likely to fail.

Cao et al. (1999) suggested a generic critical model with four interrelated types of organizational change:

- **Process change:** Change in flows and controls over flows. Typical approaches may include Total Quality Management (TQM) and Business Process Reengineering (BPR).
- **Structural change:** Change in functions, their organization, co-ordination and control. Typical approaches include contingency theory, transaction cost economics, and the configuration approach. These are reported in literature to improve the efficiency and effectiveness of the more tangible sides of an organization, but are impoverished in dealing human centred issues (Cao, 2001).

- **Cultural change:** Change in values, beliefs, and human behaviour in terms of relationship to social rules and practices. Two of the main cultural approaches are unitary culture (Kotter, 1996), and cultural diversity management (Cox & Blake, 1991; Chemers, Oskamp & Costanzo, 1995; Milliken & Martins, 1996). These approaches force attention to the human side of organizations.
- **Political change:** Change in power distribution and the way organizational issues are influenced. These can be associated with the political models of organization developed by Pugh (1978), Mintzberg (1998), Morgan (1997), Pfeffer (1992 & 1994), and Pettigrew (1985). In these models focus is on power, domination, political bargaining and negotiation processes.

A holistic view of the four types of organizational change is based on this classification.

Thr four-dimensional view of organizational change implies that managing organizational change needs diversity in approaches. Each of the four types of organizational change is the source of a particular type of problem so it needs four categories of change management approaches to deal with different types of organizational change. These approaches might be needed simultaneously, or at different stages of the overall change process.

Each of the change management approach is primarily focused on a specific type of organizational change. Therefore these approaches lack the power to deal with situations where more than one type of organizational change is required. Since different types of organizational change are interrelated, they need to be managed together through a holistic approach. This requires that multiple methods and/or methodologies are applied to a single change context. Whichever change approach or approaches are being followed, there is the need to critically evaluate whether the change is being implemented effectively. Systems thinking which is covered in other chapters of this book in greater details, therefore has a clear relevance to an holistic change management. It better enables a holistic approach to organizational problem contexts, which it sees as interdependent sub systems within the larger organizational system.

One such holistic approach (see Table 7.3) called Management of Change (MOC) is suggested by Cao et al. (1999) which relates the four types of organizational change to the three different systemic approaches: Hard Systems Thinking (HST), Soft Systems Thinking (SST) and Critical Systems Thinking (CST). The objective is to help practitioners to analyze and address diversity in organizational change systemically and critically. The key idea of the MOC framework is to help manage the diversity and interactions in organizational change and the change management methods. The framework is explicitly based on CST, and is intended to help through a critical process, determine the organizational change context and scope, participative issues, and the use of multiple methods, to facilitate and inform decision-making related to change management.

The power of this approach lies in its ability to relate different change management methods to each other through a systemic framework. The framework represents something deeper than just the use of different methods to address (say) a mixed process/cultural context, but actually enables the managers applying it to see a single context differently. For example, if a change management problem is process specific, HST can provide general principles for the effective and efficient design of organizational processes, focusing, most likely, on approaches such as BPR and TQM. But what if there are different views about implementing this change process? In this case, SST can be utilised to help gain better understanding of these views. Further, if there are disagreements where one view is dominating over others, CST may help reveal who will benefit from or be disadvantaged by the implementation of change (Cao et al., 1999).

Similarly with structural change, there is rarely a consensus on the design of vertical and horizontal organizational structures, decision systems, and human resource systems, and SST can be used to help understand the values and beliefs underlying the change decisions, whilst CST can help uncover political issues of power and conflict.

Cultural change is particularly complex. Whilst HST might be useful to help develop a unitary or strong organizational culture, such approaches must be used with care. It is all too easy to *assume* a consensus where in truth there is strict control

Table 7.3. Systematic framework for the management of change (adapted from Cao et al., 1999)

	Hard Systems Thinking	**Soft Systems Thinking**	**Critical Systems Thinking**
Process	Efficient process design and change	Interpreting the ideas, beliefs and values underpinning the process design and change	Challenging the ideas, beliefs and values underpinning the process to achieve better balance
Structural	Efficient design of vertical and horizontal structure, decision systems, and human resources system	Interpreting the ideas, beliefs and values underpinning the structure design and change	Challenging the ideas, beliefs and values underpinning the design of organizations to develop efficient structures
Cultural	Strong culture development	Encouraging diverse ideas, values and beliefs	Challenging dominant ideas, values and beliefs to reveal who is disadvantaged
Political	Conflicts of different values and interests are minimised by legally accepted power	Conflicts of different values and interests are balanced through various sources of power	Revealing coercive influences and effects, improving the positions of the disadvantaged

over expression of views. SST (perhaps applying cultural diversity management) is more likely to be of value in such circumstances, receptive environment for diverse ideas, values and beliefs, and thereby helping develop a ideas rich organization. Where disagreements are found, with one view is dominating , CST might help at least to understand, and at best to neutralize the dominant culture.

This framework can be applied in practice to help develop a holistic view of the change context. What types of organizational changes are needed? What are the possible interactions between them? Is it possible that the one organizational change may results in other types of changes? This type of questioning aims to help develop a better understanding of the change situation.

Availability of too much information or advice can also be problem as stated here:

Managers end up immersing themselves in an alphabet soup of initiatives. They lose focus and become obsessed by all the advice available in print and on-line about why organizations should change, what they should try to achieve, and how they should do it. This proliferation of recommendations often leads to confused approach and mixed results when change is attempted (Beer & Nohria, 2000).

To manage these issues, a detailed change management strategy and plan is often required to facilitate the adoption process. This plan is likely to include detailed evaluation of which part of the organization and which employees are likely to be affected. A great deal of care will be needed in actual execution of change to minimize disruptions.

Old organizational structures are often a barrier to implementing the changes required for a dynamic service delivery channel, such as e-banking. To create a smooth and efficient experience for customers, business processes often need to be re-engineered, and the number of management hierarchies reduced to speed up decision making. Changing an organization from a bureaucratic organization to an agile/responsive one opens up a number of risks; risks which should be managed with careful change management.

Trust Issues

Lack of consumer trust is a major hurdle in the growth of e-banking. Although winning consumer trust is more important in online environment, online trust does share a number of characteristics with the offline trust. Wang (2005) categorised these characteristics in the following categories:

- **Trust and trustees:** The two parties, truster and trustee, are vital for establishing a relationship. In an online environment, a website, or rather the trader behind it, is a trustee and a consumer is a truster.
- **Vulnerability:** Offline traders usually have a physical presence which reduces the sense of vulnerability but the anonymity associated with the online world leaves consumers feeling more vulnerable. This is not just about vulnerability to fraud but also loss of privacy, because every move made by a consumer can be recorded and analyzed to assess their behavior. In some cases, this information is sold to other parties without consumers' prior knowledge, further fueling online mistrust.
- **Produced actions:** A consumer action may include just visiting a website for information or purchasing a product, often providing credit/debit card as well as other personal information such as home address. Both of these action benefit traders in terms of a potential sale or an actual sale. To provoke these actions, a trader must do a number of things – discussed below – to create trust in consumers' mind.
- **Subjective matter:** Trust is a subjective matter. Some people will trust easily whereas others will not trust no matter what. The majority of consumers, however fall, somewhere in between, and can be persuaded to trust even a virtual trader. Basically, trust is a psychological state of mind when the person is willing to accept the risks involved. When the perception of benefits outweigh the risks in the relationship, the person enters into a trusting relationship (Carr, 2007). Therefore the onus is on organizations to promote e-banking benefits and minimize the related risks (provision of institutional and structural safeguards) to facilitate trust.

The above characteristics of trust show that trust is a complex issue needing careful consideration to understand what helps in formation of online trust. These elements can be described as integrity of a trader, his ability to deliver quality products/services and owning up the consequences of a near future failure (guarantees). The element of integrity also includes a trader being seen as making legitimate profits without undermining consumer interests. The presence of a privacy policy or statement on the website also inspires confidence.

Kim et al. (2003) conducted a comprehensive study into the determinants of online trust and found that the following six elements or dimensions play a key role in formation of online trust. These are information content, product, transaction, technology, institutional, and consumer-behavioral dimensions. These elements, which were further broken down into many sub-categories, formed a theoretical framework of online trust, covering the different stages that a consumer went through to complete an online transaction. Many customers seem to face a usage barrier because they perceive e-banking to be unsuitable for them. This usage barrier arises from the thinking that there is no relative advantage in switching from branch banking or ATMs to Internet and prefer the old routine of ATM use or consider Internet an unsafe, inefficient or inconvenient channel. Fear of costly mistakes due to pressing wrong key, security fears also plays a role in deterring customers from use of e-banking.

Brand name plays an important role in formation of trust and as customers use a brand, if their experience is positive, they tend to come back for repeat purchase. Their recommendations as well as carefully crafted marketing campaigns play a vital role too. Having some sort of physical presence or having an already established brand name often proves to be an invaluable asset in inspiring consumer trust. Consequently, banks with well trusted brand names which also keep high street branches are performing better in e-banking than their rival online only banks.

It appears that e-banks are relatively easy to set up in comparison to traditional branches based banks. E-banking will give customers much more choice but the ease of switching means they will be less likely to remain loyal. Experience has also shown that start-up costs are high, as establishing a trusted brand is costly and takes time (Sergeant, 2000). This is in addition to the purchase of expensive technology and integration costs. But it has to be done as a bank's strength and performance now very much depends on its ability and capacity to provide value by re-aggregating and tailor-making services to suit individuals and offering these services quickly, efficiently and securely.

Approval by third parties such as governments, financial service authorities, professional associations or by other trusted brands also plays a big part. However, banks need to take active steps to promote trust in e-banking. These steps may include:

- Purchase of similar web domain names so it becomes difficult for fraudulent traders to set up similar websites.
- Being pro-active in combating online crimes and cooperating with other banks and other regulatory/professional bodies to detect and prevent crimes.
- Taking proper care in protecting consumer's information and taking particular care in using it for marketing purposes.
- Providing appropriate guarantees against consumer losses in the event of fraud.

In addition to the above steps, website design can incorporate a number of features which contribute to the formation of online trust. Online traders can take many managerial measures to build and enhance trusting relationships before, during, and after any online interaction. Online traders depend primarily on their electronic storefront or website to attract potential customers and to communicate their message. Applying trust-inducing features to the web sites of online merchants is the most effective method of enhancing online trust. Wang (2005) proposed a framework to explain these trust-inducing features. The framework classifies these features into four general dimensions as shown in Table 7.4.

All these dimensions have the potential to facilitate or undermine trust in a website. Simple things such as use of color can be used by consumers to decide whether to trust this trader or not. Generally speaking, orange color website indicate a cheap/no frills operation whereas use of light blue may be taken as a high-end trustworthy business. Most consumers like a simple and easy to navigate structure as it creates a smooth and positive experience which is a key dimension in winning trust. Provision of the human touch such as customer service representatives if things go wrong in online environments is now considered to be vital for winning trust.

Adoption/Acceptance Issues

Within this new set of market possibilities provided by online environment, there are risks as well as opportunities for consumers. However, owing to the security

Table 7.4. Trust inducing features (adapted from Wang, 2005)

Dimension	Explanation	Feature
Graphic design	Includes graphical design features on the web site that create a first impression	• Use of three-dimensional, dynamic, and half-screen size clipart • Symmetric use of color of low brightness and professional impression
Structure design	Plan of overall structure of the website	• Easy-to-use navigation (simplicity, consistency) • No broken links or missing pictures etc • Use of navigation training tutorials • Application of page design techniques (e.g., white space and margin, strict grouping)
Content design	Actual contents in the form of text or other media such as images, sounds or movies	• Display of brand-promoting information (e.g., prominent company logo or slogan, main selling point) • Up-front disclosure of all aspects of the customer aspects of the customer relationship (e.g., company competence, security, privacy, financial, or legal concerns) • Clear display of third-party approval/certificates etc • Use of comprehensive, correct, and current product information • Use of a relevant domain name
Social-cue design	Includes social cues, such as face-to-face interaction and embedding feel of social presence in website	• Inclusion of representative photograph or video clips • Use of synchronous communication media (e.g., messengers, chat lines or video conferencing)

and trust issues discussed above, consumer take up of online services including e-banking has been much lower that many people expected. In addition many customers lack the required IT skills, or access to a computer or the Internet. Even when all of these issues are resolved, there will be people who will simply not use these new ways of conducting business and banks need to provide for them, perhaps keeping physical branches and call centers for foreseeable future.

From an organizational point of view, failing to successfully adopt e-business initiatives originate from a combination of unclear business vision for e-business and lack of technological expertise amongst other factors. Other factors include: uncertainty of financial benefits, limited size of target market, lack of time/resources to start new projects, and high costs of computing technology, organizational issues like top management short-sightedness and longstanding internal barriers.

Clash With Other Services Delivery Channels

Although e-banking promises to be more cost effective and efficient than other channels such as branch or phone banking, it may also cannibalize these other channels. In the short term a cheaper channel replacing an expensive one looks attractive, but in the long run it may cost banks an established and loyal customer base. For this reason many banks treat e-banking as only an extra channel, a factor which could mean that growth of e-banking is much slower than many expected.

Many banks have invested huge resources in their branch networks and in many ways view it as one of their core competencies. New technologies can enhance these core competencies but at the same time may destroy them. This could mean that entry barriers for new entrants keep coming down and increasing competition from new and lower cost rivals can erode profits. Banks need to be pro-active regarding new distribution channels, and should allocate resources in order to integrate them in the existing organization. Chandy and Tellis (1998) point out that the willingness to cannibalize is a desirable trait, because it promotes innovation and is necessary for the long-term survival of the firm.

Change Management Issues

One of the main problems established organizations encounter when considering e-banking adoption is organizational change. The responses of organizations that are reluctant to change but willing to compete in the new economy is summarized in Table 7.5.

Technology adoption is usually slow if too much attention is paid to technical aspects, rather than business processes and social issues. Some companies sell their e-commerce projects as 'pilot' or 'learning' vehicles and leave it's development to the IT department and many senior executives equate 'going online' with a specific technology in mind rather than using digital technologies to implement their organization's strategic objectives. Going online is about serving customers, creating innovative products/services, leveraging organizational talent, achieving significant improvements in productivity, and increasing revenues. High start up cost of e-banking also deters some banks to delay its implementation. Lack of a well defined e-banking strategy that is aligned with general business strategy is also one of the most common problem in e-banking adoption. Adoption of e-banking initiatives can also be derailed by the absence of clearly defined performance measures (this topic is discussed in detail in Chapter VIII). An e-banking initiative, just like any other business project should be undertaken within a strategic framework.

Ethical Issues

Consideration of the ethics of e-banking have mainly focused on areas relating to the use/abuse of information collected through analyzing online customer behavior. In this context the main issues may include security/privacy of information about individuals, accuracy of information, ownership of information and intellectual property, accessibility of information held and what uses of this information are ethically acceptable. These relate to: freedom of choice; transparency; facilitating fraud (ethical/illegal activities of others).

One of the main benefits of e-banking is that organizations can improve service and potentially generate more profits for shareholders and job security for employees.

Table 7.5. Common e-business impediments identified from the literature (adapted from Dubelaar et al., 2005)

Strategic factors	Structural factors	Management-oriented factors
• Creation of e-banking without major changing the core business • Duplication of traditional business practices online • Comparison of performance with traditional industry competitors in the physical world and dismissal of online competitors • Perception that Internet is an opportunity for company to communicate with customers, not for customers to communicate with the company	• Internet is adopted and related activities are sprinkled throughout the company with no direct connection to the core business • E-banking division is kept separate and disconnected from the rest of the organization or e-banking is part of another department and bogs down with other priorities	• Under-commitment of resources and assignment of e-banking responsibility to executives with no subject expertise • Lack of in-house technical expertise results in choosing inappropriate vendors for development of e-banking systems • Insist that an Internet venture meet every corporate standard, without committing sufficient resources • Initiating conversion to e-banking by requiring changes from skeptical people

On the other hand, job losses are one of the methods of cutting costs and this has numerous negative implications for those effected. The displacement of job opportunities away from face-to-face and back-office service roles to information system professionals is a common feature of the electronic commerce revolution (Turban et al 2000). How banks deal with this issue often raises ethical issues which may be mitigated by a careful and considerate approach to change management.

In business to business banking, access to sophisticated e-banking often comes hand in hand with the need for 'plumbing in' of software and hardware, which means that business customers are locked into one bank's facilities. This is a form of restriction of free choice (Harris & Spence, 2002). The main ethical issue here is that the business customer should be aware that a particular choice could mean that there are significant implications for future freedom of choice.

Fraudulent activity by individuals and businesses is both illegal and unethical but what about the *facilitating* of fraudulent activity? How much responsibility do banks have to prevent their services being used to aid unethical or illegal activities such as money laundering or depositing money made through corruption? The Swiss banking system of confidentiality has always been condemned in this regard (Harris & Spence, 2002), but many banks in other countries have been found wanting in connection with these activities.

Taking personal relationships out of responses to credit applications has the effect of dehumanizing the process. A client's relationship with a bank or a manager may have developed over years of loyal customer commitment. Reducing this to boxes ticked and computer-generated numbers/models would, according to an ethic of care, result in the loss of the development of individual relationships, the human touch and the use of intuition (Harris & Spence, 2002). Such aspects may be viewed as necessay to the new electronic economy, but human networks are just as important a part of business practice as the efficiencies associated with e-banking.

Electronic commerce also allows for the concealment of the real identity of suppliers of a product or service. This white labeling (products sold without clearly labeling the source/supplier) may offer extraordinarily misleading information about the source (Harris & Spence, 2002). This and many other ethical issues remain to be address to date and progress seems to be slow.

Small banks also have to overcome impediments related to investment, technical skills, ethical issues and understanding of organizational issues involved. All these obstacles need to be identified, and then minimized through active learning and collaboration with customers, management, and people within organization as a whole.

CHAPTER SUMMARY

This chapter presented and discussed a number of problematic issues in e-banking implementation and how they create barriers to success. We suggest that the major issues include:

- Lack of proper integration of related systems
- Culture of achieving only short-term targets
- Non web-enabled business processes
- Lack of understanding and knowledge, within the organization, about e-commerce
- Lack of product differentiation and categorisation
- Lack of understanding customer community
- Difficulties in personalisation of products
- Limited research and development
- Lack of e-commerce promotion within the organization
- Lack of understanding that the e-banking initiative is a business critical area and not just a technical issue.

Existing organizational structure and unwillingness to change amongst employees is also often seen as one of the biggest hurdle in the implementation of e-banking and we recommended a carefully planned and implemented change management strategy (see Chapter VI) to manage this.

These concerns are generic and reasonably well known. It is important that institutions embarking on e-banking are fully aware of them, so that strategies can be developed to minimise their adverse effects. Additionally, each institution has its own set of organizational barriers that it needs to deal with when deciding to make a change in the way it operates and provision of online services.

Organizations that have successfully adopted e-banking demonstrate that a combination of strong customer focus, clearly defined performance measures and incorporation of those measures in strategic planning process, a clear link between value proposition and measures, and careful change management, work in most cases. Such organizations are also able to measure how well they are delivering their value proposition to the customers and are flexible enough to quickly address any shortcomings.

REFERENCES

Becker, S. A. (2005). Technical opinion: E-government usability for older adults. *Communications of the ACM, 48*(2), 102-104.

Becker, S.A. & Nowak, L. (2003). *User profiling in an automated environment to promote universal web usability.* Paper presented at the 2003 Proceedings of the Information Resource Management Association, Philadelphia, PA.

Beer, M., & Nohria, N. (2000). Cracking the Code of Change. *Harvard Business Review,* (3), 133-141.

Black, N.F., Lockett, A., Winklhofer, H., & Ennew, C. (2001). The adoption of Internet financial services: a qualitative study, *International Journal of Retail & Distribution Management, 29*(8), 390-8.

Blount, Y. Castleman, T. & Swatman, P. (2005). E-Commerce, Human Resource Strategies, and Competitive Advantage: Two Australian Banking Case Studies. *International Journal of Electronic Commerce, 9*(3), 74–89. http://mesharpe.met-apress.com/app/home/contribution.asp?referrer=parent&backto= issue,6,8;journal,14,32;linkingpublicationresults,1:106045,1

BSI (1999a). *Code of practice for information security management,* (BS7799 part 1). London: British Standards Institute.

BSI (1999b). *Specification for information security management systems,* (BS7799 part 2). London: British Standards Institute.

Cao, G. (2001). *Contemporary systems thinking and organizational change management.* Unpublished PhD thesis, The University of Luton.

Cao, G., Clarke, A., & Lehaney, B. (1999). Towards systemic management of diversity in organizational change. *Journal of Strategic Change, 8*(4), 205-216.

Carr, M. (2007) Adoption and Diffusion of Internet Banking. A chapter in Ravi, V (ed) Advances Banking Technology and Management: Impact of ICT and CRM. IGI Global.

Chandy, R. K., & Tellis, G. J. (1998) Organizing for radical product innovation: the overlooked role of willingness to cannibalize. *Journal of Marketing Research,* XXXV (November), 474-487.

Chemers, M., Oskamp, S. & Costanzo, M. (Ed.) (1995), *Diversity in Organizations: New Perspectives for a Changing Workplace.* Thousand Oaks, CA: Sage.

Cox, T., & Blake, S. (1991), Managing Cultural Diversity: Implications for Organizational Competitiveness, *Academy of Management Executive, 5*(3), 45-56.

Cunliffe, D. (2000). Developing usable Web sites: A review and model, *Internet Research: Electronic Networking Application and Policy, 10*(4), 295-307.

DoD (1987). US Department of Defense Trusted Computer System Evaluation Criteria (*The Orange Book*). Washington, DC: U.S. Department of Defense.

Drake, P., & Clarke, S. (2001). *Information Security: A Technical or Human Domain?* 2001 IRMA International Conference: Human-Side of IT Track, Toronto Canada.

Dubelaar, C. Sohal, A. & Savic, V. (2005). Benefits, impediments and critical success factors in B2C: E-business adoption. *Technovation, 25*, 1251–1262.

EC (1991). *Commission of the European communities, European information technology security evaluation criteria (ITSEC),* European Commission.

Harden, G. (2002). E-banking Comes to Town: Exploring how Traditional UK High Street Banks are Meeting the Challenge of Technology and Virtual Relationships. *Journal of Financial Services Marketing, 6*(4), 323-332.

Harris, L. & Spence, L. (2002) The Ethics Of E-banking, *Journal of Electronic Commerce Research, 3*(2), 59-65.

Hirsh, L. (2002, May 17). The Case for e-Business Outsourcing. *E-Commerce Times.* http://ecommercetimes.com/perl/story/17802.html

Holland, C. P., Light, B., & Gibson, N. (1999b, June 23-25). A Critical Success Factors Model for Enterprise Resource Planning Implementation. In Pries-Heje, J., Ciborra, C., Kantaz, K., Valor, J., Christiaanse, E., Avison, D., Heje, C. (Eds.) *Proceedings of the 7th European Conference on Information Systems,* (pp. 273-287). Copenhagen, Denmark: CBS.

Kim, D. J., Ferrin, D. L., & Rao, H. R. (2003). A Study of the Effect of Consumer Trust on Consumer Expectations and Satisfaction: the Korean Experience. *Proceedings of the 5th international conference on Electronic: A literature review of online trust in business to consumer e-commerce transactions, 2001-2006 VIII, No. 2, 69 Issues in Information Systems commerce,* (pp. 310-315).

Kotter, J. P. (1996). Transforming organizations. *Executive Excellence, 13*(9), 13.

Liao, Z., & Cheung, M.T. (2005, March 29-31). Service Quality in Internet E-banking: A User-based Core Framework. In *Proceedings of the 2005 IEEE International Conference on E-technology, E-commerce and E-service,* (pp. 628-631).

Loh. L., & Venkatraman, N. (1994). Information technology outsourcing: A cross sectional analysis. In Galliers, R. D., Baker, B. S. H. (Eds.) *Strategic Information Management*, (pp. 263-281). Oxford, UK: Butterworth-Heinemann Ltd.

McDougall, P. (2007, February 13). Credit Suisse outsources to bt in deal worth $1.1 billion. *Information Week*.

Midgley, G. (1992). The sacred and profane in critical systems thinking. *Systems Practice, 5*(1), 5-16.

Midgley, G. (1996). The ideal of unity and the practice of pluralism in systems science. In Flood, R. L. and Romm, R. (Ed.), *Critical Systems Thinking - Current Research and Practice*, (pp. 25-36). Plenum Press.

Milliken, F. J. & Martins, L. L. (1996). Searching for Common Threads: Understanding the Multiple Effects of Diversity in Organizational Groups. *Academy of Management Review,* 21(2), 402-433.

Mintzberg, H. (1998). Politics and the Political Organization. In Mintzberg, H., Quinn J. B. and Ghoshal, S., *The Strategy Process*, (revised European edition), (pp. 377-382). London: Prentice Hall .

Mohamed, M., & Al-Jaroodi, J. (2003, October). Highly-Available Application Integration in proceedings of the 2003 IEEE International Conference on Information Reuse and Integration (IRI'03). (pp. 370-376) Las Vegas, NV, , . http://faculty.uacu.ac.ae/Nader_M/papers/IRI2003_APPLICATION_INTEGRATION.pdf

Morgan, G. (1997). *Images of Organization*, (New edition of the international best-seller). Thousand Oaks, CA: Sage.

Pettigrew, A. M. (1985). *The Awakening Giant.* Oxford, UK: Blackwell.

Pfeffer, J. (1994), *Competitive advantage through people: unleashing the power of the work force*, Boston: Harvard Business School Press.

Pfeffer, J. (1992). *Managing with power: politics and influence in organizations.* Harvard Business School Press, Boston Mass.

Pugh, D. (1978), Understanding and Managing Organization Change. *London Business School Journal, 3*(2), 29-34.

Schneider, I. (2004, July 6). Italian bank taps accenture and e.piphany for marketing muscle. *Bank Systems & Technology.* Retrieved June 12 2008, from http://banktech.com/rdelivery/showArticle.jhtml?articleID=22103823

Sergeant, C. (2000, March 29). E-Banking: Risks & Responses – UK Financial Services Authority. http://www.fsa.gov.uk/pubs

Shah, M. H. Braganza, A. & Morabito, V. (2007). A Survey of Critical Success Factors in e-Banking: An Organisational Perspective. *European Journal of Information Systems, 16*(4), 511-524. http://www.palgrave-journals.com/ejis/journal/v16/n4/index.html

Shah, M. H. & Siddiqui, F. A. (2006). Organizational success factors in e-banking at the woolwich. *International Journal of Information Management*, 26, 442-456.

Turbin, E., Lee, J. King D. and Chung, H. M. (2002). *Electronic Commerce: A Managerial Perspective,* (International edition). London: Prentice Hall.

Wang, Y. D., & Emurian, H. H. (2005). An overview of online trust: Concepts, elements, and implications. *Computers in Human Behavior,* 21, 105–125.

Chapter VIII
Key to Success:
Cases and Practical Solutions

INTRODUCTION

This chapter builds on previous chapters and brings together the technical, managerial and social issues discussed in this book so far, to offer practical solutions to the e-banking related problems. We have also included two detailed e-banking case studies of medium sized banks to illustrate our propositions. The chapter covers a number of practical dimensions such as common tools used to evaluate e-banking initiatives, real reasons for banks to implement e-banking, factors which led to their success as well as the ones which caused considerable problems.

FINDING THE ROOT CAUSES: KEY TECHNIQUES

To investigate strategic and managerial issues associated with e-banking in order to develop practical solutions, many approaches could be used, such as Key Indicator System, SWOT Analysis and Cost/Benefit Analysis. These approaches are briefly covered below (for more detail see the referenced texts).

Key Indicator System

Rockart (1979) presented this system as a substitute to critical success factors for investigating strategic issues and providing executives with the information they require. The approach is based on three concepts. The first concept is the determination of a set of key indicators concerning the general health of the business. Information is collected on each of these indicators. The second concept is exception reporting, regarding the availability of information to executives on areas where organizational performance is different from predetermined criteria. The third concept is based on expanding the availability of better, cheaper and more flexible visual display techniques to help executives digest vast quantities of information.

This technique is useful in e-banking, as implementation and operations related to it are very information intensive. It could be used to conduct detailed analysis of the information needs of e-banking managers, as well as to conduct detailed evaluation of the business as a whole, in order to determine what changes can be made in business model, structure or other aspects of management to facilitate the growth of e-banking.

SWOT Analysis

Strengths, Weaknesses, Opportunities and Threats (SWOT) analysis has been a useful tool for many business related problems. The purpose of SWOT analysis is to isolate key issues and to facilitate a strategic approach. The process of using the SWOT approach requires an internal survey of strengths and weaknesses of the program and an external survey of opportunities and threats (Balamuralikrishna & Dugger, 1995).

SWOTs can be performed by individual managers or by groups. Group techniques are particularly effective in providing structure, objectivity, clarity and focus to discussions about strategy which might otherwise tend to wander or else be strongly influenced by politics and personalities (Glass, 1991). Groups dynamics can also be affected by these factors if the process is not managed carefully.

In e-banking, SWOTs can be used to determine internal strengths such as flat organizational structures and relevant in-house skills, or weaknesses such as lack of integrated back end systems and employees' resistance to change. External opportunities such as increase in market share or image enhancement as well as threats such as potential new entrants and negative publicity if things go wrong can also be identified. Although examples given here may sound obvious and superficial, a detailed application of this approach often throws up surprises for even the most experienced managers.

Cost /Benefit Analysis

This is one of the most commonly used techniques. Cost/benefit analysis is used to analyze feasible alternatives in terms of the major costs involved together with the major benefits that are expected to accrue. There are a number of assumptions behind cost/benefit analysis:

1.   All feasible alternatives have been examined;
2.   All costs and benefits can be identified and measured and
3.   The costs and benefits can be expressed in common (usually financial) units.

In practice, these assumptions rarely hold true and managerial judgement is required in order to incorporate all elements of the analysis into the decision making process. One common difficulty in applying this technique in technology led initiatives such as e-banking is that many benefits such as enhancement in image are difficult to quantify. Some costs are also well hidden and sometimes the true costs of a project become apparent only several years after completion.

Critical Success Factors (CSFs)

CSFs have been defined in several ways depending on the purpose for which they are used. However, Rockart's (1979) original definition still remains most comprehensive. He defines CSFs as 'the limited number of areas in which results, if they are satisfactory, will ensure successful competitive performance for the organization."

CSFs is one of the major techniques used in academia as well as in industry. Evidence from the literature shows the numerous ways in which this technique has been used, for example, Ang and Teo (1997) recommended CSFs for strategic IS planning. They stress that by identifying CSFs, key managers can be assigned to the critical tasks. They further point out that CSFs, when formally identified, implicitly communicate top management's priorities, and thus direct organizational efforts in the desired direction.

Jenster (1987) sees CSFs as a framework against which employees can make sense of priorities, assumptions and environmental conditions, and are then able to better contribute to the execution of long-range plans. He further points out that, by providing a bridge between the firm's objectives and management strategy, the isolation of critical factors also provides a vehicle for the design of an effective system of performance measurement and control.

Slevin et al. (1991) used CSFs to develop specific performance measures and to track performance in a complex IS environment. According to Slevin et al. (1991),

CSFs are the basis for identifying the performance indicators used in measuring short-term progress toward long-term objectives. The process of developing CSFs has been shown to have a generally positive impact on organizations in terms of enhanced communication patterns and better understanding of goals and objectives. Holland et al. (1999a) recommend CSF method for enterprise resource planning systems implementation.

Daniel et al. (1999) used CSFs to analyze the development of marketing information systems. Averweg and Erwin (1999) used CSFs to examine the implementation of Decision Support Systems in South Africa. A study of 128 firms by Jenster (1987) in mature manufacturing industries found that the firms that had a higher return on equity: formally identified their CSFs and used these factors to monitor their progress in the implementation of strategic changes. Julta et al. (2001) states that the identification of core competencies is essential to strategy creation at every level. This provides a firm with a potential competitive edge in the offline world which can be extended to e-commerce.

Having mentioned the benefits of CSFs it is important to stress that in an ill –structured, complex social context like an organization, CSFs will be social constructs and consequently subjective. They may also change with time as the context and the participants' understanding of the context evolves (Williams & Ramaprasad, 1996). Some of the other causes for variance among CSFs are changes in environment, the stage of firm development, the management team, the stage of firm growth, the firm size and the strategy type being employed. Biases on the part of researchers, managers or methods used to elicit CSFs may also cause considerable variance.

Our inability to achieve the ideal for these reasons should not however discourage us from moving in that direction. A constant review of the criticality of the factors identified in a given situation is desirable in order to maximise their benefits. Our aim should be to seek a set of factors which are adequate and operationally feasible with respect to control (Williams & Ramaprasad, 1996). Case studies presented below in this chapter also used CSFs to evaluate the e-banking at two banks.

HOW WAS IT DONE: REAL SUCCESS STORIES

The following two case studies were conducted by us using a case study research approach. We used Interviews (with senior and middle managers involved in e-banking projects), observations and analyzed internal documents such as memos, consultation and planning reports, information given on the banks' website, media releases and annual accounts reports.

Case Study 1- Bank A

Background

This case was developed from a research conducted by the one of the authors of this book. For confidentiality reasons we call it Bank A. The Bank A is one of the UK's leading providers of personal financial services and products It is a very innovative company and its enthusiasm for new technologies means that it is in forefront of providing financial services through its e-banking channel.

It is one of the medium sized banks in United Kingdom with over 400 branches nationwide. Initially it was opened as a small building society and remained so until World War One. Following the development boom of the '30s, the Bank A was able to expand rapidly and by mid nineteen thirties it was the third largest building society in the country with assets of over £38m.

Growth continued during the 1940s and 50s. The 1960's saw the transformation of the Bank A into a modern financial services institution, with the opening of a new dedicated administration centre. By 1970, half of all UK families owned their own homes and the strong demand for mortgages enabled the Bank A to establish itself as a national building society, with high street branches in most of England. The Bank A was one of the first financial institution to network its branches, using countertop on-line terminals linked to the central mainframe.

Deregulation in the mid-1980s enabled building societies to compete in many new areas that had previously been the traditional preserve of the banks and insurance companies. The Bank A took a lead in this through diversification into new areas. It developed several subsidiary companies offering a wide range of services including life assurance unit trusts, estate agency, insurance and direct sales. Abroad, the Bank A has established it's subsidiaries in many European countries such as Italy, France and Germany. In late 1990s, like any other building societies it floated in London Stock Exchange to become a Public Limited Company

E-Banking at Bank A

Most of the financial services at the Bank A are designed to be accessible through a variety of different channels such as branches, telephone, the Internet, digital televisions and mobile phones. This means that many customers (those with right equipment of course) have all-time access to their finances. This gives a flexibility to customers to manage their finances wherever they are, and whenever they want, instantly. Using any of the e-Channels available at the Bank A, customers can view their current account and saving accounts; view the balance/valuation of any Bank A account including mortgage; savings, current account, personal loan, and unit trusts; pay bills; arrange to pay bills or transfer funds on future dates up to six weeks ahead; move money between their accounts and mortgage; change their pin; apply for personal loans, new accounts or mortgages.

To provide this kind of access and flexibility, the Bank A continuously invested heavily in technology and has gone through many organizational changes, which are discussed in a later section.

Reasons for Participation in E-Commerce

Since becoming a PLC, Bank A's strategy has been focused on adapting to the new world of multiple distribution outlets beyond the traditional branches network. The main reason behind this was top management's belief that winners will be those organizations which combine new technologies with traditional business to provide integrated solutions which meet customer needs Another reason was the fast changing environment in the retail banking industry with new entrants, such as Egg and Smile providing financial services using innovative business models and technologies. Relative maturity of Internet technologies meant provision of convenient services (via Internet, mobile phones and iTV) to customers was now more feasible with a promise of much lower transaction costs. Taking these factors into account, the Woolwich decided to be an innovation leader in the area of e-commerce rather than drag behind its competitors. Enhancement of the company's image for both customers, as well as investors, was another key objective.

Increasing customer retention through depth of relationship and service was also an important objective. Internet technology was seen as a key enabler for this purpose because it can provide rich information about customers, enabling the Woolwich to personalise financial services according to the needs of the individual customers, thus enriching the relationship and as a result achieving greater loyalty. Very early into the e-banking implementation, they noticed that customers who have signed up to Woolwich e-banking service are 65 per cent more profitable for the bank because these channels were attracting high-income customers. They were also getting customers from the remote areas of UK, where they had no penetration in past.

CSFs in E-Commerce at the *Bank A*

E-banking has been a very successful initiative for the Woolwich winning the approval of existing customers (many of them have signed up the online banking channel) and attracting new ones. The following is brief description of the factors which were reported (by our research participants) to be critical to the success of e-banking.

Understanding Customers

This factor has been seen as a key to success at the Bank A. They invested heavily in relevant technologies, which enables them to gather and analyze extensive customer information. At a basic level they used a systems called QuickStream which helped them to analyze (by providing the record of customer's clicks in the form of a stream) customer's behaviour during their visit to the Bank A's website. *"This information is very useful for both design and marketing purposes"*, said the Manager for Customer Support for e-Channels. They also used a software tool, called 'Webtrend', which records where people enter the home page and how they navigate through it and how they leave the site. According to the e-commerce Enhancement Manager, *"This enables us to evaluate our advertising campaigns as well as get continuous feedback on our services and accessibility issues (design of website etc.)"*.

They also used a software web-collaboration tool, which was a call agent that could see where a customer is on their website. It could record how long they have been on each individual page. Viewing this information on screen in real time, a sales agent could type in a message on customers' screen, offering help and advice. This initiative was aimed at improving their customer services and increasing sales. This combined with other factors has helped them expand current customer base by acquiring new customers as well as enriching existing relationships.

Organizational Flexibility

The Bank A has changed considerably in terms of departmental structures and business process in order to web-enable itself. There are new teams such as the e-commerce development team, which they did not have before but also other business processes behind that team have been significantly changed. According to e-commerce Enhancement Manager *"we did it the wrong way, the re-engineering of business process followed the introduction of e-commerce rather than other way round"*.

There are many processes which have now been totally integrated and automated such as delivering check or deposit books on customer's request. Staff number has not reduced, instead their role has changed and they all are very much geared towards sales. The ability to focus on sales has resulted in 3.6 products held by each customer, which is much higher than its competitors. This radical transformation from being a mortgage centred building society to a customer focused and integrated bank was another reason for its takeover by the Barclays. Bank A's Principal Technical Specialist, pointed out that *"Barclays want to utilise the experience of the Bank A's managers to transform themselves in similar ways. That is why there have been number of senior appointments within Barclays from the Bank A's staff.*

Web-Specific Marketing

The Bank A is aware of the power and uniqueness of the Internet medium. The Internet requires a different way of marketing to sell products. Their Manager for Customers' Support for e-Channels stated that, "*e-Channels have opened up a whole new way of communicating with customers and we have a dedicated area within our marketing function that deals with the e-Channels. This means that e-commerce has changed the way the marketing department works in order to cope with new ways of marketing. Now the focus is on understanding customers and using that understanding to enrich relationships with them*". Their home website presents adverts on the right hand side of the screen which keep asking customers about their requirements for other financial services. If a customer clicks on any of those advertisement windows, they are led to the relevant page. According to e-commerce Enhancements Manager "*from next year we're going to start tailoring advertisements to personalise them. For example, when a customer logs into our system, we will be able to conduct a quick profile of his/her account, look at what he/she hasn't got with us and that's what we would start advertising*". This profiling ability is also likely to enable them to assess the requirements of individual customers and offer services accordingly. The main idea behind this is replacing high margin products with smaller margin – multi-product relations with customers. The management believes that e-banking is key to success in relationship marketing. So far this strategy has resulted in 65% increase in the average income per e-banking customer.

Rapid Delivery of Services

E-commerce has raised people's expectations regarding the time it takes to deliver services. Whereas in past, people were ready to accept a couple of day's delay in funds transfer, now it has come down to real time. As indicated by e-commerce Enhancement Manager "*people move money between their accounts and walk straight to the branch to draw it out. WAP service is heavily used for this purpose on Saturdays*". People want other services such as loan or mortgage approval quickly too. This demand for instant services is becoming a critical success factor and the Bank A see it as an opportunity to gain more business.

Integration

Instant delivery required extensive integration of business processes and Information Systems (IS). One of their senior IT Manager explained that, "*the Bank A uses a middleware layer for integration of different systems and channels. This allows a host of different clients (front end systems) to access a whole lot of back-end systems".* This middleware layer which provides common interface to all existing systems, enables them add new systems quickly as the interface has to be implemented just once, to the middleware rather than to the all range of different systems. In addition, said Head of e-commerce at the Bank A, *"this middleware enabled us to implement a component-based architecture. Tasks such as checking accounts are available as business objects in the middleware and can be used by all channels".* This makes the channels interchangeable and allows the bank to add new channels or services without disrupting core services. As shown in Figure 8.1 the middleware allows access to all services through all channels. The downside is that if the middleware goes down, it can have quite a lot of effect on all channels.

The technology architecture shown in Figure 8.1. has enabled the Bank A to easily adapt its business model to the new requirements of e-banking, without touching the legacy mainframes used in the back-end environment. This ensures that the system will evolve over time and the resources allocated for e-banking will not drain into upgrading legacy systems. This architecture also allows the Bank A to add new off-the-shelf systems to quickly increase the capacity of the systems.

Another aspect of integration is helping customers to see the whole financial picture. This means providing customers with information about all products with the Bank A, analyzed and summarised on a single page. For example a customer may have a current account, a saving account distributed into many pots, mortgage and credit card with the Bank A. It would be useful for him to know at a glance, his financial position to make informed decisions. Another word used for this type of services is account aggregation. The Bank A was one of the first bank to offer this kind of services to its customers.

Figure 8.1. Channels and services integration at the Bank A

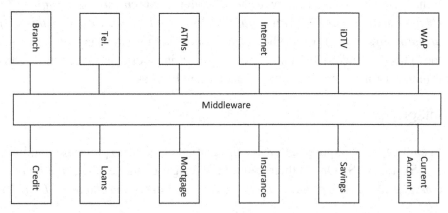

Availability of Resources

Availability of human and financial resources is critical in all types of projects. In new technology projects such as e-banking, shortage of readily skilled human resources can be a severe handicap. The Bank A got round this problem by implementing a very intensive training programme for some carefully selected members of the existing staff. As an example, their e-commerce Enhancements Manager stated that *"when we implemented Wireless Application Protocol (WAP), there was no one in the country who knew about the implementation of WAP technology for financial services so we decided to send seven of our people to Helsinki for training. They were the people who implemented WAP technology on their return from that training. Where need dictated, people from other organizations such as Unisys were also brought in"*. Regarding financial resources, they did not have any considerable problems as top management was firmly behind this project and providing sufficient resources for uninterrupted progress.

Support from the Top Management

Support from the top Management is widely considered to be a key success factor in technological projects (Turban et al., 2000). In the Bank A's case, its chief executive at the time of implementation of project, worked out the open plan, came up with finances for it and participated in day- to-day implementation of the project. *"Without his absolute commitment we wouldn't have done it"* (e-commerce Enhancements Manager).

Security

Security is a mentioned as very critical success factor by almost everybody in e-banking field. In fact, lack of it, or consumers' fears about it, is one of the biggest obstacles in the growth of e-banking. The Bank A uses highest levels of encryption to secure their system. Their Analyst/Programmer further elaborated on this point by saying, *"we use secure layer technology which encrypts all of the information, from a customer logging in or filling in an application form to storage and feedback to the customer"*. Costs of this high level of security are very high but they see it as necessary evil.

Established Brand Name

Having an established brand name was also cited by many informants at the Bank A as a critical success factor. The main reason for this given by most informants was that, a household name such as the Bank A gives customers added confidence to conduct business online. Other reasons may include their previous positive experiences with the company and the non-substantial nature of the online medium which makes trust in a well-known name even more important than when more traditional channels are used.

Bank A's approach to using their brand name to enhance trust in online environment is well supported in e-commerce related literature. For example, Turban et al. (2000) proposed branding as a transferable resource across physical and social barriers to entry for customers in a new and perceptibly daunting environment. The importance of brand factor is widely recognised now and some virtual financial organizations are opening or considering to open some high street branches to enhance their brands.

Having Multiple Channels

This factor is also related to the non-substantial nature of the online medium. Most of the informants at the Bank A stated that e-banking by an organization, which is also accessible through other channels such as branches and phone banking, is most likely to successful in the long run. This is because customers can use the most desirable channel suitable for task in hand. For example, a customer may use the Internet for checking account balances or transfer money between accounts but may ring in to settle a dispute or go to a branch for a face to face discussion on complex matters such as mortgages. To fully utilise multiple channels advantage, channel integration is required which may include: sharing of business rules and other components across channels, a common set of interfaces into core systems for use across all channels, high quality customer-centred functionality across all channels, ability to deliver all products and services through all channels and customer services which are able to support all channels. The Bank A was very close to these ideals for channels integration.

Fast Responsive Customer Service

There is usually higher expectation for customer service from the e-Channels. Also, to support 24 hours e-Channels, customer service has to be available 24 hours too. Before the arrival of e-commerce at the Bank A, customer services were not available 24 hours a day. To meet these expectations and requirements, support to customers has improved considerably, with this all- time availability of customer services and increased choice for customers to use whichever channel they wish to use at any time. The technical help desk to solve technical problem experienced by the customers' support services helpdesk at the call centres. According to the Bank A's Technical Support Analyst *"our aim is to develop seamless integrated architecture that will allow the customer to view, access and interact with the set of services that the Bank A is offering and a few technical problems are preventing us from this ideal, but we'll get there soon*". To minimise these technical problems, every new component has to be tested across numerous hardware and software platforms resulting in very high testing costs. However, it is also a necessity to reduce load on customer services and to reduce any inconvenience to the customers.

Mixed Strategy for Selection of Vendors

In information technology projects, choice of vendors is generally an important issue. Some companies go for a single vendor solution to ensure easy integration whereas others chose best of breed products to find products, which meet their requirements better. At the Bank A, they have adopted a mixed strategy. They try to get most of the components from Microsoft but where requirements dictate, they also get some components from other vendors or develop themselves. They have a Microsoft consultancy team operating within their headquarters and in many projects, their expertise of Microsoft products is heavily utilised. Therefore, they try to use Microsoft products as their first choice. Another reason for this may be the easier integration of different components from same vendor.

Systematic Change Management

The Bank A paid special attention to this issue from beginning. They consulted most of the employees on major decisions. E-banking was quite aggressively promoted within the organization in a number of ways. First, they made sure that every employee has access to the Internet. Second, they encouraged them to open "open plan" accounts by putting £100 in the accounts of those who did, so they can actually experience new e-Channels. Third, when mobile phone banking was launched, they provided everyone who wanted, with a mobile phone. Fourth, they put Internet booths in branches so staff can experiment with it and promote it to the customers. As stated by the Bank A's Principal Technical Specialist, *"changes are communicated to the Bank A's staff in weekly or monthly team talks, where staff get a chance to discuss all aspects of a change. In addition the company's intranet and monthly newsletters are used for this purpose"*. This strategy helps make staff feel an important part of the change and eases resistance to change.

A major benefit of this strategy they experienced was useful feedback, which was invaluable for improving services and system interface. Another major benefit of promotion of e-commerce within the organization was that most members of staff were willing to go along with the changes it brought with it. Their Principal Technical Specialist stated that *"we've seen a massive change in technologies and work practices during the last few years, active promotion of e-commerce helped us get the required commitment from our people"*.

General Comments about Bank A's E-Banking

They did not consider incentivising e-Services (i.e. cheaper loans or higher interest rates on savings in the Internet accounts) was necessary to attract customers to their new channels. The main reason cited by them for this was that, their brand name, customer service and technological leadership was enough for this purpose. Another reason cited by their Customers Support Manager for e-Channels was that *"we don't differentiate products for e-Channels because our main target is customers who prefer a multi-channel solution rather than hunt for bargains from Internet only banks"*. While this may be true, in our opinion product differentiation (offering higher value products on e-Channels) would attract even larger numbers of customers because many of them expect this from e-Channels.

Their website design and operational functionality was a rare weak link in the Bank A's e-commerce approach. The following criteria was used for evaluation of the Bank A and other websites: the homepage, online quotation, online application, pricing information, clarity of explanations, ease of navigation, on site resources, return visit incentives and overall ease of doing business. On many occasions, the Bank A's financial calculator was 'down for upgrade' and the table of typical examples of their financial products was just one long page and was difficult to read. Application forms were also a touch too long and difficult to fill in. A positive aspect of the Bank A's website operations is that they are keeping it fairly fresh with regular changes on a monthly basis to its look and feel.

Another area in which they can build on their existing successes is to broaden the scope of their information gathering and analysing technologies across all channels. Whereas it's true that e-Channels are better suited to this kind of activity, understanding customers' interaction patterns with all channels would be very useful as it would provide a fuller picture to be utilised to further enhance their relationship with customers.

The Bank A's attitude and approach to e-banking is very impressive. In the beginning, they made the mistake of jumping on to e-banking without much planning and realisation of its organizational impacts. However they learnt from their mistakes quickly and followed e-banking with the organizational changes required for e-banking, such as the re-engineering of business processes and some modifications in the organization's management structure to speed up decision-making process.

Case Study 2 – Bank B

Background

This case was also developed from a research conducted by the one of the authors of this book. For confidentiality reasons we call it Bank B. The Bank B is one of the

UK's medium sized financial services groups. It offers a broad range of financial services to personal, commercial and small business customers. It can trace its origins back to mid nineteenth century. Its amalgamations with other local societies commenced, culminating at the end of the 2nd World War with a name change and the opening of a national branch network in 1940s.

During 1950s the Bank B, undertook a major initiative to establish itself on a national basis by opening a number of new branches beyond its home territory. While Bank B programme of mergers continued, resulting in it becoming one of the 'Top 10' largest UK Building Societies.

In mid 1990, Bank B announced its intention to convert from a mutual building society to a Public Limited Company. Bank B successfully converted from a mutual building society to a bank and became a listed FTSE 100 plc a few years later. Bank B's distribution network consist of: a network of over 300 branches provides UK-wide coverage, call centres for phone banking, a network of over 2500 ATMs, with plans for a significant expansion, their website which is continuously improving in terms of functionality. It is widely considered to be a very conservative organization which is usually slow in embracing changes (Hughes, 2007).

E-Banking at the Bank B

E-banking at Bank B was launched early in 2001. It came after a project to launch a new Internet bank was cancelled, as management at Bank B decided that launching e-commerce under their existing brand, which is well established and trusted in the market place, would be better than building a completely new brand. After its cancellation, the project team re-joined Bank B, that is when e-commerce was given high profile. Most of the disparate parts of the group that were working on e-commerce were brought together to give it a central focus. E-banking at Bank B has achieved considerable successes in terms of growth in revenues from this new channel. According to the Marketing Research Manager, "*the Internet has quickly become a main stream channel for delivering services to Bank B's customers along with branches, call centres and ATMs*".

Why they wanted E-Banking?

In early 2000s Bank B set out a strategy based on building a customer-focused business. Its main objective was to provide superior shareholder returns by better identifying and meeting customer needs. They set out many strategic targets including e-banking, and the steps needed to meet them. Their customer base of almost six million personal customers makes them a major UK brand. They are big enough to be powerful, but also small enough to be agile, innovative and to deliver simplification and change more effectively than larger competitors. Having these characteristics, offering online services was an obvious next step with following objectives:

Retaining Customers for Longer

Their main strategic objective was to increase the loyalty of customers. This meant delivering them the service and products they want. *"Bank B has a large and diverse customer base and many of them wanted us to offer our services online"* said the Head of Credit Cards & Personal Loans at the Bank B. The convenience offered by e-commerce was seen to be essential for retaining those customers. According to their e-commerce Research and Development Manager *"what we are trying to do is to give customers the choice of whichever channels they wish to come into the bank. We know that some customers have preference for e-Channels so we are giving them what they want to win their loyalty"*.

Offering electronic services with very basic functionalities, as was the case at the Bank B, could be a risky strategy. For example if a customer cannot transfer his funds from saving accounts to current accounts online, which was the case until recently, in frustration he/she might switch to a competitor who offers such convenience. When asked about this, one informant said *"our calculation was that most of the Internet channel customers use it for basic functions such as checking accounts or downloading product information. So instead of waiting for full functionality to materialise and letting those customers go, we started offering basic services as soon as we were able to. This was a customer retention exercise and we have been largely successful in this"*.

Selling More to Existing Customers

The UK financial services market has matured considerably and there is very limited scope for creation of new markets. This means that the most common route to growth is to sell more products to existing customers. At Bank B, e-banking was intended to play a key role in this regard. Revenue growth by this type of relationship marketing was a key objective when e-banking was launched. Early signs are encouraging as both the volume and value of new business generated from the Internet channel are growing all the time.

Building a More Cost Efficient Business

By better understanding customers, and better understanding which channels they prefer to buy from and to use, offering those channels and by consistently simplifying their business processes, they aim to grow their business whilst also significantly improving cost-efficiency. To do this they have heavily invested in technology and process changes needed to deliver cost efficiencies in the long term.

E-Commerce Became a Hygiene Factor

As many organizations in the retail financial services industry begun offering their services on electronic channels such as the Internet, Interactive TV and mobile phones. *"Many customers begun to expect online access from their banks. Not playing in this space meant losing business"* said the website Development Manager. In this situation, management of Bank B felt that it was necessary to start offering their services which would also convey a positive message to shareholders and potential new investors that the bank is dynamic, aggressive and strategically focused.

CSFs in E-Banking at the Bank B

The e-banking project is a widely considered with Bank B to be successful in achieving most of the objectives stated at start of the project. It has helped many existing customers to conduct their business online as well as attracting new ones. The following is a brief description of the factors, which our research found to be critical for e-banking success at the Bank B.

Formation of E-Banking Specialist Team

Right from beginning, the management of Bank B decided to form a specialist e-commerce team. This was done to avoid the situation where e-banking is pushed aside by the other priorities in the IT or marketing department, which were leading candidates to develop e-banking. The team started its work three years ago with only three members. It has since grown to almost thirty members and works closely with other departments. Almost all informants from the e-commerce team agree that this factor played a critical role in the success of e-commerce at the Bank B. However, the lack of a broader perspective, because few team members had any exposures to the e-commerce outside the Bank B, means that they have no benchmarks to compare their performance against. In some cases the team relies heavily on the Marketing and IT departments for some of its operations, such as security testing, which often causes delays. Communications within the team is very good and most of the informants agreed that the e-commerce director and other senior managers within the team are very approachable and encourage new ideas.

Security

Some informants rated security of front and back-end systems to be a critical success factor. Two reasons for this were cited by informants (i) being a bank, there is an obligation for Bank B to be secure and (ii) public tolerance for any security breaches is very low and any such instance may result in huge negative publicity and financial losses. Bank B is using very high-level encryption technology and various other measures to achieve their goal of keeping their systems secure.

Established Brand Name

As in the Bank A case study presented above, most of the informants at the Bank B also consider having an established brand name as one of the most critical success factors. The reasons given by them were also similar to the one given by the informants at the Bank A, such as customers' previous positive experiences with the company and the non-substantial nature of the online medium which makes trust in a well-known name even more important than when more traditional channels are used. Some other informants argued that, while this factor may not be critical, it does provide established providers with a built-in advantage over new comers, especially in the context of e-banking. New online businesses have to spend a much higher proportion of their financial resources on advertising and often offer much higher value products to attract new customers. This means it may take them years to become profitable.

Having Multiple Channels

The importance of this factor is also related to the non-substantial nature of the online medium. Some informants at the Bank B expressed a view that a combination of services delivery channels is most likely to be successful in the long run. This is because customers have the choice to use the most desirable channel for task in hand. This implies that other channels if effectively utilised can help increase the use of online channels by customers. Channel integration is about sharing of business rules and other components across all service delivery channels, a common set of interfaces in core systems for use across all channels, high quality customer-centred functionality across all channels, the ability to deliver all products and services through all channels and customer services which are able to support all channels. At Bank B their multi-channel strategy worked very well. Customers have access to all channels and e-banking is growing in prominence all the time.

Good Products

The Bank B has a range of good products and services. According to the e-commerce Director, "*if your products are poorly designed or wrongly priced then electronic channel will not help you much in terms of sales. Bank B has always been an innovative company in terms of product design and online channel should help us use this strength to speed up the process of product design and delivery*". Product differentiation for the online channel is another important aspect as generally people expect better value on this channel. Bank B has begun this process by introducing lower (than other channels) interest rate loans on the Internet and offering high interest rates on Internet only accounts.

Internet Specific Marketing

e-commerce has enabled the implementation of a new marketing strategy which is designed to enrich the relationship with their existing customers (selling them more products). One example of this approach is the Alliance's Premier Products which consists of a competitively priced current account which also gives customers incentives to buy a full range of the company's other products, including discounted mortgages, low interest credit cards and personal loans, higher than usual interest rates for savings accounts, and free annual travel insurance. Figures show that premier product customers purchase over four products on average. Comparing this with their overall average of 1.5 products per customer, it looks a remarkable achievement. By offering financial services and other products through their partners on new electronic channels, Bank B is trying to maximise its revenue streams.

One problem area in this regard was the meagre relation between marketing and e-commerce departments. Some informants in e-commerce thought that people in the marketing department do not understand the marketing requirements for e-commerce channel and spend far too much (per sale). Whereas informants from marketing department laid blame for this situation on e-banking department which, according to them, has failed to live up to its promises (especially in terms of cost effectiveness).

Integration

Integration has been a key factor in the success of e-commerce at the Bank B. They have taken many steps to achieve this by restructuring the group to enable significant cost and efficiency improvements. They are implementing a new group-wide technology architecture, which they hope, will deliver integrated customer access, provide better customer service and reduce costs. Even at its current levels, they are able to give decisions on most of the applications received through the Internet within 24 hours. However, there is a considerable scope for improvement. For example "*process of applications processing can be automated in many cases to make it almost instant and that's where we will be able to deliver the promise of cost reductions*" said the e-banking Marketing Manager. Another improvement under consideration, according to their Internet development manager, is to provide customers with up-to-date details of all their Bank B accounts on a single web-screen.

Old information systems called 'legacy systems' are the biggest hurdle in the path to integration. Bank B's Senior e-commerce Manager, pointed-out that "*We have separate systems for maintaining and managing our current accounts, separate systems for maintaining and managing our loan etc. Significantly, only one of these systems is real-time*". The reasons for this situation cited by some informants were: lack of investment in the technical infrastructure in the past, shortage of human resources in IT department and scarcity of project management skills within the organization which resulted in some major project failures. To address this situation Bank B is implementing middleware called 'ROMA', which will enable them to integrate all legacy systems to all channels. It would also enable them to plug and play new applications. Figure 8.2 represent the new Bank B technology architecture being developed at present.

Lack of process integration is another hurdle in this path. According to R & D Manager "*we would quite often build technology and then tell people about the process that goes with the technology, but we should start with the process which says what does the customer experience need to be from end-to-end, therefore what are the processes and which technologies will be supporting this process*". Also, there are some old business processes still in operation, which were designed for

Figure 8.2. A representation of new technology architecture at Bank B

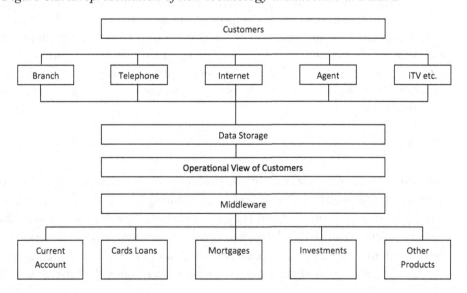

an off-line world when customers' expectations were much lower. *"Strategy 2000 recognised this problem and situation is improving gradually"*, said their website enhancement manager.

Another aspect of integration is channel integration to offer inter-linked services solution. Bank B has already got country-wide Web of branches and ATMs, an even bigger network of Girobank post offices (its subsidiary) and 24 hours telephone banking. *"With the addition of Internet banking Bank B is striving for even greater integration of these channels to offer greater convenience to its customers"*, said Head of Credit Cards and Loans Marketing Department.

Regarding inter-links between different teams and departments, e-commerce has made it necessary for many departments to work closely together. R & D manager mentioned an example of this effect *"e-commerce is bringing closer e-commerce and IT departments. Other changes are also taking effect gradually"*. Currently, Bank B is spending around hundreds of millions in restructuring to enable the integration of services. According to the Group's chairman *"We have a new organizational structure, with the emphasis on having profit and loss responsibility with customer segment managers"*. The aim is to reduce the management layers and speed up decision-making process.

Availability of Project Management Skills

Many informants believe project management skills to be a critical success factor and cited the shortage of large-scale project management skills within the organization, which has lead to many project failures in the past. Some of them went as far to suggest the outsourcing of major technical projects. According to Head of Credit Cards and Loans, *"in early days of* e-banking *we set ourselves very ambitious targets while not understanding our limited IT and project management capabilities, has led to many disappointments. When we start setting targets at the level of our capabilities, the situation will change"*. As a direct result of these recent failures, the confidence in the success of large-scale project management is very low. Some projects have been divided into small manageable pieces, which is making the managers' job easier and reduces the risks from failure. However, the company may be losing the economies of scale and slowing its growth, as many small projects usually take longer and consume greater resources to complete than one large project divided into various activities.

Organizational Change Management

E-banking can and should bring about organizational changes, which may include, the re-engineering of business processes and less structured and agile business processes. This is already happening at Bank B. R & D Manager pointed out that *"business processes have to be re-engineered first and organizations should be structured to support those processes. We are going through that transition process".* Bank B's website Development Manager emphasised this by saying *"e-commerce requires a different culture and a different mindset to a traditional banking environment which is very resistant to change".* Most informants cited the 'systematic internal communications' (discussed as a separate point below) as the key to the success of change management.

Many ways of communication are being used to re-assure branch staff. The main message is that success in e-commerce would only mean a change of role for them, not redundancy of their jobs. Instead of them being engaged in routine transactions, e-commerce would enable them to assume the role of advisors. Therefore, the aim is to turn branches into customers' service centres and encourage customers to conduct their routine transactions online.

Internal Communications Management

The company paid special attention to this aspect of change management. Regular staff involvement was achieved through a two-way dialogue between staff and their managers, and consultative and negotiating committees, including discussion with trade unions. Regular meetings, group wide team briefings, circulars and newsletters helped to ensure that staff were aware of the organization's performance and objectives. In addition, the Managing Director regularly addressed the Group's top managers on key issues, signposting future directions and responding to questions from around the company.

The company encourages the involvement of employees in the performance of the company through the employee Share Award Schemes. The annual sales conference is another way in which company interacts with its front-end employees (people involved in sales, usually in branches).

Regarding communications related to e-commerce, there are regular updates on the Intranet and whenever there is significant event, for example launching a new website, people from the e-commerce team tend to go out to communicate with staff. Staff are able to access e-banking through the company's Intranet, which also helped promote e-banking within the organization.

Enrichment of Website

Bank B is adding additional functionality to its website at a very fast pace. In addition to normal financial services such as account management, it has many extra features which make it attractive for a wide variety of people. For example, they launched an innovative share dealing service through their website where customers can use a service called share portfolio service. This enables them to see how their chosen stocks would have performed, without actually investing any money, which makes it attractive for people new to this type of investment.

For small businesses, Bank B teamed up with WorldPay, a provider of e-commerce technology, to create 'Netshop Solutions'. This gave small business the chance to build their own website and start trading on-line quickly and cheaply. Additional services available there include the design of a company logo, domain name registration, free registration with hundreds of Web search engines, and free management reports on customer transaction details to help collate useful market information and analysis. These types of extra services generates Web traffic on the site, raising possibilities to cross-sell to its visitors. They also need to reduce the length of their online application forms, which are much longer than many other e-banking organizations' forms.

In terms of the design of their website, Bank B is continuously changing the look and feel of their website, *"basically to attract more visitors and to improve the visitors to applications ratio"*, said their Website Development Manager. This, again demonstrated the importance of website design and content richness in attracting business.

Support from Top Management

The chairman of the company has been a very keen supporter of e-banking, right from beginning. Many informants in the e-commerce department see him as an e-commerce champion. The importance of getting their support was stressed by e-commerce Development Manager, when he stated *"the support from top management is crucial for success but what determines the pace of progress is the support from rest of the organization. We are not 100 % there yet"*. The ways to address this problem, he suggested, were to spend some time in building relationships and educating people about e-banking.

Availability of Resources

In the beginning of e-banking project, the company did not have sufficient human resources to build e-commerce systems. Therefore, they outsourced the development of the new websites while the company continued to look for and develop relevant skills of its own. As a result, they were able to roll out other advanced electronic services, mainly on their own. Now, websites originally outsourced have been brought in-house for improvements and maintenance, which indicates the availability of increased human resources to their e-banking team.

Systems which actually run the products (back-end systems) are still not fully integrated mainly due to the lack of enough human resources in the IT department. The Director of e-commerce puts it this way *"big banks such as Barclays have got thousands of people working on their IT systems, whereas we are doing essentially same thing with only few hundred. This sometime causes problems such as delays in completion of projects.*" For this reason, there are some time delays in the e-commerce team's operations too, as one informant puts it, "*if we need the Security Department to help us in testing a part of our website so we can launch it, it may take four or five months for them to do that because they're doing other things*". He suggested that, more resources should be available to the e-commerce team to outsource any urgent work to avoid delays. In terms of skills resources, some respondents cited the shortage of multi skilled people, which is hindering the integration of business and technical processes.

Focus on Customers

When customers conduct their financial management on-line, there is an expectation that the process would be much quicker than off-line processes. For example, if a customer applies for a loan online, they expect a decision straight away and completion of process within a couple of days simply because they have applied through a fast channel. The findings of their internal research suggested that in 80% of cases, Bank B is not delivering against these expectations and in only 9% of cases, it is delivering above expectations. These findings suggest that, despite bringing customer services to the centre of the attention, Bank B is not very successful in this regard. They have made considerable efforts during recent times to focus their efforts on serving customers, including setting targets for response within specified time (usually within 24 hours) and considerable improvements in the above figures are expected as a result.

The customer focus is the focal point of Bank B's strategy to offer services on many channels. Their executive chairman said "*By using the Internet technologies to web-enable the bank, we will simplify internal processes, and give those customers who want to transact with us over the Internet the means to do this*". He further stressed this point by saying, " *the strategy we chose to pursue is, in many ways, a simple one. Through the effective, integrated deployment of new technology and the rigorous simplification of our business, we intend to become the most customer-focused financial services organization*".

Another example of their endeavour to better customer service is the provision of extensive information about major purchasing decisions faced by customers such as buying house or car, on their website. The site provides a wide range of information on questions, issues and problems faced by customers when faced with such major purchasing problems. This type of enhanced customer service is mainly aimed at evoking an emotional interest in their brand and enhancing their image.

One aspect of the customer service at the Bank B, which needs improving, is to simplify the application process. To do this, application forms will have to be drastically shortened and for existing online customers, most of the fields of an online application form should be filled automatically when they apply for another product. Customers should also be able to monitor the progress of their application online.

Some other General Points about E-Banking at Bank B

Integration of systems and processes, or rather lack of it, seems to be the most critical issues for most of the informants for this study. Lack of adequate systems integration is continuing to be a key obstacle in improving the functionality of their website and integrating channels. Shortage of human resources and project management skills was commonly cited to be the main reason for this. However, some informants blamed poor planning for recent projects failures. For example, one informant has put this in these words, *"we should have had a plan for delivery of technology very early on and because of the very high risk involved we should have alternative plans in place but we didn't. As a result when technology failed to deliver, business is suffering with almost stalled growth"*. Regarding process integration, the situation is not much better either. According to one informant "what we have done to date about processes integration, has been a whole series of quick fixes, using Sellotape to make things work. There has been no organised effort to study current processes and re-design them to Web-enable them."

It seems that Bank B is making the same mistakes as some other banks were making a few years ago. In this respect it has not learnt much from others or from its own mistakes. It is mainly focused on achieving short-term sales targets. This strategy creates an atmosphere of competition between different teams and between different channels, reducing the prospects of mutual co-operation. The reward system need be re-designed to encourage people, teams, departments and channels to co-operate with each other.

Lack of understanding about e-banking in other departments is pretty evident. For example, the marketing department still insists on using direct mail or phone calls for marketing purposes. Whereas some people in e-commerce believe that email marketing is best for e-commerce because its much cheaper to send thousands of emails at once and the message can contain direct links to the Bank B's website. They also want to establish business partnerships with other popular websites to attract more visitors which has begun to happen now but Bank B has long way to go in this regard.

Gathering information about customers is not considered to be very important at the Bank B, largely due to the lack of systems integration. Some informants disagreed with the idea of using this information for the personalisation of financial services, arguing that financial services are not like computers or music CDs where personalisation is fairly common. The main reason given for this was that an average customer only buys a financial product almost once in five years, limiting the scope for use of historical financial information for personalisation purpose. Another reason cited by a Senior e-commerce Manager at Bank B was the time pressure to launch new products, which leaves little room for an organised effort to gather and analyze data about customers. Even where Bank B can easily capture useful data it makes little effort for it. Probably, as a result of these reasons, efforts to understand customers are generally limited to some product testing or monitoring the effects of various marketing activities.

While the scope for personalisation in standardised financial services such as current accounts or saving accounts is very limited in comparison with, say, book retailing, an improved understanding of customers enabled by e-banking and data-mining technologies can greatly enhance the prospects of cross selling their products. The figure of around 1.6 products per customer is not great in comparison with some of Bank B competitors and shows a weakness in Bank B's efforts of gathering, analysing and utilising information about customers.

A considerable number of applications for various financial services are now coming in through the e-banking channel. However, a large number of these applications get rejected on the ground of the low credit score of the applicants. Low credit scoring is typical of the Internet enthusiastic customers segment as they tend to be younger than average applicants with perhaps a bit less careful attitude to their financial management aspects resulting in their low credit scores. With some flexibility in product differentiation, Bank B can sell its products to them at higher prices or with payment protection plans, instead of rejecting these applications altogether. Criteria for accepting applications need to be reviewed to accommodate this new younger online customers segment. *"Another possibility is to sell other providers' products who may be willing to take higher risks and earn commission"* (Commercial Manager). However, this may be a too radical departure from their current business model which has a focus on selling its own products.

Research and Development (R & D, is another area identified by some informants, which needs greater attention. They suggested that, this function should have its own budget so that it can explore or develop new technologies; try them out on a small sample set of customers and help positive findings to be implemented across the organization. They should also be responsible for monitoring the activities within and outside the financial sector for new ideas and technologies and explore them further to evaluate their usefulness for Bank B. In other words, R & D should be a multi-disciplinary team and should act like a think tank within the organization and enable it to take a long-term strategic view of technical and business developments and facilitate successful innovation.

They have made little noticeable effort to promote this initiative to the their employees in general. As a consequence, lack of enthusiasm for new e-Channels amongst managers outside the e-commerce department may be one of the reasons for a relatively slow speed of improvement in their e-commerce functionality. Once evidence of this came from the Head of Credit Cards and Loans when he said "*I think if we want to drive a strategy for the business, which includes e-commerce as a strong part of the channel mix then we need to develop some quick ways and prove that there are strong benefits to either consumer or to the organization and until we do that, there will be plenty of cynics around".*

Other areas which need improvements at Bank B include: integration of different service delivery channels such as Internet, branches and call centres so each of them complement each-other rather than remain largely ignorant or feel threatened, reduction in number of management layers speed up decision making process, developing a group-wide e-commerce strategy with its objectives clearly defined and communicated to all employees, improve systems documentation with e-commerce department and building partnerships with other financial and non-financial (i.e. technology firms) companies to maximise the benefits from e-commerce.

Case Study 3 - Salem Five Bank
(Case adopted from Marlin, 2005)

Since launching one of the first Internet banking sites 10 years ago, Salem Five Bank (with $1.8 billion in assets) has continually melded technology to meet fast changing business requirements. Like many banks, at the time of my arrival in 2000, Salem Five had been aggressively pursuing the Internet as a new business platform - Bank One created WingspanBank, Citibank created CitiFi - everybody was creating these re-branded Internet banks. Nobody was sure whether the Internet was going to be a separate business from traditional banking or a complementary delivery channel. It soon became apparent that the Internet was going to be a channel, not a distinct business in its own right. For those banks that didn't have an established retail presence, the Internet represented a tantalizing business model. But for those that did have a presence, the costs of marketing and supporting two distinct brands outweighed any business benefits.

They want to run e-banking as complementary to the existing channels and not as businesses that compete with each other. That represented a fundamental change in direction. Instead of building a separate brand and business model around the Internet, they embraced e-commerce technology throughout the institution. E-banking became a catalyst for changing the way they interacted with and sold products to all of our customers - consumers, small business and commercial banking customers. It also had an effect on the nature of the institution itself. Up until then, Salem Five had pretty much had a reputation as being in the thrift business - i.e., the business of selling mortgages or certificates of deposit. With the coming of e-commerce, their reputation began to change to that of a more traditional commercial bank, with a focus on current/saving accounts, rich relationships with customers and full channel integration.

With this major change in business strategy, each channel became a project in itself. They had a detailed look at the ATM network and upgraded it to operate in high security needs environment. They also refreshed their phone banking and upgraded Internet banking to a new platform. At one time, the Internet banking platform had its own database; now the bank operates a single integrated database for all retail channels. Whenever or wherever a transaction takes place, it updates the core processing system in real time.

The bank found that, once people used to the e-banking, it becomes the channel of their choice. The branches however, continue to get traffic and people. One of the most striking developments has been the decline in check processing, due primarily to debit cards, but also to things like electronic check conversion.

In last five year, the e-banking technology boom years of the early 2000s have been replaced by a much stricter regime around security and compliance. Back then, technology drove the changes that transformed banking from a traditional bricks-and-mortar business into an e-commerce business. Today, the primary focus is on security and privacy. Those two issues occupy a lot of management's attention at Bank Five. No one could have envisioned five years ago the importance they would have today. And the need to comply with regulations such as the Bank Secrecy Act has taken its toll in areas such as opening new accounts, where they now have to be much more cautious and deliberate. There's also more overhead in ensuring that they have appropriate policies and procedures in place to meet these more-rigorous legal/regulatory requirements. In terms of fraud detection and prevention, banks have to become more proactive in implementing technology to monitor transactions.

The three case studies mentioned above highlight a number of practical issues faced by banks as well as solutions they implemented to address those issues. These solutions however shouldn't be taken as a prescribed best practice but as a helpful guideline for problems which would be unique to that organization. Some of the key lessons learnt are presented below.

Brand Management

The above cases suggest that having a well known and trusted brand is an asset for any business but its value rises dramatically in an uncertain and insecure online environment. Owing to the security and trust issues associated with the Internet, developing a new brand is much more difficult than in non-Internet environment. However, despite many difficulties, a number of companies such as Google, Yahoo, Amazon have managed to create very high value brands.

The speed at which people can move from awareness to action on the Internet is much greater - a unique advantage over other business channels. To utilise this advantage business need to be innovative in website design and in Internet related marketing communications.

Developing an Internet brand requires a two-part strategy. The first part is about how a company finds, serves, and satisfies its customers. The second focuses on how a company utilizes media and communicates a clear message in competitive and confusing online markets. The Website is first tool of e-brand making. A good

Figure 8.3. Different aspects of e-branding (Verma & Agarwal, 2004)

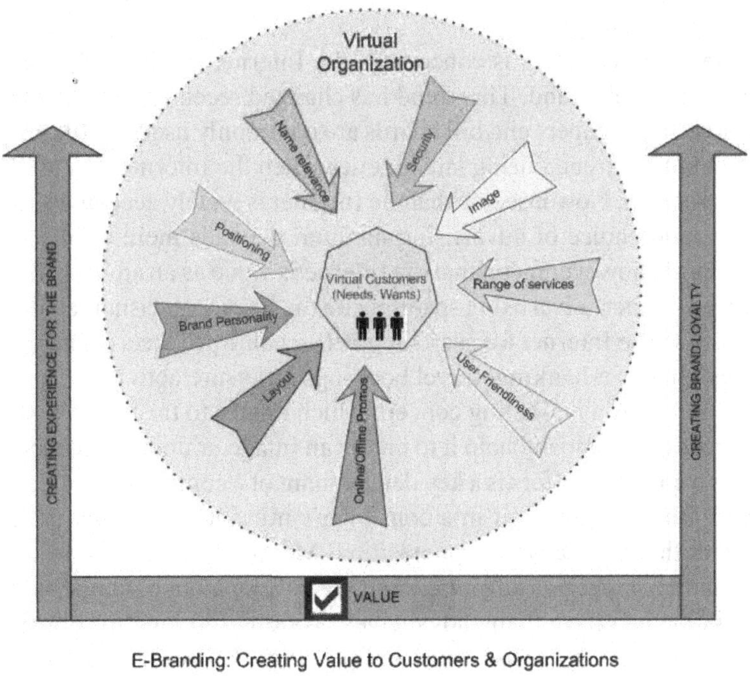

E-Branding: Creating Value to Customers & Organizations

website doesn't just require technical skills but also expertise of marketers and marketing literate artists.

It is important to consider and plan for various dimensions of e-brand development. These dimensions, as shown in Figure 8.3 include: website design, promotion, positioning, security, easy to remember name and quality service delivery in different market environment. Of course many of these aspects are also present in traditional marketing but with a unique Internet specific flavour.

The issue of developing a website which inspires trust is covered earlier in this book so we concentrate here on other aspects of e-brand development. The next issue is brand name. A golden rule is that it shouldn't be too long so that it becomes hard to type and it should be easy to remember. For this reason some banks chose names such as Egg or Smile for their e-banking arm whereas others chose to keep their existing brand name such as http://www.alliance-leicester.co.uk. They argued that utilising an already trusted brand name is better than changing it to make it short, and that a new brand name will take resources and effort to establish.

Advertising for web business may simply start with mentioning the URL in all company correspondent. This mainly applies to businesses which already have a well known physical presence. For those organizations which are not well known or are virtual organizations, much more intensive marketing methods are needed which may include: registration with search engines, providing cash incentives, discounted products, locating entertaining activities on the site, and developing advertising campaigns.

As far as advertising is concerned, the Internet has been the main choice for advertising a web brand. This trend has changed recently and other media such as TV, Radio, Newspapers and bill boards are commonly used for this purpose. This is a reversal of the trend during late nineties when the Internet was used to advertise offline products. Now it seems that the Internet is widely accepted as a mainstream medium, and choice of advertising medium depends more on the target market. This does not however mean that the Internet's value as an advertising medium had decreased. In fact, advertising spending on the Internet is rising rapidly as more and more people use Internet for searching better value products (such a electronics) or services such as e-banking, travel bookings or leisure activities.

Positioning is a marketing concept which relates to the ways in which products or services of a company help it to create an image or market position. The type of services a company offers is a key determinant of a company's positioning strategy. A brand which comes first in a consumer's mind for a product or service would mean that that company has top position. Moving first to offer an innovative service to gain competitive advantage and the development of image as an innovating organization can have many advantages. Waiting too long for offering similar or superior choices may cause considerable harm. However, first mover advantage can easily turn into disadvantage as doing so before being fully ready harmed the reputation of many banks in late nineties. Their failure to integrate services, content and advice prevented customers from realising their time-tested goal of trust and convenience resulted in loss of customers.

Creating a smooth and pleasant experience is considered important in e-brand development. It can be achieved through creating a dynamic content environment, creative design and flawless functionality which creates that experience and often results in customer attraction, satisfaction, retention and profitability.

Word of mouth or a recommendation to use a particular website by customers to other customers is still a key determinant of success. To get that recommendation, companies need to create the positive experience mentioned in previous paragraph, as well as providing incentives for these recommendations.

Other aspects specific to e-branding include dealing with the issues of trust and privacy. With privacy and security rating high on the list of concerns of Internet shoppers, companies must clearly indicate, through their e-brands, their position and policies on these issues. This way, all the products and services offered under the brand name will inherit that reputation. As new concerns or values emerge in the e-marketplace, e-brand managers must reposition their brand dynamically to meet their customers' expectations, needs or wants.

PLANNING FOR INNOVATION AND SUSTAINABLE GROWTH

Innovation has always played a key role in human as well as businesses survival but the need to be innovative has become much more significant in the Internet era, simply because fast paced changes in the market place often require the quick and innovative use of existing resources. Different people define innovation in many different ways. According to Teece (2001), innovation is a process where knowledgeable and creative people and organizations frame problems and select, integrate and augment information to create understanding and answers. Porter and Cunningham (2005) provided another general definition of innovation: "to include both improvements in technology and better methods or ways of doing things. It can be manifested in product changes, process changes, new approaches to marketing, new forms of distribution, and new concepts of scope…[innovation] results as much from organizational learning as from formal research and development". Tidd et al. (1997) clarify that innovation is not same as invention; it is about developing new ways of doing things or developing products using a combination of new and old ideas.

Advances in information technology (IT) have made possible so much innovation in many industries, such as banking, logistics, communications and automation. Lee and Kim (1998) argue that IT innovation is different from a typical innovation as it is usually based on the use of IT to achieve innovation and stresses information enabled innovation. Therefore, Lee and Kim (1998, p. 289) offered a different definition of IT innovation: "the overall process of initiation, adoption, and implementation of new information technology to improve organizational performance." This implies that managers should know how to integrate emerging ICT with their

Figure 8.4. A model for IT innovation implementation (adapted from Lee & Kim, 1998)

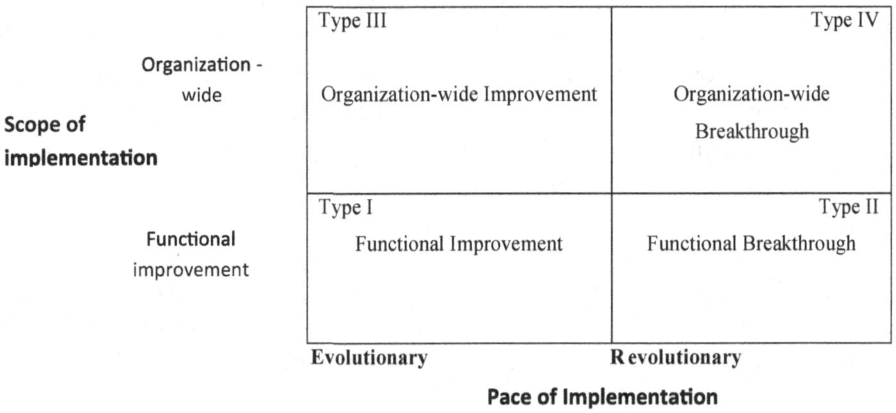

Scope of implementation		Pace of Implementation	
		Evolutionary	**Revolutionary**
Organization - wide		Type III Organization-wide Improvement	Type IV Organization-wide Breakthrough
Functional improvement		Type I Functional Improvement	Type II Functional Breakthrough

business objectives to achieve the desired business benefits (for more on how to do this, see the chapter on Strategy).

There are many types of IT innovations. For example Lee and Kim (1998) examined the effects of contextual factors on the implementation of client/server systems and interrelated IT innovations (given in Figure 8.4). They classified four types of IT innovation according to the dimensions of 'implementation scope' and 'implementation pace':

1.   **Type I - Functional Improvement:** The scope of implementation is functional and the pace of implementation evolves according to the organizational circumstances. The functional improvement is not unsettling (for organizations and employees) as it would typically be implemented in the form of a staged process in one or just a few parts of an organization. The introduction of PCs to operate a new imaging application in a personnel department is an example of functional improvement.

2.   **Type II - Functional Breakthrough:** The scope of implementation is limited to one or few organizational functions but the pace of implementation is quick. For example, some Korean banks implemented a foreign asset-liability-management system rapidly because of the forceful instructions from the Korean banks association.

3.   **Type III - Enterprise-Wide Improvement:** The scope of implementation is organization-wide, while implementation evolves slowly. An innovation is typically implemented in the phased mode. It may start from a single application or department and gradually spread to the other parts of the organization. For example, a centralised system can be migrated to the distributed system in the phased mode, starting from a single application or department and gradually spreading across an organization coving all applications.

4.   **Type IV - Enterprise-Wide Breakthrough:** The scope of implementation is enterprise-wide and implementation is revolutionary. This is the most radical option, which is likely to result in many organizational changes and may result in strategic level repercussions. Using this option, organizational changes and innovative technology implementation are likely to occur together. For example, a distributed computing system or a groupware technology may be implemented at the same time as an enterprise-wide business-process reengineering project is underway.

The above discussion implies that an IT innovation may be in the form of a new type of system to better solve existing problems or innovative use of IT to create new markets and revenue streams. Lyytinen and Rose (2003) provided some specific examples of IT innovations, which are summarised in the Table 8.1.

*Table 8.1. Some examples of IT innovations in services (adapted from Lyytinen &
Rose, 2003)*

Applications for adminis-trative core	Internet Web-based enterprise reporting tool – system is used to track items such as human resource related information (turnover, sick time, etc.) across an organization independent of client location, access point, or platform.
Applications for functional integration	Intranet Web-based balanced scorecard system -Tracks key perfor-mance indicators that are considered core to business line of a company
Applications for Customer Process integration	Business to customer Internet computing applications - e-Government applications. Services of government were expanded to allow tens of thousands of citizens to concurrently submit documents and request public services over the Internet independent of client platforms or the time of day.
Applications for inter-or-ganizational integration	Business-to-Business (B2B) Extranet applications - B2B digital market-place application for e-procurement in newspaper industry. Application aggregates purchases of such items as newsprint and link across the entire newspaper industry in order to lower transaction fees and prices. System is available 24 hours a day and is independent of location, cli-ent, and a platform.

IT is seen as a key enabler of knowledge support to the innovation process (Green-halgh et al. 2004). The management of innovation is the most knowledge-intensive organizational process; therefore it often requires support from IT. Adamides and Karacapilidis, (2006) acknowledge, however, that organised information cannot be a substitute for human understanding and learning, but can help to fill existing gaps in knowledge. They further point out that, in filling these gaps, the role of IT is to enable transformation of information into practical knowledge.

Adamides and Karacapilidis (2006) provide a useful and practical insight for IS managers, into the innovation process and role of IS as an enabler. They present an **Information Systems** oriented framework that aims at integrating different stakeholders' perspectives and technology development tools across different ac-tivities. The framework consists of a systemic problem representation scheme and an evolutionary problem solving methodology (called Group Model Building by Selection and Argumentation) that supports the whole innovation process, helping the development of innovative ideas. Their paper also presents the structure, func-tionality and use of Knowledge Breeder, a web-based software system that helps implementing the above methodology. The model consists of various components such as definition of context, knowledge storage and retrieval process, which it-eratively interact with innovation and product development tools to help solve a particular problem in innovation process.

In line with the research mentioned above, the important role IT plays to sup-port innovation was also emphasised by Brown and Eisenhardt (1995) and Tidd et al., (1997) when they suggested that knowledge and information flows are the key determinants of successful innovation and new product development processes.

Similarly, some concepts such as 'absorptive capacity' and 'complexity studies' see knowledge as the key enabler in organizational innovation. Absorptive capacity is about measuring an organization's ability to value, assimilate, and apply new knowledge. Measuring is done at multiple levels (individual, group, firm, and national level) (Zahra & George, 2002). 'Complexity studies' is derived from general systems theory and regard innovation as the continuity and transformation of patterns of interaction, understood as complex responses of humans relating to one another in local situations (Fonseca, 2001). These frameworks help organizations to understand the usefulness of information, assimilate it through systematic interactions, and apply it to achieve success at innovation through technology.

From an organizational point of view, innovation may be viewed as a new product, a new process or a new business model likely to make an organization more profitable. Organizational innovativeness is regarded as primarily influence by structural determinants, especially size, functional differentiation, resources, and specialisation (Greenhalgh et al. 2004). This implies that an organization's size, resources level and area of specialisation influences its ability to innovate. For example, an organization specialising in pharmaceuticals will have to continuously innovate to survive, and the level of its resources and size usually determine its effectiveness at innovating.

Kumar and Mulchandani (2005) presented a case study conducted at Wipro, a leading IT company in India, which is a good example of business innovation, (see Box 2 for a summary of the case). The case demonstrated the process of development of an IT innovation, organizational preparations for its implementation and the organizational structure and business processes used in managing innovation process. Their main conclusion was that the development of innovative ideas into viable product or service requires developing appropriate organizational processes, structures and systems.

Having established the importance of Innovation and role of new technologies, which may include e-banking technologies, it would be helpful to discuss some of the main barriers to the innovation process. Kuisma, (2007) lists a number of barriers which he classified as usage barriers, value barriers, risk barriers, tradition barrier sand image barriers. He further elaborated on this and listed the following factors which are often cited as common barriers to Innovation:

- Innovation's incompatibility with consumer's practices or habits
- Innovation's inability to produce economic-or performance-based benefits
- Physical risks and innovation overload
- Magnitude of change caused by the innovation
- Negative image related to the innovation

For any of the above reasons, resistance or even total rejection by employees or consumers may occur. However, resistance or rejection cannot be just attributed to

Box. 2

Box 2 – How innovation is done within technology companies? The Case of Wipro
(Source: Kumar and Mulchandani, 2005)

Wipro Technologies is one of India's top three software services companies. The company has pioneered several firsts in its journey towards excellence: it was the first company in India and the first software services company in the world to achieve SEI-CMM Level 5 certification and also the first company to achieve CMM Level 5 certification.

In year 2000, it formally launched a company-wide innovation programme. Two years earlier, in an attempt to reinvent itself for the globalised economy, Wipro re-launched its brand. The innovation initiative had its roots in the brand re-launch effort. The company aimed to institutionalise a climate for continuous innovation, which until then was a sporadic activity.

Wipro's successful experience with the Six Sigma and CMM certification programmes had taught them the importance of running a mission critical programme as a focused initiative with the close attention of the top management. Therefore, Wipro's top management deferred the programme to a point in time when the innovation initiative would be the main focus of the management and the organizational process. Top management also provided required resources for the innovation team to study the whole domain of innovation and to develop an appropriate programme according to the company's objectives.

A high-powered two member team, entrusted with the task of carrying out an extensive study and preparing the blue print for the innovation initiative, held discussions with companies and academics. At the end of this consultative process, the team concluded that there were no ready models of innovation that could be replicated at Wipro and hence an entirely ground up approach had to be adopted, according to their own specific needs. The team also realized the importance of involving customers in the process, primarily for validating ideas.

Wipro defined innovation as 'the implementation of new ideas resulting in a marketable product or service', emphasizing the need to align the innovation programme with business needs and avoid the trap of innovation for innovation's sake. A structured programme was conceived, with clear focus areas and targets, to direct effort towards promising areas. These preparation prior to launching an innovation initiative provides the clarity and focus.

Wipro followed a Stage Gate process that consisted of six gates wherein market validation was the requirement at every gate prior to movement to the next stage. This process defined how ideas for innovation were to be generated, evaluated and supported through the different stages of evolution till they reached the stage of commercialization. The process also specified the rewards and incentives for those who generated the ideas as well as those who worked on the ideas in their subsequent stages of evolution.

Wipro has enjoyed a fair amount of success with innovation process based ideas as well as industry specific solutions in finding customers. While focusing the organization's attention on innovation as a strategic priority, the innovation process was helpful in handholding to the organization's members in their pursuit of innovative ideas. The Wipro experience also makes clear that each organization has to uniquely address its needs of innovation and there are no ready templates of successful innovation programmes that would fit the bill for all.

---

the above reasons, it could also be due, for example, to the lack of a proper change management process. In an online environment, the speed of new innovations may overwhelm many employees or consumers, and proper change management strategies become more important than in conventional situations.

CHAPTER SUMMARY

Banks have heavily invested in the internet, but the returns so far have been less than expected. As shown in the case studies presented in this chapter, this is mainly due to inexperience with e-banking. E-banking requires an integrated ICT infrastructure using powerful collaborative technologies that integrates all the different channels, rather than promoting one over the other. Branch and call centre staff alike need better information about customers, and more powerful real-time analysis and advice tools to help them match products and services to the right customers. This requires good understanding of the e-marketing concepts which have been covered in this chapter.

The task of winning consumer trust becomes easier if a proper e-branding strategy is followed. E-branding needs less efforts if an offline brand already exists, but creating a new Internet only brand is an uphill task and needs considerable time, resources and effort. In both cases, creating a positive experience for customers is key, and implementing strategies to gain recommendations from customers is often viewed as one of the most effective marketing strategy.

Another key strategy for the success of e-banking is to promote innovation in organizations. There are many ways in which innovation can be promoted in an organization including: creating room for experiments, tolerance to failure of good ideas, implementing a reward system to encourage individuals as well as teams to innovate. There are also many barriers to innovation, including: short term results culture, resistance to change, low acceptance rates of new ideas. These barriers can be overcome by promotion of an innovation culture in organizations and careful change management.

REFERENCES

Adamides, E. D., & Karacapilidis, N. (2006, January). Information technology support for the knowledge and social processes of innovation management. *Technovation,* 26(1), 50-59.

Ang, J., Teo & T. S. H. (1997). CSFs and Sources of Assistance and Expertise in Strategic IS Planning: A Singapore Perspective. *European Journal of Information Systems*, 6(3), 164-171.

Averweg, U. R., & Erwin, G. J. (1999, January 5-8). Critical Success factors for implementation of decision support systems in South Africa. In Sprague, R. H. J. (Ed.) *Proceedings of the 32nd Hawaii International Conference on System Sciences: Minitrack on Information Technology in Developing Countries,* Hawaii, USA.

Balamuralikrishna R., & Dugger, J. C. (1995). SWOT Analysis: A Management Tool for Initiating New Programs in Vocational Schools. *Journal of Vocational and Technical Education*, 12(1), 1-7.

Brown, S. L., & Eisenhardt, K.M., (1995). Product development: past research; present findings, and future directions. *Academy of Management Review*, 20(3), 343-378.

Croft, J. (2006, Jun 28). Barclays and Woolwich have failed to bond. *FT.com*. 2006.

Daniel, E. (1999, November 3-4). Who Dares Wins? On-Line Banking Services and Innovation Types. InHackney, R. (Ed.) *Proceedings of 9th Annual Business Information Technology Conference,* (Paper No. 34), Manchester, UK.

Fonseca, J. (2001) *Complexity and Innovation in Organisations*. London: Routledge.

Glass, N. M. (1991). *Pro-active Management: How to Improve your Management Performance.* East Brunswick, NJ: Nichols Publishing.

Greenhalgh, T., Robert, G., Macfarlane, F., Bate, P., & Kyriakidou, O. (2004). Diffusion of Innovation in Service Organisations: Systematic Review and Recommendations. *The Milbank Quarterly*, 82(4) 581-629.

Holland, P., Christopher, P., Light, B., & Kawalek P. (1999a, June 23-25). Beyond Enterprise Resource Planning Projects: Innovative Strategies for Competitive Advantage. In Pries-Heje, J., Ciborra, C., Kantaz, K., Valor, J., Christiaanse, E., Avison, D., Heje, C. (Eds.) *Proceedings of the 7th European Conference on Information Systems*, (188-301) CBS, Copenhagen, Denmark.

Hughes, C. (2007, Feb 22). COMPANIES UK: Time for A&L to build on its safe legacy. Retrieved May 05 2007, from http://search.ft.com/ftArticle?sortBy=gadatea rticle&queryText=woolwich&y=6&aje=true&x=13&id=070222000983&page=3

Jenster, P. V. (1987) Using Critical Success Factors in Planning. *Long Range Planning*, 20(4), 102-109.

Julta, D. N., Craig, J., & Bodorik, P. (2001, January 3-6). A Methodology for Creating e-Business Strategy, in Sprague, R. H. J. (Ed.) *Proceedings of the 34th Hawaii International Conference on System Sciences: Minitrack Infrastructure for e-Business on the Internet,* Maui, HI.

Kuisma, T., Laukkanen, T., & Hiltunen, M. (2007). Mapping the reasons for resistance to Internet banking: A means-end approach. *International Journal of Information Management*, 27, 75–85.

Kumar, K., & Mulchandani, M. (2005, September). Getting an Innovation Initiative off the Ground: The Experience of Wipro. *IIMP Management Review*, 41-48.

Lee, G.H., & Kim, Y.G. (1998). Implementing a Client/Server System in Korean

Organizations: Interrelated IT Innovation Perspective. IEEE *Transactions On Engineering Management*, 45(3), 287-296.

Lyytinen, K., & Rose, G.M. (2003, December). The Disruptive Nature of Information Technology Innovations: The Case of Internet Computing in Systems Development Organisations. *MIS Quarterly*, 27(4), 557-595.

Marlin, S. (2005, July 01). Banking for the 21st Century. *Bank Systems & Technology*.

Porter, A.L., & Cunningham, S.W. (2005). *TECH MINING: Exploiting New Technologies for Competitive Advantage*. Hoboken, NJ: Johan Wiley & Sons.

Tidd, J., Bessant, J., & Pavitt, K. (1997). *Managing Innovations: Integrating Technological, Market and Organisational Change*. Chichester, UK: Wiley.

Rockart, J. (1979). Chief Executives Define Their Own Data Needs, *Harvard Business Review*, 57(2), 81-93.

Slevin, D. P., Stieman, P. A., & Boone, L. W. (1991, October). Critical Success Factor Analysis for Information Performance Measurement and Enhancement, *Information & Management*, 21, 161-174.

Teece, D.J. (2001). Strategies for managing knowledge assets: the role of firm structure and industrial context. In Nonaka, I., Teece, D. (Eds.), *Managing Industrial Knowledge: Creation, Transfer and Utilisation* (125-144)., London: Sage Publications..

Turban, E., Lee, J., King, D., & Shung, H. M. (2000). Electronic Commerce, a Managerial Perspective. London: Prentice Hall.

Verma, S.Y. Agarwal, N. (2004). Cyber Branding: An Exploratory Study Of Virtual Organizations. *Journal of Internet Banking and Commerce*, 9(3), http://www.arraydev.com/commerce/jibc/2004-12/Nikhil.HTM.

Williams, J. J., & Ramaprasad, A. (1996). A Taxonomy of Critical Success Factors. *European Journal of Information Systems*, 5(4), 250-260.

Zahra, A. A., & George, G. (2002). Absorptive Capacity: A Review Re-conceptualisation and Extension. *Academy of Management Review*, 27(2), 185-203.

Chapter IX
E–Banking Project Management

INTRODUCTION

Project management is an important concept in business development. Often, the development of information technology or managing change will be run as projects, and managed using various well established project management techniques and tools. E-banking is often treated like a large scale project and broken into several small scale projects to manage various different aspects (called project portfolios), ranging from BPR to make the organization ready for online operations, to actual implementation of e-banking technologies.

PROJECT MANAGEMENT OVERVIEW

Project management methodologies offers a systematic approach to all stages of a project by providing guidance on how to plan, monitor, and measure every step in a project.

Project management is defined by the Project Management Institute (PMI, 2008) as the application of knowledge, skills, tools and techniques to a broad range of activities in order to meet the objectives of a project. Another relevant concept in this context is Programme Management. PMI (2008) defines Programme Management as the coordinated management of a portfolio of projects to achieve a related set of business objectives.

A project may involve a number of steps such as feasibility study, determination of objectives, planning, execution as well as end of project evaluation. A number of project management tools such as MS Project or PRINCE are available to support these steps.

Traditional project management methodologies offer a structured, low risk and rigid approach to project management, but this approach may not be most appropriate in e-banking, which is often implemented in external, customer facing environments. Shah et al (2007) states that e-banking managers seem often to be willing to take greater risks and use flexible and unorthodox approaches. This is mainly because e-banking projects are close to the core activity of the bank (promoting and selling financial services) so they are likely to use an approach which leaves a highest number of options open and allows for quick adjustments to respond to the fast changing technologies, market place and customer preferences. In this chapter we describe the traditional project management methods but with a flexible approach used in e-banking projects.

PROJECT PLANNING

E-banking is often a large scale business initiative requiring large scale financial investment as well as the availability of a pool of human resources with a range of specialist skills such as technological, marketing, change management and project management. Aladwani, (2001) suggests that offering an e-banking system proceeds through three generic phases, pre-development, development, and post-development. The pre-development stage is the period before the development of a bank's online services. At this phase, the idea of implementation of e-banking attracts top management and the benefits/pressures of initiating e-banking become irresistible. The development phase includes implementation of e- banking related systems and necessary changes in the organizational structure and culture. The second phase involves several managerial and technical issues, discussed in previous chapters that need to be addressed. The last phase, post-development, includes a number of activities such as maintenance of systems, continuous update of the website, evaluation of services, and implementing any necessary changes. For this phase, bank's management needs to understand a range of new marketing, product development and innovative delivery methods to ensure the success of the project.

A number of e-banking development, implementation and management activities become independent projects themselves so that e-banking as a whole requires programme management rather than just project management. For example, the e-banking adoption process has to be carefully planned and executed and is often seen as a project in its own right. From an IT project point of view, time and budget constraints could prove to be serious problems, as would be the handling of any organizational transformation processes. To deal with these issues, support from top management is seen as a key ingredient for success of an e-banking project. E-banking needs a champion amongst top management (generally the board of directors). Lack of senior management support is a major restriction to e-banking because, without it, obtaining the required resources to bring about the necessary changes in an organization can prove impossible.

In late 1990s there was acute shortage of e-banking related skilled people, and this still persists, partly owing to continuous changes in technologies. The situation is worst in developing countries, owing to the lack or poor provision of education, training and exposure to these technologies. Dealing with these issues is an integral part of any project management process.

SETTING SUCCESS CRITERIA

Success or failure can often be just a matter of perception, so that project evaluation is essential in understanding and assessing the key aspects of a project that make it either a success or failure (Wohlin & Andrews 2001). Jiang et al. (2002) state that assessment of a project's outcome is important to most of those involved in development projects - whether as a developer, customer, manager, or any other stakeholder - for different and, possibly, conflicting reasons. For example, a developer may regard good functionality of a system as a success, whereas for a senior manager, impacts of a project on organizational productivity may be the only measure of success. Thus there is a clear need for some comprehensive success indicators to be agreed before the start of the project. Existing literature proposes a number of different frameworks for evaluation of success in technological projects, which are discussed below.

The concept of project success has been an intensely debated issue. Freeman and Beale (1992) state that success means different things to different people. An architect may consider success in terms of aesthetic appearance, an engineer in terms of technical competence, an accountant in terms of dollars spent under budget, and a human resources manager in terms of employee satisfaction. A review of the project management literature does not provide any consistent interpretation of the term 'project success'. This is consistent with many other researchers, such as Jiang et al. (2002), who point out that often success is defined in general terms (e.g. cost, completion time, or savings). They further state that, from this perspective, projects are frequently deemed failures upon delivery because few are completed on time and within budget.

There are numerous problems associated with evaluating/assessing the effectiveness of technology projects. However, many researchers have proposed a number of models to measure project success. For example DeLone and McLean (1992 and 2003) proposed a model for IS success in 1995 and later amended it to be used in e-commerce projects.

The DeLone and McLean (1992) model (see Figure 9.1) was an attempt to bring many success measures into one model and suggests an existence of interdependencies between its components. By studying the interactions among these components of the model, as well as the components themselves, a clearer picture should emerge as to what constitutes information systems success. They also proposed an update of their model recently (See DeLone & McLean, 2003). The updated version of their framework is mainly specific to evaluating e-commerce information systems.

Seddon (1997) criticised this model and suggests that "DeLone and McLean tried to do too much in their model and as a result, it is both confusing and misspecified". He proposed a revised model (see Figure 9.2). In his model he replaced 'use' which he argued is a type of behaviour not a success measure, with 'perceived usefulness' and added 'society' as a stakeholder, which he argues, is impacted by the success or failure of a system. Seddon's model also consists of several complicated relationships and is very much IS specific.

Figure 9.1. The DeLone and McLean model of information systems success (adapted from DeLone and McLean 1992)

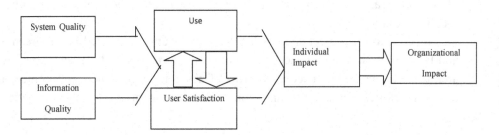

Partial Behavioural Model of IS Use

The feedback loop from perceptions (user satisfaction) back to expectations recognises the importance of learning. The model asserts that expectations are continuously being revised in the light of new experiences with the system. In a clockwise fashion, revised expectations lead to revised perceptions of IS success and ultimately, to revised expectations.

Goldenson and Herbsleb (1995) also gave a list of success indicators that were adopted by El Emam and Birk (2000). Goldenson and Herbsleb (1995) used six measures, listed in Table 9.1, to evaluate the success of systems development projects. Two of the measures, ability to meet schedule and budget commitments, address process predictability. The others are product quality, staff productivity, staff morale/job satisfaction, and customer satisfaction. El Emam and Birk (2000) proposed six measures that are similar to Goldenson and Herbsleb (1995) with the exception of 'ability to meet specified requirements'. Table 9.1 presents a summary of these two sets of criteria.

The main difference between Goldenson and Herbsleb (1995) and El Emam and Birk (2000) is that the former refers to a broad concept 'product quality' while the later refer to a concept of 'ability of product to satisfy specified requirements' (highlighted in bold font). Both of the authors have proposed these success mea-

Figure 9.2. Seddon model of IS success (adapted from Seddon, 1997)

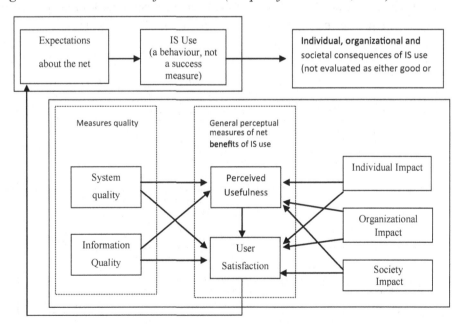

Table 9.1. General success measurement guidelines (adapted from Goldenson & Herbsleb, 1995; El Emam & Birk (2000).

Goldenson and Herbsleb (1995)		El Emam and Birk (2000)
1.	Ability of meet budget commitments	1. Ability of meet budget commitments
2.	Ability to meet schedule commitments	2. Ability to meet schedule commitments
3.	**product quality**	3. Ability to achieve customer satisfaction
4.	customer satisfaction	**4. Ability to satisfy specified requirements**
5.	Staff productivity	5. Staff productivity
6.	Staff morale/job satisfaction	6. Staff morale/job satisfaction

sures as general guidelines and do not suggest any formal methodology for project success evaluation.

Shenhar et al. (2001) propose a multidimensional framework for assessing project success. In this approach, projects are classified according to the technological uncertainty at the project initiation stage and their system scope, which is their location on a hierarchical ladder of systems and subsystems. The approach presented in Table 9.2 It has thirteen success measures, arranged into four dimensions such as project efficiency, impacts on customer, business success and preparing for the future.

The first dimension is concerned only with efficiency of the project management effort. This is a short-term dimension expressing the efficiency with which the project has been managed. It simply tells us how a project met its resource constraints, was it finished on time and within the specified budget. The second dimension relates to the customer, addressing the importance placed on customer requirements and on meeting their needs. The third dimension addresses the immediate and direct impact the project may have on the organization. In the business context, did it

Table 9.2. Project success framework (adapted from Shenhar et al., 2001)

Success Dimension	Success Measures
Project Efficiency	Met project schedule Stayed on budget
Impacts on customer	Met functional performance Met technical specifications Addressed most customer needs Solved a customers' problem The product is used by customers effectively Customer satisfaction
Business success	Commercial success in terms of profit or growth Creating a large market share
Preparing for the future (Long term benefits)	Creating a new market or segment Creating a new product line Developing a new technology (or new type of system)

provide sales, income, and profits as expected: did it help increase business results and gain market share. The last dimension is aimed at measuring long-term benefits from a project and it addresses the issue of preparing the organizational and technological infrastructure for the future.

Shenhar et al. (2001) suggest that:

- The first dimension can be assessed only in the very short-term, during a project's execution and immediately after its completion.
- The second dimension can be assessed after a short time, when the project has been delivered to the customer, and the customer is using it. Customer satisfaction can be assessed within a few months of the moment of purchase.
- The third dimension, direct success, can be assessed only after a significant level of sales has been achieved, usually one or two years.
- The fourth dimension can be assessed only after a longer period, probably two, three, or five years.

The application of this framework's different dimensions would vary from project to project, and emphasis on different dimensions would also change. For example, in a complex project, the emphasis may be on meeting requirements rather than meeting the project schedule. In a relatively simple project, the emphasis may be on the efficiency dimension and less tolerance on cost or schedule overruns. Emphasis also changes according to technological uncertainly. For example, greater uncertainty may mean greater importance of future potential, whereas low uncertainty may mean greater importance placed on budget and schedule aspects.

Shenhar et al. (2001) proposed this approach with a premise that projects are part of the strategic activity of the organization, and must be executed with an organizations' short-term as well as long-term objectives in mind. They stress that project managers should act strategically, with their activities focused on business needs and on creating competitive advantage with winning products. Thus assessing project success would relate to both performance during execution and success of the end results. For this reason, unlike Baccarini (1999), they do not distinguish between project success and product success. Shenhar et al. (2002) also claim that this framework could be helpful not only to all parties (project managers, teams and top management), but also throughout the entire life cycle of the project (selection, definition and execution).

Some of the criteria would help in the task of evaluating success in e-banking projects, but it is important to remember that, even with a sophisticated success measurement framework, success will not be easy to measure. Baccarini (1999) recommends that the following factors should be considered when interpreting success.

- **Success has hard and soft dimensions.** Some project success criteria are objective, tangible and measurable (hard), such as budget or schedule, and others, such as benefits to an organization or to society. are usually subjective and often difficult to quantify.
- **Success is perceived**. Different stakeholders may have their own particular subjective perception of success, depending on their needs and how well these needs are satisfied by the project. For one group, a project may be a huge success and for another group, a total failure.
- **Success criteria must be prioritised.** Success criteria can be conflicting, which means there will often be trade-offs that must be agreed to by all parties before the project is started. In many projects there may be a large number of stakeholders, consequently there is a need to identify the stakeholders who are going to have the most influence in determining project success. Their criteria should have higher priority, and should be emphasised (Lipovertsky et al., 1997).
- **Success is affected by time.** Each success criterion has its own timescale for measurement. For example, time and budget aspects can be measured as soon as a project is completed, whereas product usefulness may only become clear after several years.
- **Success may be partial.** Project success may be partially achieved, or projects may be measured in varying degrees of success. The determination of project success can be ambiguous and it becomes extremely difficult to give an unequivocal verdict of success or failure when some criteria are successfully met, and others are not.

Common Reasons for Failure of Technology Projects

IT has changed almost every aspect of our life, but there is strong indications to suggest that not all IT projects are successful. A study by Beynon-Davies & Lloyd-Williams (1999) argued that 60%-70% of all software projects fail. Raz et al, (2002) also reported that "Most of projects failed to achieve their business objectives, costs were well over budget, and support costs were underestimated for the year following implementation. Other studies like the Reel (1999) and Roby et al. (1993) have all reported that success rates in IT projects are quite low.

Doherty et al. (2000) argue that few information systems can be considered a success. The reason for claiming success is, they argue, largely based on an erroneous methods of measuring success. These methods they say are usually focuses on the extent to which a system meets the requirement specification agreed at the start of a project. The main measures of success are often negative in nature, basically the so-called correspondence failure, whereby the system objectives are stated in

Figure 9.3. Types of information systems failure (Adapted from Lyytinen & Hirschheim, 1987)

Failure Type	Explanation
Correspondence	The failure of the final 'system' to correspond with the requirements/objectives determined in advance
Process	Failure in the development process, usually in the form of a cost/time overrun or inability to complete the development
Interaction	Users fail to use the 'system' sufficiently or effectively meaning it has failed
Expectation	Failure of the completed 'system' to meet the expectations of participants

advance, and failure is defined in terms of these objectives achieved or not achieved. Lyytinen and Hirschheim (1987) suggest the notion of expectation failure, or the failure of the system to meet the expectations of stakeholders and propose four dimensions of failure (presented in Figure 9.3).

In most instances, the systems development life cycle emerges, implicitly or explicitly, as an important control element, resulting in success measures adhering to the functional engineering model, taking a structured, problem-solving approach: human complexity in the system is viewed as something which can be analyzed, and toward which a requirement specification can be written. But many disagree with this view. Beath and Orlykowski (1994), for example, criticise the interaction between users and systems professionals when systems are built, and argue that users participation is seen as ideological rather than actual, with users often taken to be passive rather than active stakeholders in the process.

As discussed in the previous section, just like success, failure could also be matter of perception if the success measures were not clearly spelt out right at the start of the project. Some of the common reasons for the project failures are outlined below.

Organizational structure: Deficiencies in the apparent organizational structure such as a lack of a performance-measuring subsystem or a control/decision-making subsystem can cause major problems in project management (Fortune & White 2006). There are many different types of organizational structures, bureaucratic, hierarchical, and matrix are most commonly cited organizational structures. Jackson and Schuler (1995) suggests alternative views of organizations, and looks at four particular views: organizations as machines, organisms, cultures, and coercive systems. A mechanistic view takes organizations as machines, within which rule-based systems can be used to control operations in a controlled manner. So if the inputs to the process are known, the outputs can be predicted with a fair degree of precision.

An organization as an 'organismic' is seen from a systems perspective. The organization is a collection of sub-systems organised to maintain a 'steady state' within their environment. Organizations as cultures sees their functioning as a social structure. In this view there are no fixed structures and composition of people changes to reflect business objectives. Finally, organizations as coercive systems views them as functioning according to power structures, adding a unique element which is not present in the other three views. This view promotes the notion that organizations support the status quo or maintaining existing power structures.

There are some other ideas on organizational structures such as Mintzberg (1998), which suggest that organizations are subject to seven forces; direction, proficiency, innovation, concentration, efficiency, co-operation and competition. Detailed discussion of these structures in outside the scope of this book and a flavour of thinking about organizational structures given above demonstrates the complexity of the situation under which the projects have to be managed and problems present in organizational structures such as too many layers, extreme politics can influence the project success or failure.

Lack of clear purpose: Objectives were not clear at the beginning or became blurred in the passage of time. This can happen especially in large projects which are completed over a long period of time. Over a long period organizational priorities can change or lack of clarity about long-term objectives may lead to stating wrong directions at the beginning.

Setting unrealistic targets: This issues is one of the most common cause of a project failure. Project objectives should be: set with realistic estimates of time and resources available, specific and measurable description of a specific performance, describes the intended result "how much or what by when", jointly agreed and prioritised with consultation with stakeholders, set at the beginning of the project, reviewed regularly to ensure they remain realistic and relevant.

Lack of communication: Communications are not clear between different stakeholders or groups of stakeholders. This is often the case in technology related projects when managers do not understand the technology and technologists do not understand business resulting in misinterpretation of objectives/requirements.

Lack of proper planning: Without proper and detailed planning it is easy to underestimate the time or resources required to achieve desired objectives. Successful deployment of IT projects should be based within and guided by a realistic time frame. Often the time scale for a project will be too short, as a result of which projects overrun. This may come to be seen as a failure in the project, and in some cases may lead to abandonment (Procaccino, 2005).

Misunderstand environment: Due considerations not given to the environment under which the project will be managed or the product will be used. This could lead to insufficient resources or efforts allocated to deal with the environmental factors.

Poor requirements specification: Vague specifications often affect project success. Organizational IT projects are often complex systems, but initial specifications may sometimes be vague and unclear. This may result in relative lack of progress in deployment of the systems.

Imbalance priorities: An imbalance between the resources applied to the basic transformation processes and those allocated to the related monitoring and control processes, perhaps leading to quality problems or cost increases or delays (Fortune & White 2006).

Scope creep: Clients sometimes have additional demands after a project contract is finalised or even when a system is close to completion, which may be beyond the scope or resources allocated of the project. This, in many instances, can hamper project progress. As Petrie et al. (1999) points out that when design changes cause plan and schedule changes, the problem is worse than simply modifying the design.

Lack of support from top management: Technology projects such as e-banking have high uncertainty in terms of time/cost and objectives attached to them. Therefore support from top management is essential to deal with problems resulting from such uncertainty such as cost overruns.

Poor project control: In many cases management wants to avoid change and hence faces paradoxical situations when change occurs. Control systems that are guided by a rigid traditional mindset may require that systems adhere to initial requirement specifications, instead of adapting to changes in the environment (Coley, 2006). This may be counter-productive to project success. Changing requirements however should be managed by having flexibility built into the initial project plans and resources allocated.

Lack of good leadership: Projects go through many good and bad periods and require good leadership skills to keep all stakeholders motivated and the plans on track.

Poor testing: Tests, conducted during project planning may be incomprehensive and incomplete. This is common with regard to planning project finances. Project managers are often satisfied if they have a fixed source of funds, and may not want to explore other options. The problem occurs when committed sources of funds face challenges and fail to deliver according to their promises (Coley, 2006). Poor testing can also be a major problem in technological projects when a number of bugs are left in the systems and it fails to perform when exposed to the pressures of real business environment. Bugs are not the only problem however, scalability and adoptability of systems must also be thoroughly tested.

Lack of users' participation: New technologies often face resistance from most user groups which includes employees as well as customers. IT projects require all users of the system to be involved. Lack of user involvement and stakeholder participation may hamper the success of IT systems (Coley, 2006). It is not an easy issue to deal with, especially when users are customers and hierarchical structures and top-down management practices may often come in the way of desirable levels of user involvement.

Unsupportive organisational culture: A project can fail if the project team, the system it is developing or desired outcome do not fit well in that organization's culture. Organisational culture can be described as the collective will or consciousness of an organization, based on certain patterns of beliefs shared by all its members. Culture emerges from the social interaction of all organisational members.

When developing and implementing systems such as e-banking, culture needs to be understood, so that an organization is in a better position to incorporate its e-banking strategies which are in line with the existing culture and any cultural change seen to be in progress.

This essentially emergent view presented by Clarke (2007) sees culture as embedded in the symbols, myths, ideologies and rituals of the organisation (Figure 9.4). Symbols are the shared codes of meaning within the organisation, and may appear as language (particularly evident in information technology), corporate offices, company car schemes, logos, or simply stories about the organisation that are passed down over the years. Myths are evident in all organisations, commonly appearing as founder myths or creation myths. The ideology is an organization's systems of knowledge or set of beliefs about the social world, key among which will be the ethical position. Too often, organisations are seen to have one ideology, but

Figure 9.4. The components of organisational culture (adapted from Clarke, 2007)

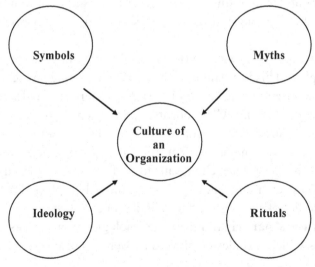

actually all organisations have sets of consonant and conflicting ideologies. Rituals within organisations help to cement the underlying values. Most sales conventions have acceptable behaviours, dress which are not prescribed, but are known and followed: wear a suit and tie; clean your company car; support some speakers and not others. To be successful at implementing a major initiative such as e-banking project with far reaching implications, the organization needs to determine what its 'culture' is, how it is changing, where the major influences are coming from.

Insufficient attention to change management: Many organizations invest heavily in technologies but fail to allocate sufficient resources for dealing with change management issues. This could result in lack of motivation as well as slow business processes which are unable to support the speed required for operations in online environment.

Managing change is a difficult and complex. Change management is dominated by 'manipulative' assumptions, with cultural factors, through which an organization deals with the underlying beliefs. Early approaches to dealing with human issues, in which the views of participants were seen as barriers to be overcome, have partially given way to a cultural perspective through which change is perceived as a participative rather than planned or structures process. There is a need to combine methods aimed at dealing with change from both planning (revolutionary or transformational) and incremental (evolutionary) perspectives. In particular, whilst evolutionary change is valuable in the short to medium term, revolutionary change may be necessary in the longer term, and may be hampered by an evolutionary or incremental process.

Arguably, in the context of banking sector, the situation regarding project management is even more problematic. Apart from the issues discussed above, the nature of the banking setting is also multi-dimensional and extremely complex due to regulations and financial risks involved. IT-based systems have existed for many years, but have not largely been integrated into the core business processes.

Typical Steps in an E-Banking Project

All e-banking projects will have unique features in terms of size, market environment, technological or organizational change needs. Having said that they will also have a number of common aspects, and the following is a guide to the typical phases an e-banking project will go through.

Feasibility study: Top management is convinced that e-banking will bring many benefits to the bank but is not clear about Return On Investment (ROI), suitability/ability of the organization to take such giant step or availability of required resources so they conduct a feasibility study to address these issues.

Decision to go ahead: This decision is often taken by the top management, followed up by initial top-level plans.

User requirements definition: The Customer service department and information systems department will collaborate on the creation of customer surveys and interviews which will be used to determine e-Banking project requirements. The Customer service and Information Technology Department interview customers. The Customer service department will conduct surveys and forward replies to Information Technology department. The Information Technology department conducts internal surveys and interviews for requirements gathering. Information Technology Department will synthesize the requirements from the surveys and interviews.

Risk analysis: The risk analysis will be carried out in collaboration with all involved departments. Risk analysis will produce a risk management plan which will be used to manage risks of e-Banking.

Project planning: Detailed project plans are developed for development of systems, testing, deployment and handover. Dealing with organizational change management issues will also be planned at this stage.

Pilot project: Pilot systems to be developed and evaluated to refine project plans and systems requirements.

E-Banking system development: The e-banking systems will be developed in house or by the outsourcing vendor under the guidance of banks. The bank and the outsourcing vendor will conduct the acceptance/functionality testing jointly.

Training: Training in use of e-Banking facilities will be managed by all parties involved. The training will be conducted in parallel to the most phases of the project but to be completed before services go live.

Evaluating: Regular evaluations are required especially at the beginning of the services going live to address any problems, to assess benefits and to learn from the experience so that the next iteration brings better results.

Project Management Methodology/Tools

A typical project will involve hundred of activities which would roughly fall into the following categories.

1. Cost estimating and preparing budgets
2. Planning for effective communication and deciding on which communication tools will be used. Some project management tools such as PRINCE 2 offer group working facilities to enable effective team working
3. Setting goals for individuals and project teams
4. Implementing change and process improvement

5. Quality assurance and controls
6. Risk assessment and management
7. Scheduling and time management etc.

The project management methodologies help plan and keep track of the above activities. There are many project management tools but most commonly used methodologies include PRINCE 2 and Microsoft Project.

PRINCE2

PRINCE2, or **PR**ojects **IN** Controlled Environments, is a comprehensive methodology for project management. It was developed and owned by the Office of Government and Commerce (OGC) in the UK. The PRINCE 2 manual is now in its 4th edition and has a dedicated accreditation body (APM Group Ltd) with over 15 accelerated consulting organizations.

PRINCE2 describes eight components which need to be present for a successful project (Murray, 2008):

1. **Business case:** The business reasons for the project
2. **Organization:** helping in planning the roles and responsibilities of the stakeholders
3. **Plans:** defining the project's products, how the work should be carried out, when and by whom
4. **Controls:** how the project managers exercise control
5. **Management of risk:** identification and management of risk
6. **Quality in a project environment:** Management of quality issues and procedures
7. **Configuration management:** how the project's products are developed and configured
8. **Change control:** how to manage changes to specification or scope of the project/product

Prince 2 is a process driven methodology rather than rigidly staged, so it offers the flexibility required for e-banking projects.

Microsoft Project

This is another common project management methodology as well as a software tool. It is a useful and popular project management tool used for business project planning, scheduling tasks, managing resources, monitoring costs and generating reports. Its main features include:

- Helps defining the content and building the project plan
- A calendar to reflect the work schedule
- Allocation of tasks
- added sub-tasks, linked related tasks and set task dependencies
- Milestones to identify significant events
- Lag and lead times and constraining dates
- A resource list and created resource calendars for the resources
- A critical path to reflect the core project processes
- Comprehensive reporting tools to keep track of the progress.

There are other tools to complement these methodologies and details of such tools can be obtained from www.pmi.org or other related websites. In addition to these tools/methods we also recommend a system 'approach to project management' (Clarke et al., 2007) for an example of its implementation) which can be used in conjunction with the above described tools/techniques.

A SYSTEMS APPROACH TO PROJECT MANAGEMENT

It has been argued earlier that banking is a complex domain and the management of systems might be seen as attempts to control variety and complexity through a reductionist approach. Reductionism seeks to understand systems in terms of their constituent parts, assuming that these parts operate independently. This approach, which sees organizations as rigid structures, with departments working in an isolated manner, is not suitable for the banking industry, with its mix of professionals working toward common objectives but often within fairly loose forms of organization. This approach is especially undesirable in e-business environment where systems and organizational integration is vital for success. Here, a more holistic and systemic approach might be seen as more likely to be successful, and such an approach is fundamental in systems approaches to project management.

As discussed in other chapters of this book, the central idea behind systems thinking is that organizations are constituted of sub-systems, or elements, that are in interrelationships with one another, and which exist within a boundary. What is important is not the elements per se, but the interrelationships between them, because it is the nature of the interrelationships that give character to the system. Inputs to the system are transformed within it, and go out as output, which in turn informs further input with feedback (Figure 9.5).

Figure 9.5. The systems perspective (adapted from Flood & Jackson, 1991)

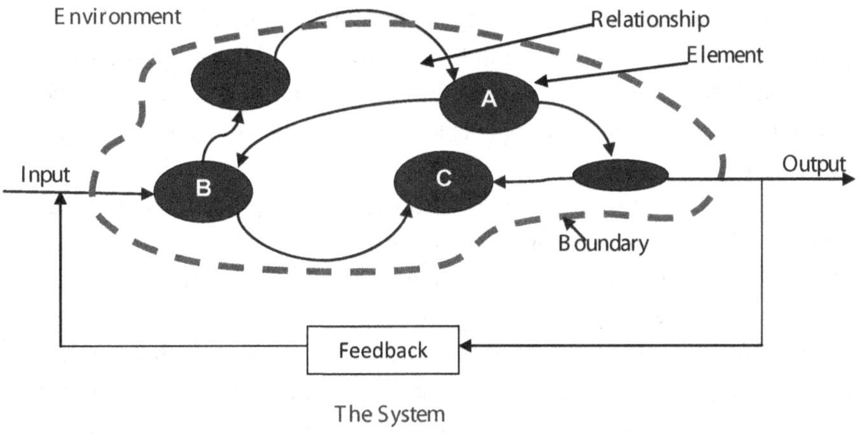

Organizations constantly interact with their environment, and modern modes of working mean that often members of organizations work as temporary networks, multi-disciplinary and virtual teams, and sometimes even as temporary organizations in themselves for the achievement of particular business objectives.

The environment outside the system are often a challenge to be addressed by the variety within it. The discipline of cybernetics (Ashby, 1956) has forwarded the idea that variety can only be addressed with variety. Organizations normally create departments to deal will specific business aspects like sales, personnel, marketing, procurement, finance and so on. The danger is that these departments can become closed systems operating in themselves, not interacting with one another. As a result of this, very often short term project goals are maximized at the cost of long term interests of an organization (Dooley, 1997). In effective organizations, people have to work across departments in a systemic way so that planning is done with a holistic perspective of where the organization currently is and what it wants to achieve. In project management field, this process is sometimes called programme management. For instance, Xerox, the first company in the US to win back market share from the Japanese in the 1980s (Guns, 1996), adopted a new strategy to fight Japanese competition. The then CEO of Xerox, Allaire, split the company into eight divisions each focusing on a particular product or a product group (Guns, 1996). This was probably an attempt to overcome departmental barriers and provide a product-specific platform, bringing together members of different departments to share diverse knowledge and work together for a specific product or common organizational objectives.

Systems thinking promotes the understanding that departments may contain boundaries, but not barriers. Whereas boundaries allow permeation of ideas and opinion, and facilitate team working, barriers do not. Hence, whereas boundaries can be facilitative, barriers are prohibitive. Senge et al., (1994) argues that perception plays a crucial role here as it basically depends upon the observer who perceives what causes the system to work together. Therefore, the systems thinker is continually negotiating and re-negotiating through boundary critique: a process where organizational knowledge as well as from its' environment may be continuously synthesized.

Systems thinking can provide significant philosophical and practical underpinnings for technological projects. E-banking needs to be perceived as a network of activities, rather than as stand-alone technological projects managed by the IT department. For effective planning and deployment of e-banking related systems, people should work across departments forming networks, the members of which can then be enabled to think more systemically about the organization as a whole, instead of perceiving their own responsibilities in an isolated manner. Merali (2004) notes:

> ... *in order to engage effectively in the discourse of the network society, there are two shifts necessary in the 'classical' understanding of the systems (such as e-banking):*
> - *A shift in the focus of 'systems thinking': from focusing on discrete bounded systems to focusing on networks; and from focusing on structural properties of systems to engaging with the dynamics of systems.*
> - *A shift in ontological assumptions about information: from focusing mainly on discrete entities (individuals, organizations or applications) as loci for information creation and interpretation to drawing the role of the network as a focus for these processes* (pp.436-7).

All of this understanding is important for e-banking projects which often need collaborations across an organization or even outside an organization to be successful. Unsystemic way of working, within an organization defined by departmental and other barriers could result in failure of the whole project.

MANAGING HUMAN ISSUES

An e-Banking project will have significant economic, organizational and social impact on the organization. Therefore, well defined goals combined with a communication strategy will reduce any resentment amongst the bank's staff. Such resentment may create a negative atmosphere that will have considerable consequences on the progress of the project. Other social issues and ways to deal with them, discussed in Chapter VI, are also relevant here.

In multinational companies, cultural differences often exacerbate communication problems. For example, a message from someone where communication tends to be more direct might seem rude to someone from a different background. Misalignment of expectations can be the source of major problems in large scale projects. To avoid such mishaps, we suggest ongoing communication to manage each other's expectations. Communication can build trust, and this greater trust can often lead to improve formal and informal communication levels. Hence, meaningful communication is a necessary antecedent of trust. There are two types of communication, formal and informal. Formal communication is often about hard data such as legal, technical or commercial. Informal communication is more personal and requires greater degree of trust and understanding between different stakeholders in a project.

E-Banking systems often result in significant impact on the organization, and require people throughout the organization to learn new behaviors and skills. Negative effects of change are inevitable when people are forced to adjust to fast paced change. Organizations need to proactively recognize the effects of change and develop skills amongst its staff to enable the change. Without this proactive approach, the risk of resistance to change increases significantly and reduces the chances of achieving expected benefits.

Change management is a well developed concept and a number of methods exist for managing technology related changes. Detailed discussion of these change management methods is outside the scope of this book. Most common themes include:

- Create the vision to inspire people.
- Create the plan to manage change.
- Communicate exact changes to affected parties.
- Cultivate motivated and empowered affected parties using training as well as incentives to embrace change.
- Cement the change in the organization's culture gradually.

Managing social issues must be taken seriously as mismanagement of these issues is often cited as a key reason for the failure of the projects.

CHAPTER SUMMARY

It is becoming common in the financial sector to manage the organization, and in particular strategic change, through projects or project portfolios, termed programme management. E-banking is often considered a major change and requires careful management of its projects.

A very high number of technological projects fail because of poor project management. To gain competitive advantage and create value through adoption of change management strategies, companies can implement business processes that allow efficient and effective enterprise project management.

It is important to understand that success in projects is largely a subjective concept. Any success evaluation should take into account both the hard (tangible and measurable) and soft (subjective and difficult to quantify) dimensions of success. Success is perceived differently by different stakeholders, and success criteria must be prioritised to address any possible conflicts. Success is also affected by time, with some measures being short-term and others long-term. Finally, success may be partial, as some criteria may be successfully met whilst others may not.

Project managers must agree the criteria with the stakeholders as early as possible and apply appropriate factors to deliver agreed dimensions of success. The rate of success may also be improved if all parties involved keep expectations at a realistic level and place importance on a quality product and organizational congruency.

To be successful, any complex project needs to work across departments at both the planning and operational levels. The implementation of e-banking projects needs to address long term organizational benefit and sustainability as well as short term gains. There is a difference between seeing the separation of departments as barriers to interaction, and seeing them as boundaries to be permeated. Staff from different departments need to be brought together to work together towards common objectives. Stakeholders' participation in decision making from the earliest stages of a project is needed to ensure that there is a common will to collaborate rather than resistance to open up.

REFERENCES

Aladwani, A. M. (2001). Online banking: a field study of drivers, development challenges, and expectations. *International Journal of Information Management*, 21, 213–225.

Ashby, W. R. (1956). *Introduction to Cybernetics*. London: Methuen. http://pespmc1.vub.ac.be/books/IntroCyb.pdf

Baccarini, D. (1999, December). The Logical Framework Method for Defining Project Success. *Project Management Journal,* 25-32.

Beath, C. M., & Orlikowski, W. J. (1994). The Contradictory Structure of Systems Development Methodologies: Deconstructing the IS-User Relationship in Information Engineering. *Information Systems Research,* 5(4), 350-377.

Beynon-Davies, P. & Lloyd-Williams, M. (1999). When health information systems fail. *Topics Health Inform Manage,* 20(1), 66-79.

Chowdhury, R. S. Clarke, S., & R. Butler. (1994). Healthcare IT Project Failure: A Systems Perspective. *Journal of Cases in Information Technology,* 9(4) 1-15.

Clarke, S. A. (2007). *Information Systems Strategic Management: An Integrated Approach, (2nd Ed.).* London: Routledge.

Coley Consulting. (2006). *Why Projects Fail.* Retrieved April 08, 2006 from http://www.coleyconsulting.co.uk/failure.htm

DeLone, H., & McLean, E. R. (2003, Spring). The DeLone and McLean Model of Information Systems Success: A Ten-year Update. *Journal of Management Information Systems,* 19(4), 9-31.

DeLone, H., & McLean, E.R. (1992, March). Information Systems Success: The Quest for the Dependent Variable. *Information Systems Research,* 3(1) 60-96.

Doherty, N., Shantanu, B., & Parry, M. (2000, April 26-28). Factors Affecting the Successful Outcome of Systems Development Project. In Beynon-Davies P. Williams, M.D. Beeson I (Eds.), *Proceedings of the UKAIS conference on Information Systems, Research,* (pp. 375-383). Teaching and Practice, Cardiff, UK.

Dooley, K. (1997). A complex adaptive systems model of organizational change. In *Nonlinear Dynamics, Psychology and Life Science.* 1(1), 69-97.

El Emam, K., & Birk, A. (2000). Validating the ISO/IEC 15504 Measure of Software Requirements Analysis Process Capability. *IEEE Transactions on Software Engineering,* 26 (6), 541-566.

Flood, R. L. & Jackson, M. (1991). *Creative problem solving: Total systems intervention.* Chichester, UK: Wiley.

Fortune, J., & White, D. (2006). Framing of project critical success factors by a systems model. *International Journal of Project Management,* 24(1), 53-65.

Freeman, M., & Beale, P. (1992). Measuring project success. *Project Management Journal,* 23(1), 33-38.

Goldenson, D.K. & Herbsleb, J.B. (1995) *After the Appraisal: A Systematic Survey of Process Improvement, its Benefits, and Factors that Influence Success* (Tech. Rep. CMU/SEI-95-TR-009-ESC-TR-95-009). Software Engineering Institute. http://www.sei.cmu.edu/pub/documents/95.reports/pdf/tr009.95.pdf

Guns, B. (1996). *The Faster Learning Organization: Gain and Sustain the competitive edge*. San Diego, CA: Pfeiffer & Co.

IT Cortex. (Date not available). Failure Rate: Statistics over IT projects failure rate. Retrieved January 23, 2006, from http://www.it-cortex.com/Stat_Failure_Rate.htm

Jackson, S.E. & Schuler, R.S. (1995). Understanding Human Resource Management in the Context of Organizations and their Environments. *Annual Review of Psychology*, *46*, 237-264. http://arjournals.annualreviews.org/doi/abs/10.1146/annurev.ps.46.020195.001321

Jiang, J. J., Klein, G., & Discenz, R. (2002). Perception differences of software success: provider and user views of system metrics. *The Journal of Systems and Software*, 54, 17-27.

Lipovertsky, S., Tishler, A., Dvir, D., & Shenhar, A. (1997). The relative importance of project success dimensions. *R & D Management*, 27(2), 97-106.

Lyytinen, K., & Hirschheim, R. A. (1987). Information Systems Failure: A Survey and Classification of The Empirical Literature. In Zorkoczy, P. I. (Ed.) *Oxford Surveys in Information Technology*, 4 (pp. 257-309), Oxford, UK: Oxford University Press.

Merali, Y. (2004). Complexity and Information Systems. In Mingers, J. and Willcocks, L. (Eds.), *Social Theory and Philosophy for Information Systems*. Chichester: John Wiley & Sons.

Mintzberg, H. (1998). Politics and the Political Organization. In Mintzberg, H., Quinn J. B. and Ghoshal, S., *The Strategy Process*, (Rev. European Ed.), (377-382), London: Prentice Hall.

Murray, A. (2007, March). *Everything you wanted to know about PRINCE2 in less than one thousand words* (White Paper). Retrieved June 25 2008, from http://www.best-management-practice.com/gempdf/PRINCE2_White_Paper_v2.pdf

Petrie, C., Goldmann, S. & Raquet, A. (1999). *Agent-based project management*. Stanford University. Retrieved September 18, 2005, from http://www-cdr.stanford.edu/ProcessLink/papers/DPM/dpm.html

PMI (2008). *What is project management.* Retrieved March 8, 2008, from http://www.pmi.org/Pages/default.aspx.

Procaccino, J. D., Verner, J. M., Shelfer, K.,M., & Gefen, D. (2005). What do software practitioners really think about project success; an exploratory study. *The Journal of Systems and Software.*

Raz, T., Shenhar, A. J., & Dvir, D. (2002). Risk Management, Project Success, and Technological Uncertainty. *Research & Development Management*, 32(2) 101-109.

Reel, J.S. (1999). Critical Success Factors in Software Projects. *IEEE Software* (May/June), 18-23.

Robey, D., Smith, L., & Vijayasarathy, L. R. (1993). Perceptions of Conflict and Success in Information Systems Development Projects. *Journal of Management Information Systems,* Summer, 10(1), 123-139.

Seddon, P. B. (1997, September) A Re-specification and Extension of the DeLone and Mclean Model of IS Success. Information Systems Research, 8(3), 240-254.

Senge, P.M., Roberts, C., Ross, R.B., Smith, B.J., & Kleiner, A. (1994). *The Fifth Discipline Fieldbook: strategies and tools for building a learning organization.* London: Nicholas Brealey.

Shah, M. H., Braganza, A., & Morabito, V. (2007). A Survey of Critical Success Factors in e-Banking: An Organisational Perspective. *European Journal of Information Systems,* 16(4) 511-524, http://www.palgrave-journals.com/ejis/journal/v16/n4/index.html

Shenhar, A. J., Tishler, A., Dvir, D., Lipovetsky, S., Lechler, T. (2002). Refining the search for project success factors: a multivariate, typological approach. *Research & Development Management*, 32(2), 111-126.

Shenhar, A.J., Dvir, D., Levy, O., & Maltz, A. (2001). Project Success: A Multidimensional Strategic Concept. *Long Range Planning*, 34, 699-725.

Wohlin, C., & Andrews, A. A. (2001). Assessing Project Success Using Subjective Evaluation Factors. *Software Quality Journal*, 9, 43-70.

Chapter X
Systems Thinking and Knowledge Management for E-Banking

INTRODUCTION

As has been shown to be the case with information systems, it can be argued that the perception of knowledge seen as either a purely technical or purely social phenomenon is insufficient. This argument will be developed within this chapter, the aim being to answer the question: 'what kind of system is an e-banking system, when seen from a knowledge management perspective?'

We begin by looking at organisations and their management, initially establishing a historical frame. Systems thinking, and its relationship to KM, is then reviewed, followed by a more in depth analysis of social systems philosophy and theory, and the domain of epistemology. All of this points to a theoretical grounding on which to base the application of KM to e-banking in the philosophy and theory of Kant and Habermas, and in order to further develop this theme, social theory, and particularly critical social theory, is discussed. The outcome is an argument for social systems theory, and, more particularly, critical social theory, and for theories of communicative action to provide the grounding for e-business. A discussion then follows of what this means for the application of KM to e-banking, incorporating the concepts drawn from social theory.

ORGANISATIONS AND THEIR MANAGEMENT

Our study of organisation theory begins with Frederick Taylor's scientific management (Taylor 1947), initially formulated at the turn of the nineteenth to the twentieth century. Major subsequent developments have been administrative management theory (Fayol 1949), where the management process is defined (to forecast and plan, to organise, to command, to co-ordinate and control), and bureaucracy theory (Webber; see Gerth and Mills 1970).

Taylor's work may be loosely classified as time and motion or work study, and this, as well as the other theories noted above, adheres to the rational model, which views organisations mechanistically, seeing the attainment of maximum efficiency as achievable by putting together the parts in an effective way under the control of management. Hierarchy, authority and rational decision making are fundamental to this.

In the 1920s, as evidenced by the Hawthorn experiments, the human relations model began to gain ground, based on social structures of people at work and motivation. This model pointed to democratic, employee centred management. More recent developments have seen the growth of the systems model of organisations, where they are viewed systemically as open systems responding to environmental changes and maintaining a steady state (Selznick 1948; Katz & Kahn 1978). This systems approach links well with empirical research in socio technical systems (Pasmore & Sherwood 1978), and contingency theory (Lawrence & Lorsch 1969).

Broadly, the systems model recommends that if an organisation is not functioning properly the sub-systems should be examined to see that they are meeting organisational needs, and the organisation examined to see that it is well adjusted to its environment. These tasks are charged to a management sub-system.

From a systems perspective, business organisations today may be characterised as complex, adaptive, human activity (micro-social) systems. In so far as such systems are devoid of human interaction (in, for example, a robot assembly plant), focus on a purely mechanistic approach may yield valuable results. As system complexity, and particularly the degree of human activity, increases, this approach is seen to break down, and human viewpoints need increasingly to be considered. There can be little doubt that this "micro-social" view of an organisation is highly relevant to e-business. As has already been discussed in earlier chapters, in e-banking we have a situation in which technology and human activity are increasingly integrated, with the whole "socio-technical" system becoming the key focus of attention. The systems perspective on management offers insights into this which are not available through alternative views. The following section investigates this perspective more fully, as a precursor to applying systems thinking and knowledge management to e-banking.

Systems Thinking

In common usage, the term 'system' has come to mean very little. How, for instance, are we to make sense of a single definition of 'system', when it is applied to such diverse objects as 'a hi-fi system', 'the railway system', or 'the system of planets and stars we refer to as the Universe'? Clearly, before the idea of a Knowledge Management system is investigated, we need a common definition of 'system': this is what this section aims to achieve.

To begin with, a system is more than a simple collection of components, since properties 'emerge' when the components of which systems are comprised are combined. So, for example, we may gather together all of the components that make up a bicycle, but only when they are assembled do we have the emergent property of a mode of transport. Further, all systems must have a boundary – try to envisage a system without a boundary, and it soon becomes clear that the concept is meaningless. When considering the nature and properties of any system, care should be taken when looking at the components of the system in isolation. These parts, or sub-systems, interact, or are 'interdependent', and so need to be considered as a whole or 'holistically'. In addition, there is likely to be a discernible structure to the way sub-systems are arranged – in a hierarchy, for example. Finally, there need to be communication and control with the system, and it has to perform some transformation process. So, in summary, a system may be defined according to its:

- Boundary
- Emergence
- Holism
- Interdependence
- Hierarchy
- Transformation
- Communication and Control

Further to this, and following Checkland (1994), it is possible to conceive of a typology of systems divided into:

- Physical systems, which are either natural or designed; and
- Human activity systems.

Generally, whilst physical systems might be *complicated*, and require significant skill and expertise to construct or even understand (hence the modern-day interest in the Universe), only human activity systems exhibit *complexity*. In essence, human activity systems are complex adaptive systems. In order to relate this understanding to Knowledge Management, it is necessary to determine how, according to the above classifications, organisational systems should be categorised. Are they designed physical or human activity systems, or some combination of the two?

Designed physical systems are mechanistic or deterministic, requiring a view of the World that is mechanical or technical, and typically rule-based. By way of an example, think of an aeroplane. It is clearly a designed physical system, whose design depends on the laws of aerodynamics. Construction of, arguably, this most complicated of all machines requires considerable skill and knowledge, but it all accords to a set of rules, most of which are well known. It is these properties that have led to such systems being seen as closed in relation to their environment. By contrast, organisational systems, whilst they might make use of designed physical or even natural systems, are made up of human actors. They are open, complex adaptive systems of activity.

Following this line of thought, Knowledge Management systems emerge as fundamentally systems of human activity, exhibiting voluntary behaviour (or 'free will'). Such systems take an interpretivistic or subjective view of the World: a view which sees not 'objective reality', but a series of human perspectives and opinions. They are probabilistic rather than deterministic. However, whilst KM systems may be primarily human activity systems, they may also contain sub-systems which are technological or organisational, and these sub-systems may have a role in better enabling the KM to function. A way of conceptualising this is to think of a KM system as a human activity 'lens' through which all knowledge activity is viewed, and in accordance with whose characteristics and properties that activity is interpreted (Figure 10.1).

Knowledge management and knowledge acquisition therefore consist fundamentally of human activity, and as a consequence are subject to human perception and agreement. The whole, bounded KM system which this is seeking to manage or interpret may contain technological and structural elements, but the purpose of these is simply to better enable the human activity system to function. By seeing KM in this way, we move ever closer to a new viewpoint from which to observe, implement and manage e-business systems which, after all, we have posited as socio-technical.

This view is supported by research that highlights the complexity of social systems, and the inappropriateness of studying such systems using scientific methods. In effect, in the social sciences, there is a complexity that stems from the introduction of human activity. Such activity is not absolutely predictable, being based on intended and unintended actions that do not easily lend themselves to study by the reductionist rules of repeatability and refutation.

Systems thinking, then, may be seen as fundamental to an understanding of KM and, hence, e-banking, which may be recast as a human (social and cognitive) activity, supported or enabled by structural and technological sub-systems. By way of a summary, each of the properties of systems can now be related directly to issues in KM (Table 10.1).

Figure 10.1. The nature of knowledge management systems

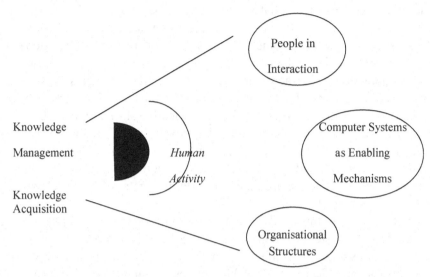

THE PHILOSOPHY AND THEORY OF SOCIAL SYSTEMS

This is a section which some readers will find interesting and others may wish to avoid. We include it here for completeness, and because we see it to be of immense importance. Much of our research has focused in this area, with the aim of providing a sound foundation for the ultimately practical issues, which, in our view, need to be underpinned by significant philosophical and theoretical principles.

Some Philosophical Issues

The philosophical and theoretical perspective on which this study is grounded sees the World as socially constructed, and therefore argues that human issues are best seen from a socially constructed viewpoint. This section describes that viewpoint in more detail, and sets the context for the study.

Philosophically, this study is grounded in critical social theory, as derived specifically from the work of Kant (1724-1804), particularly as described in *The Critique of Pure Reason* (Kant 1787). Whilst it might appear odd to underpin a twenty-first century study of Knowledge Management with the work of an eighteenth century philosopher, we contend that Kant's work has particular resonance for the domain of KM, and ask only that you bear with us for the time being, and suspend judgement until the end of this chapter. By tracing a route through philosophy and theory, we hope you will see the relevance of the underpinning chosen for this study.

Table 10.1. Systems of knowledge management and e-banking

System Property	Implications for Knowledge Management — Human Activity Systems	Enabling Mechanisms: Designed Physical Systems	
		Structure	Technology
Boundary	The limits of that which can be known	The organisation, or relevant part of it	Bounded technological sub-systems which enable the whole system of Knowledge Management to function more effectively: e-banking technology.
Emergence	Emergent properties of a knowledge system: e.g. decision making	Structure and technology must be seen in terms of their contribution to the emergent properties of the whole KM system: e-banking as more than the "sum of its (human and technological) parts".	
Holism	Encompasses technical, human (cognitive and social), and organisational factors	Must not be viewed in isolation, but only as part of the whole KM system: guards against viewing e-banking as, for example, a solely technological issue.	
Interdependence	Changes in part of the system (e.g. human knowledge acquisition) effect changes in other parts (e.g. the use of enabling technologies)	Technology, organisation, and human activity working together are the source of success in any KM system: in e-banking, the technology affects the people interacting with it; people affect structure; and so on.	
Hierarchy	As human beings we see structures in knowledge systems (hence the data structures in computerised systems)	Organisational structures help facilitate human knowledge acquisition and sharing: important to see e-banking structures as enabling mechanisms to the whole e-banking system.	Technologies support the organisation and/or human actors: as with organisation, technologies enable, they are not an end in themselves.
Transformation	The acquisition of knowledge always leads to changes, which may be perceived in organisational terms as transformation processes	The key in transformation achieved through Knowledge Management: technology and structure are enablers: an overview of what is to be transformed by the new e-banking system is a powerful image.	
Communication and Control	These are fundamental to knowledge systems, and once more require understanding of the interactions between human, technical, and organisational issues	Used as aids to communication and control in the overall KM system: this is not about power and control, but about facilitating the enhanced use of the e-banking system to gain competitive advantage.	

KNOWLEDGE MANAGEMENT FROM ITS PHILOSOPHICAL AND THEORETICAL ROOTS

Information from literature and empirical evidence suggests knowledge management (KM) to be a domain still at a rather immature stage of development. One of the key reasons identified for this is that the concept of *knowledge* lacks a clear definition. This chapter lays out an approach to underpinning the concept of knowledge, and thereby KM, from philosophical and theoretical perspectives, and from this underpinning reframes the domain of KM. The work is presented, not as a definitive study, but as something to promote what we see as an essential debate. Comments on the issues discussed here will be gratefully received by the authors.

It is common to come across ideas of knowledge that categorise it according to: explicit or implicit; explicit or tacit; more than data or information and less than wisdom; and so on. Whilst of value in themselves, such definitions lack something fundamental, as is evidenced by the fact that they commonly give rise to self-referential definitions (for example: 'knowledge is made up of explicit and implicit knowledge'). What seems to be happening here is that we are learning something about the nature of knowledge, having assumed that we already understand what it is *in its essence.*

In this study we meet the problem head on, but first a word of caution! There is no intention in a single book chapter, to attempt a once-and-for-all definition which will satisfy everyone on the question of knowledge as a concept. We, as authors, would like to think that we can achieve the task of setting in motion an important debate, which will yield satisfactory outcomes to its participants: this chapter aims to be the beginning of that debate.

So to the question 'what is knowledge?' To answer this, our research has been on two complementary dimensions: philosophical and theoretical. First we have undertaken a very brief review of the KM literature in order to determine a rationale for the study. Following this, the chapter looks at what we might learn from epistemology, with the explicit aim of determining what the theory of knowledge has to tell us about its management. This particularly addresses how an understanding of such theory helps unravel the problem of what knowledge *is*, without which we argue that *management* of knowledge is impossible. We next take a deeper historical perspective on philosophical developments in the understanding of knowledge. Beginning with concepts taken from Greek philosophy, this history covers the thinking of early Western philosophers through to the most recent ideas of contemporary epistemology. Issues covered include scientific versus alternative forms of knowledge, knowledge as objective reality or subjective understanding, and Kant's transcendental philosophy. Where relevant, specific philosophical positions are addressed, examples being Locke's definition of knowledge according to its source in intuition, reason or experience, and Hume's concept that knowledge is limited to sense experience.

A review of pre-critical philosophy is used as a backdrop to the philosophical perspective which forms the basis of this research, grounded on Kant. Specific theoretical developments seen to be relevant to an understanding of Knowledge Management are then reviewed, including work by Habermas on the 'subject-knower-object' problem, through which knowledge is defined both in relation to objects of experience and to the so-called *a priori* categories that the knowing subject brings to the act of perception. Through this and other theoretical perspectives, the social and reflective dimensions of knowledge are investigated in more depth.

The aim throughout is to relate these ideas to an understanding of knowledge that will inform contemporary Knowledge Management studies, and the final section of the chapter looks at the practical guidance for knowledge and its management which might be derived from these perspectives, and how this relates to selected recent approaches to KM.

A BRIEF REVIEW OF THE LITERATURE

The knowledge management (KM) literature seems, from our perspective, to lack certain fundamentals, which a review of some of the more recent publications will serve well to illustrate. There seems to be only a limited attempt to base the development of organisational KM systems on any explicit foundation. So, for example, in an otherwise excellent paper partially targeted at unearthing the 'conceptual foundations' of Knowledge Management, Alavi and Leidner (2001) discuss views of knowledge taken from IT and other literature, commenting that:

"The question of defining knowledge has occupied the minds of philosophers since the classical Greek era and has led to many epistemological debates. It is unnecessary for the purposes of this paper to engage in a debate to probe, question, or reframe the term knowledge ... because such an understanding of knowledge was neither a determinant factor in building the knowledge-based theory of the firm nor in triggering researcher and practitioner interest in managing organizational knowledge."

It is our contention that, by any reasonable standards, such a view is unsupportable. It seems that what is being said could be characterised in any of the ways listed below, none of which seems to us to be acceptable.

1.   The philosophical and theoretical foundation for the study of knowledge has nothing to tell us about how we should manage it.
2.   Philosophy and theory is of no value to the debate.

3.   That we should accept there being no more to say about the underpinning to the domain, and it is therefore acceptable to proceed on a conceptual or pragmatic basis.
4.   That all of the philosophical and theoretical issues raised in the past have been incorporated into current approaches.

However we should interpret this statement, it is our hope that, by the end of this chapter you will be closer to our view: that philosophy and theory are central to an understanding of how to manage knowledge.

Not all writers exclude consideration of fundamental underpinning to the domain, but mostly the research can be characterised as eclectic and somewhat unconnected in character. So, for example, Sutton (2001) draws widely from philosophical and theoretical sources, including, for example, Heidegger and Wittgenstein. But the arguments and perspectives are presented in a rather disconnected manner.

For the most part, research in KM is primarily pragmatic or at best conceptual. In an essentially pragmatic study, Earl (2001) proposes a taxonomy of KM strategies. The problem is that, although the *practical* significance of the findings presented are without question of value, there seems to be nothing to tie the ideas together, with even the conceptual schema (unusually for Earl) being strangely fragmented. Other recent publications on KM seem to follow a similar tack. These include a Journal of the Operational Research Society special issue (Williams & Wilson 2003), and a range of edited texts (see, for example: Coakes, Clarke et al. 2001).

Having determined a rationale for the study, the next section now proceeds with an analysis of concepts drawn from epistemology.

What we Might Learn from Epistemology

It seems perhaps curious that so much of the writings in KM ignore (explicitly at least) epistemology, or the theory of knowledge.

"Philosophers have given a great deal of thought to ... what we can know – or mistakenly think we know – through perception or through other sources of knowledge, such as memory as a storehouse of what we have learned in the past, introspection as a way to know our inner lives, reflection as a way to acquire knowledge of abstract matters, or testimony as a source of knowledge originally acquired in others" (Audi 1998 p. 1).

What seems to be put in play here is the dependence, for an understanding of the concept of knowledge, on its generation and retention from and within a number of sources. Certainly, any idea of managing knowledge that solely focuses on material stored, for example, in databases, seems insufficient even from this initial cursory inspection. Further to this, reason (Audi 1998 p. 104) may also be seen as a source of *a priori* truths, though such an approach has been challenged by empiricist philosophers. This will be discussed in more detail below, together with the position taken on these issues by this chapter, which is essentially Kantian. Finally, from the domain of epistemology, we have to consider (Audi 1998 p. 152-175) the process of inference, by which basic knowledge is extended.

Within the limits of a chapter of this length, we will attempt to make sense of these issues and their relation to KM in our contemporary Western World. But before that, we would like to delve a little deeper from a philosophical and theoretical perspective.

Issues from Pre-Critical Philosophy

Some of the earliest and most influential Western evidence of civilisations struggling with systems of thought is to be found in Greek philosophy, which, at its most basic, might be seen as a search for *certain* knowledge. Central to this is the concept that our senses may delude us, and a questioning of whether we have any basis for believing that sense experience brings us into contact with objective reality. This led early Greek philosophers to the central question of what the world consisted of. Socrates (470-399 BC), for example, believed it possible to achieve objective knowledge through conceptual analysis. It is here that we first see the division of knowledge into *what is* and *what ought to be*: factual and normative knowledge. Seeking knowledge through conceptual analysis led Socrates to his 'theory of ideas', which was further developed by Plato (427-347 BC). In essence, Plato considered ideas to have objective reality, and knowledge to be gained by a continuous cycling between ideas and perceptions. Plato argued that whilst the objects of our knowledge do exist those objects cannot be attributed to anything in our world of perception. They existed in an ideal state in a world beyond our knowledge.

Aristotle's (384-322 BC) approach to determining knowledge takes into account the philosophies of nature, mathematics and metaphysics. Here again we see the attempt to establish absolute truths through the process of reason.

Moving forward to the beginnings of our modern age, the reawakening of interest in the ideas which had absorbed the Ancient Greeks led, during the Renaissance and beyond, into what might be characterised as arguments over method. Emerging pre-eminent during the period of the Enlightenment was scientific method, within which knowledge was seen as objectively determined. To those espousing early scientific method, we live in a world which is realistic and deterministic, and which can be understood through reductionist method, using such approaches as induction, deduction and experimentation. Truth was to be determined through repeatability, refutation, verification and falsification.

Into this world came Descartes (1596-1650) as the first of the 'Continental Rationalists'. In terms of knowledge creation, the relevance of Cartesian method is that truth is judged according to rational criteria – even sense experience should be verified through reason. In opposition to this we might cast the British empiricists. Locke (1632-1704), as with the empiricists who followed him, accepted rationalism as giving an insight into *concepts*, but did not see that this necessarily gave an insight into *reality*. For the latter, acquisition of knowledge is attained in the empirical sciences.

We thus reach a position where the concepts of knowledge production through rational and empirical processes are in opposition, and to the philosophy of Immanuel Kant (1724-1804).

A Foundation in Kantian Critical Philosophy

Kant's critical problem, as first formulated in the letter to Herz (21 February 1772), concerns the nature of objective reality. Prior to Kant, all philosophical schema took objective reality as a 'given', and sought to explain how it was that we could have knowledge of this reality. If this were taken as definitive, it is easy to see how we might build (empirical) knowledge in the way suggested by Locke (1632 to 1704): that we are born with a 'tabula rasa' or 'blank slate' on which impressions are formed through experience. This explains the pre-Kantian debate of reason versus experience as the source of our knowledge. The rationalist view was that, by reason alone, we are able to formulate universally valid truths (for example, around such issues as God and immortality); empiricists, by contrast, see experience as the only valid source of knowledge.

Kant's insight, and unique contribution, was to bring together rationalism and empiricism in his new critical transcendental philosophy. The basis of this is his 'Copernican Revolution' in philosophy. Loosely stated, this says that objective reality may be taken as existing, but that, as human beings, we have access to this only through our senses: we therefore see this objectivity not as it is, but as we subjectively construct it. Unlike Berkeley (1685-1753), Kant does not claim that objects *exist* only in our subjective constructions, merely that this is the only way in which *we can know them*: objects necessarily conform to our mode of cognition.

For this to be so, Kant's philosophy has to contain *a priori* elements: there has to be an object-enabling structure in our cognition to which objective reality can conform, and thereby make objects possible for us. This is what lies at the heart of Kant's *Transcendental Idealism*.

- Whilst objects may exist (be 'empirically real'), for us they can be accessed only through their appearances (they are 'transcendentally ideal').
- Our cognition does not conform in some way to empirical reality, rather this 'objectivity' should be seen as conforming to our modes of cognition. In this way, we 'construct' our objective world.

- Objects of cognition must conform to our sense experience. So, in this sense, knowledge is sensible, or the result of experience.
- These objects must conform to the object-enabling structures of human cognition. The resultant transcendental knowledge is (at least) one stage removed from objective reality, and is, according to Kant, governed by *a priori* concepts within human understanding.

All of this gives a foundation for determining what knowledge is, and how it might be obtained, and is the subject of the following section.

Kant and Knowledge

The thinking with which Kant was grappling in trying to make sense of knowledge is well represented by the positions of Leibniz (1646-1716) and Hume (1711-1776). In effect, both saw knowledge as either necessary and *a priori*, or contingent and experiential. Kant's unique argument is that, whilst accepting these forms of knowledge, although all of our knowledge *begins with* experience, it does not follow that knowledge all *arises from* experience: in other words, experience may be simply the cue that gives rise to knowledge claims not derived from it. One of these key non-empirical knowledge claims is the concept of freedom.

A further claim made by Kant is that knowledge can be built only through the combined interactions of sensibility and intuition:

"Without sensibility no object would be given to us, without understanding no object would be thought. Thoughts without content are empty, intuition without concepts are blind. It is, therefore, just as necessary to make our concepts sensible, that is, to add the object to them in intuition, as to make our intuitions intelligible, that is, to bring them under concepts. These two powers or capacities cannot exchange their functions. The understanding can intuit nothing, the senses can think nothing. Only through their union can knowledge arise" (Kant 1787 p. 93).

Further, that which appears to us is not simply a collection of unconnected sensations: it consists of content as well as form, and without the latter would be meaningless. Form is intuitive, and cannot arise out of the sensation – it must be *a priori*. A sequence of auditory sensations, when heard by us, becomes a tune; but the tune is not inherent in the original data (this would be equivalent to empirical data supplying its own form, and even if there is seen to be an inherent form supplied with the data, there is no reason why we should see it as such, this requires apprehension) – it must be supplied by us.

"What objects may be in themselves, and apart from all this receptivity of our sensibility, remains completely unknown to us. We know nothing but our mode of perceiving them – a mode which is peculiar to us ... Even if we could bring our intuition to the highest degree of clearness, we should not thereby come any nearer to the constitution of objects in themselves" (Kant 1787 p. 82).

In summary:

1. Objectivity is conceivable only from the perspective of a thinking subject.
2. Central to Kantian philosophy is the question of how it is possible for subject and object to be so joined – what conditions must apply in order that this might be so?
3. In the Transcendental Deduction, Kant argues that subject and object make each other possible: neither one could be represented without the other.
4. All of this rests on their being: 1) a world of objects which is unknowable to us; 2) *a priori* concepts in understanding which enable representation of this world of objects.

Kant's philosophy has been the foundation for much of philosophical debate which continues to the present day, one of the primary themes of which is pursued below.

Whilst Kant's work, even within this one text of *The Critique of Pure Reason*, is complex and extremely diverse, certain strands of relevance to KM can be drawn out. Primary amongst these is the need to take a position on the way in which we see the World. As human beings, our viewpoint is essentially made up of two factors:

1. The concepts which we are born with, which Kant called *a priori* concepts. An example of this which seems particularly relevant to our research domain, given its dependence on communication, is the idea that we are born with an ability to communicate through language. The actual language used is acquired empirically, but the ability to acquire it seems to be endemic to the human race.
2. An empirical understanding which we access through our senses. The relevance of this is that we do not have access to 'objective reality', only to that which our senses are able to show us (for Kant, this formed the basis of his theory of 'Transcendental Idealism', giving rise to 'objects for us' which differ from what objects might be 'in themselves').

Theoretically, this philosophical position leads to a grounding in those theories relevant to human understanding and interaction, which are to be found in the social and cognitive domains. Given that in KM we are seeking mutual understanding, those theories which best explain social interaction might be seen as especially relevant. Drawing again on the stream of social enquiry emanating from Kantian philosophy, this leads, through the critical social theory of the early twentieth century Frankfurt School, to contemporary social theorists such as Foucault and Habermas (see, for example, Habermas 1971; Habermas 1987). It is to the latter that the fields of management science and, now, Knowledge Management, turned for support in the 1980s and beyond, and it is therefore strands of Habermasian theory that are used to underpin this study. The detailed range of these theoretical perspectives is too great for inclusion in a chapter of this length, but the principles will show its relevance to KM. Habermasian critical social theory is concerned with issues such as social inclusion, participation, and a view of how we *ought to* undertake intervention in social domains.

A Theoretical Perspective Grounded on Kant

Critical philosophy has been fundamental to a stream of thinking in the 20ᵗʰ century to the present day, giving rise to forms of critical social theory, for which the primary contemporary theorist is Habermas (1929 -).

Habermas (1971; 1976; 1987) follows Kant in arguing that reliable knowledge is possible only when science assumes its rightful place as one of the accomplishments of reason. Whilst the achievements of scientific study are not disputed, the problem perceived through the route followed by Kant and Habermas is that the methods of science which have grown out of modernity are effectively self referential: that scientific study sets up rules and then tests itself against its own rules is a procedure which has given considerable advances to modern society, but to regard this as representing all knowledge is mistaken. Habermas refers to the worst excesses of this as 'scientism': that we must *identify knowledge with science*.

Habermas' argument is against the objectivistic illusion of unreflecting science (or otherwise modern positivism), in which, with (for example) approaches such as experimental method, rules are devised against which observations are then tested in an unreflective and self-supporting manner. Habermas argues that the scientistic (positivist) science community is unable to perceive self reflection as part of its process, and that such reflection must be built into an understanding of knowledge. As with Kant, Habermas' challenge is whether knowledge is reducible to the properties of an objective world, leading him to a definition of knowledge which is based on perception, but only in accordance with *a priori* concepts that the knowing subject brings to the act of perception.

Further, since the knowing subject is a social subject, all knowledge is mediated by social action and experience, leading to Habermas grounding his theories in communicative interaction, an issue we return to at the end of this chapter.

In essence, Habermas argues that these difficulties disappear once a scientific basis for our thinking is denied. For example, suppose science (as is suggested by

Kant and Habermas) is seen as just one form of knowledge, which in any case is simply a convenient human perception of how the world works. Now, all human endeavour becomes mediated through subjective understanding. However, this problem has been replaced with another, which may be stated as follows:

1.   Accepting all human actions as mediated through subjective understanding leads to the possibility of a basis for Knowledge Management in the universal characteristics of language.
2.   There is no longer a dichotomy between subject and object.
3.   The difficulty we are now left with is essentially a practical one, of how to incorporate these ideas into management practice.

To address this, Habermas' (1976; 1987) theory of communicative action presents a universal theory of language which suggests that all language is oriented toward three fundamental validity claims: truth, rightness and sincerity. What is most compelling about this theory, however, is that all three validity claims are *communicatively mediated*. This viewpoint is most radically seen in respect of the truth claim, where it is proposed that such a claim results not from the content of descriptive statements, but from the Wittgenstinian approach casting them as arising in language games which are linked to culture: truth claims are *socially contextual*.

In the following section, these ideas are taken forward to provide an approach to KM which is grounded theoretically and philosophically.

WHAT DOES THIS MEAN FOR KNOWLEDGE MANAGEMENT AND ITS APPLICATION TO E-BANKING?

Knowledge Management has been defined by some as the extraction and conversion of 'tacit' knowledge on an individual and organisational level into 'explicit' knowledge. Further, it is argued, this explicit knowledge often takes the form of specific electronic 'tools' or 'assets' which can be manipulated for competitive gain, examples being intranets, groupware and knowledge repositories. 'Tacit' knowledge, by contrast, is often described as the 'hunches, intuition and know-how' of people, or their 'skills, routines and competencies'. The aim of KM as regards tacit knowledge might be seen as an attempt to make this often highly subjective knowledge explicit, thereby facilitating its management through such enabling media as technology. The link to e-banking here is clear: the target of most e-banking (and, indeed, e-business) technology is the systematic recording and management of information – or, perhaps, "explicit knowledge". A deeper study of KM shows us the limitations of such an approach, which should be replaced by techniques aimed at integrating e-banking systems into the socio-technical fabric of its existing and potential users.

Additionally, a number of studies have called for a more holistic, systemic approach to KM. One such example is the division into the 'know-why, know-what, know-who, know-how' questions of KM. Know-how might be seen as technologically focused, know-who as socially constructed and depending on processes of debate, whilst know-why and know-what relate to issues of power and coercion in societal structures.

Finally, there are numerous classifications which aim to demistify KM. Included in these, for example, is the division into socialisation, externalisation, combination and internalisation.

But what does 'managing knowledge' infer from the standpoints discussed in this chapter (see Figure 10.2)?

Epistemology, philosophy and theory all have a part to play in determining the elements of a system of Knowledge Management.

Figure 10.2. Early lessons from philosophy and theory

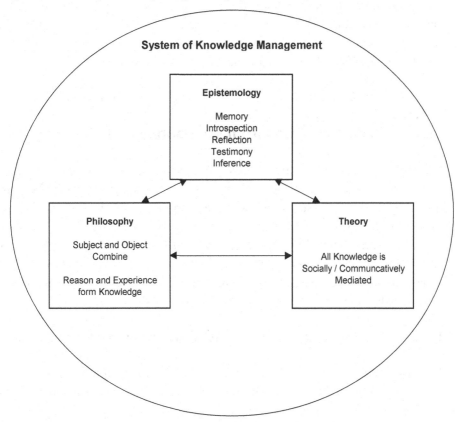

Epistemology

Knowledge derives from perception, memory, introspection, reflection and testimony. It is subject to *a priori* concepts, and is extended by inference.

Philosophy

From the time of Greek philosophy, there have existed fundamental arguments regarding knowledge being a search for truth, or for normative agreement. Initially the argument raged between rationalism and empiricism, and one of Kant's unique contributions, through the 'Copernican revolution in philosophy', was to unite subject and object in knowledge production: subject and object, according to Kant, make each other possible.

Theory

Following the thinking of Habermas, in which can be seen the echoes of Kant, science produces only one form of knowledge – believing all knowledge to be scientific is an 'objectivist illusion'. What Habermas does that is so helpful to us is he sites knowledge as mediated by social action, and subject to reflection, without which we end up with self-referential systems which are in danger of producing 'knowledge' based on disputable 'facts'. To misquote an anonymous source:

"The problem ain't so much what we know, as what we know that ain't so."

Summarising the Issues from Philosophy and Theory

The philosophical and theoretical investigation conducted in researching the content of this chapter indicates that knowledge is a human construct, inseparable from the *a priori* understanding that we, as human 'actors', bring to its formation. Epistemology shows us that, for example, 'knowledge as a storehouse' is at best a partial view, and one which, for the purpose of KM, must be supported by other knowledge sources and processes. So, as human 'actors', the *a priori* conceptual understanding we bring to the knowledge process, if omitted from the management of knowledge, leaves that management impoverished.

The primary philosophical concerns in relation to KM may be summarised as:

1.   We see knowledge both in terms of 'truth' and 'normative understanding'. Knowledge is not solely concerned with those irrefutable truths or facts which might be scientifically proven.

2. Reason and experience contribute to our knowledge store and our understanding.
3. The 'objectively real' and our 'subjective understanding' are interlaced, each providing the conditions for the other.

KM, therefore, must be addressed *through* a human perspective: there is no sense in a KM process focused only on the 'objectively real'. Following the Kantian stream of critical social theory into the twenty-first century, the most significant theorist, and one on whom much management systems development has been based, is Habermas. From Habermas' theoretical approach to communicative action, it is possible to see a way forward through knowledge derived from a communicatively mediated rationality, in which normative understanding is privileged ahead of 'objective truth'.

The remaining objective of this chapter is therefore to ground KM in a more comprehensive view of social theory. To this end, the following section discusses issues in social theory and a potential approach to KM.

Social Theory

This section is a search for the relevant theoretical underpinning to Knowledge Management research and practice, further expanding the philosophical and theoretical discussion above. Information is sought from two sources. In the first place, there is the underpinning social theory itself. Secondly, the holistic intent of Knowledge Management is pursued through a review of systems theory.

A study is undertaken of social theory, reviewing the paradigmatic arguments, and assessing potential future directions. To establish the theoretical underpinning, the relevant philosophical, ontological, epistemological and methodological issues are outlined, and placed in context with the development of the natural sciences and systems science. Difficulties encountered in management science are reviewed, providing a basis for development of the relevant theoretical underpinning to Knowledge Management.

Critical social theory has been applied extensively in information management (Hirschheim 1986; Hirschheim & Klein 1989; Lyytinen & Hirschheim 1989; Clarke 2000; Clarke & Lehaney 2002), and offers potential as a way forward for Knowledge Management. This chapter aims to determine a practical approach to Knowledge Management by exploring work already undertaken in the domain of management science, where the relevant ideas have been a subject of debate since the 1960s.

This exploration begins with an outline of the branch of critical social theory to be applied, and pursues this line of reasoning through critical systems thinking, relating each approach to the paradigm problems encountered. These views are then synthesised to produce an approach to Knowledge Management which is true to the principles of critical social theory.

Social Theory: The Paradigm Problem

This section reviews the work of Burrell and Morgan (1979), which is used to provide a framework for understanding the development of Knowledge Management within this chapter.

Burrell and Morgan positioned all social theories into one of four paradigms: functionalist, interpretivist, radical humanist and radical structuralist (Figure 10.3), according to the extent to which they were subjective versus objective or regulative versus radical.

The subjective-objective dimension can be seen in terms of four elements: an ontology, an epistemology, a view of the nature of human beings, and methodology.

The ontological debate concerns the nature of reality, the two opposing extremes of thought being realism: that reality is external to the individual and is of an objective nature; and nominalism: that reality is a product of individual consciousness. Epistemology is concerned with the grounds of knowledge, or how the world might be understood, and this understanding communicated as knowledge. The two opposing extremes are positivism: knowledge is hard, real and capable of being transmitted in a tangible form; and anti-positivism: knowledge is soft, more subjective, based on experience and insight, and essentially of a personal nature. Human beings may be viewed on a scale from deterministic: determined by situations in the external world and conditioned by external circumstances; to voluntaristic: they have free will, and create their environment.

Figure 10.3. Four paradigms for the analysis of social theory (Adapted from Burrell & Morgan, 1979)

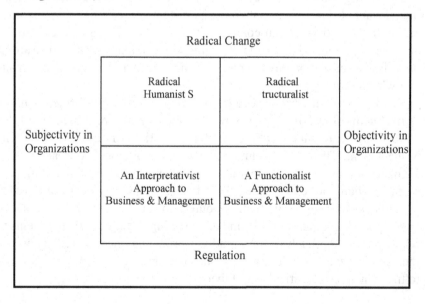

The view taken of ontology, epistemology and the nature of human beings directly influences the methodological approach which is adopted. A realist ontology, positivist epistemology and view of human beings as largely deterministic, leaves nomothetic methodologies as the appropriate choice. Such methodologies are characterised by a search for universal laws that govern the reality that is being observed, leading to a systematic approach. A nominalist ontology, anti-positivist epistemology and view of human beings as largely voluntaristic, indicates ideographic methodologies as appropriate: the principle concern would be to understand the way an individual interprets the world, with a questioning of external 'reality'.

The regulation-radical change dimension (Table 10.2) was the result of Burrell and Morgan recasting the then prevalent order-conflict debate. The sociology of regulation emphasises a view of society based on preservation of the status quo, whilst the sociology of radical change is "concerned with man's emancipation from the structures which limit and stunt his potential for development." (Burrell & Morgan 1979 p.17).

The functionalist paradigm is, in Burrell and Morgan's terms, regulative in nature, highly pragmatic, often problem orientated, and applying natural scientific methods to the study of human affairs (Burrell & Morgan 1979 p.26).

As discussed earlier, the early application of functionalism to business organisations is to be found in functionalist organisation theory, which can be traced from the work of F.W. Taylor (1856-1915). This laid the foundation for the 'classical school', contributors to which have been, for example, Fayol and Gulick. In Fayol's work, organisations are characterised in terms of a reality which can be investigated systematically, taking a highly mechanistic view of human beings, informed by an objectivist ontology and epistemology.

Functionalist organisation theory can be identified anywhere from the most objective to the most subjective margin of the paradigm, and, from a social theoretical perspective, the objective-subjective dimension does not automatically im-

Table 10.2. The regulation - Radical change dimension (Adapted from Burrell & Morgan, 1979)

Regulative organization theory is concerned with:	Radical organization theory is concerned with:
The status quo	Radical change
Social order	Structural conflict
Consensus	Modes of domination
Social integration and cohesion	Contradiction
Solidarity	Emancipation
Need satisfaction	Deprivation
Actuality	Potentiality

ply a paradigm shift. The relevance of this to e-banking goes back to the earlier arguments for e-banking as a human-centred domain. A functionalist approach to e-banking does not exclude human action, but risks functionalist issues such as structure becoming the main focus of attention: a 'real world' which is seen to exist independently of human perception. There is, of course, a real danger that, given the highly technological foundation of e-banking systems, the domain will be dominated by functionalism. The purpose of this chapter, together with the earlier chapter on human involvement, is to offer an alternative to this in order to avoid the critical problems of such a focus.

As with the functionalist paradigm, the interpretative paradigm is also regulative, seeing social reality as "…little more than a network of assumptions and intersubjectively shared meanings." (Burrell & Morgan 1979 p.29-31). Burrell and Morgan argue that the ontological assumptions of interpretative sociologists lead them to seek an understanding of the existing social world from an ordered viewpoint, and do not allow them to deal with issues of conflict or coercion. Interpretivism suffers criticism from all sides. Functionalists see it as finding out about problem situations without any means of solving problems or, in effect, producing any 'hard' output. Radical thinkers criticise interpretivism for its support of the status quo - the existing power base: interpretivism is fine for achieving consensus, provided the conditions required for consensus-seeking pre-exist; it has no means of overthrowing existing power structures or of resisting coercion.

The radical humanist paradigm has much in common with the interpretative paradigm, being nominalist, anti-positivist, voluntaristic and ideographic, but unlike interpretivism "emphasises the importance of overthrowing or transcending the limitations of existing social arrangements." (Burrell & Morgan 1979 p.32). Radical humanism aims to help humans achieve their true potential. The emphasis is on radical change and the attainment of potentiality through human emancipation, or release from 'false consciousness':

" . the consciousness of man is dominated by the ideological superstructures with which he interacts, and these drive a cognitive wedge between himself and his true consciousness. This . 'false consciousness' inhibits or prevents true human fulfilment" (Burrell & Morgan 1979 p.32).

Radical humanism is the position from which critical theory may be taken as a perspective. In relation to the earlier discussions, interpretivism offers an alternative to functionalism in so far as it does not accept there to be an objective reality but only socially constructed reality, but that its relativist stance makes it unable to view itself as the target for reflection. The radical humanist paradigm offers a way forward. Through critical social theory there is the possibility of moving beyond a debate located firmly in the sociology of regulation to a critically reflective, radical position.

Habermas (1971) provides the primary theoretical support which management science has taken to underpin interventionist approaches based on radical humanism. Habermas' Theory of Knowledge Constitutive Interests sees all human endeavour as undertaken in fulfilment of three knowledge constitutive or cognitive interests: technical, practical (in satisfaction of human interaction or communication) and emancipatory. Jackson (1993) follows the cognitive categories of Habermas, and argues that in Western industrialised society the technical interest has been accorded too much primacy. Jackson goes further in asserting, again after Habermas, that, in fact, practical questions are re-defined as technical ones, effectively blocking the separation of what we ought to do from questions of how we ought to be doing it.

The radical structuralist paradigm shows similarities with functionalist theory, but advocates radical change through structural conflict (Burrell & Morgan 1979 p.34). Whilst a tenable view for organisational theorists, its value to this study is limited, since the aim is not revolution but gradual change.

These paradigmatic considerations carry implications for an approach to e-business based on KM, which will now be investigated in more depth in the following section.

SOCIAL SYSTEMS THEORY: APPLYING KNOWLEDGE MANAGEMENT TO E-BANKING

So far in this chapter we have argued for a systems-based KM approach to e-banking, bringing together the social and technical elements of the domain in order to better balance the technology and human elements of e-banking systems. Below, we begin building a perception of these as systems informed directly by social theory, in order to further enhance their foundation.

In the study of social systems, where the key to the functioning of the system is human activity, functionalist views are therefore questioned. Experimentation is of limited value in such systems: the utility of problem solving, functionalist techniques, is diminished when dealing with ill-defined, highly complex human activity systems. As a result, 'softer' methods of approaching the issues are seen to be of value.

Social systems are therefore where the reductionist, functionalist approach meets its most severe challenges, and where systems views are seen to be of increasing relevance. Social science involves increasing complexity; a complexity which derives from the systemic nature of the objects of study and the introduction of human activity. The limitations of functionalism are demonstrated in the study of social systems, where predictive models may be seen to have only limited value. Social action does not lend itself to study by reductionist methods, but is determined by the meaning that individuals attribute to their actions.

This brings the discussion back to the functionalist - interpretivist debate, but now, with the support of social theory, this debate can be taken further and a foundation developed for e-banking. This is the direction which has been pursued by part of the systems movement, from its origins in the so called Singer/Churchman/ Ackoff school (Jackson, 1982; Britton & McCallion, 1994), through to present day systems thinkers. Jackson (1982) has shown how the soft methods of Ackoff, Checkland and Churchman all adhere to some degree to the assumptions of the interpretative paradigm, and identifies a third position which distinguishes hard, soft and emancipatory systems thinking (Jackson & Keys, 1984; Jackson, 1985). The argument is for a pluralist approach, which sees the strengths and weaknesses in each of the three areas and argues that each one must be respected for those strengths and weaknesses.

All of this is mirrored in e-banking, where the argument, which from a Habermasian (Habermas, 1971; Habermas, 1976) perspective is seen as a critical social problem, is wrongly cast within the sociology of regulation. The effect of this may be illustrated through Figure 10.3, where e-banking is best perceived from a radical humanist perspective. Seen from social theory, for example, the concept of an e-banking system consisting of only (say) the computer element might be seen as excessively functionalist, though perhaps with some evidence of interpretative analysis. But interpretative approaches alone would be seen as insufficient to deal with the complexity of human interaction, which critical social theory, whilst addressing the functionalist and interpretivist, also signals progression to a more radical approach. Much work in this area has already been undertaken in the management science domain, and it is from here that further support will be sought in formulating an alternative framework for e-banking.

Critical Social Theory: The Theoretical Underpinning

Critical social theory (CSoT) can be traced from the work of Kant, through Marx and the Frankfurt School. The two most widely accepted modern theorists are Foucault and Habermas, and it is to the latter that management science turned in the 1980s in order to develop a more human-centred view of its domain.

CSoT applied to the field of e-banking is appealing for its denial of a grounding in solely natural scientific principles. Seen through a scientific framework, e-banking appears as objective: the same for all involved since it is independent of human perception. CSoT refutes this, seeing our understanding of the world as determined by *a priori* conditions which are uncritically accepted. Critical theory seeks to expose these, and thereby release human beings from their 'false consciousness' to a position from which true potentiality can be attained. An alternative to the current functionalist and interpretivist approaches to e-banking may be found in developments based on the work of Habermas (1971; 1976), in particular his theory of knowledge constitutive interests (Table 10.3).

Habermas' three cognitive interests, technical, practical, and emancipatory, are identified in labour, interaction and power, and provide conditions for the three sciences, empirical/analytic, hermeneutic, and critical. The empirical/analytic, served by the natural sciences, is therefore seen as satisfying only the technical interest. Since, as has been argued, traditional approaches to e-banking might be seen as having their roots in the natural sciences, or at best in an interpretative ontology, they appear from a Habermasian perspective as an insufficient basis for e-banking. What is needed in addition is critical science to deal with issues of power and domination, serving the emancipatory interest.

From these roots came the development, in the domain of management science, of critical systems thinking, which is detailed below before moving on to the development of a critical framework for e-banking.

Critical Systems Thinking

Critical systems thinking (CST), it is argued, accepts the contribution of both hard and soft approaches, and, through critique, enhances awareness of the circumstances in which such approaches can be properly employed. The pragmatism of functionalist approaches and the lack of theoretical reflection in interpretivism allow CST to expose both as special cases with limited domains of application. The value of CST to e-banking can be demonstrated through the Burrell and Morgan grid (after Burrell & Morgan, 1979 p.22). Burrell and Morgan's work, together with contributions from Oliga (1991), may be interpreted as shown in Figure 10.4.

Table 10.3. The theory of knowledge constitutive interests (Adapted from Oliga, 1991)

Knowledge Constitutive Interest	Basis of Human Interest	Underlying Paradigm	Methodological Approach
Technical (control)	Labour (Instrumental action)	Functionalist	Empiricism Rule-based
Practical (Understanding)	Communicative Interaction	Interpretative	Hermeneutics Human-Centred
Emancipatory (Freedom)	Authority (Power)	Radical/Critical	Critique Human-centred with critical intent

This perspective further supports the view that traditional views of e-banking largely emerge as serving the technical interest, focusing on purposive-rational action. The alternative, evident in this domain since the 1970s but still limited in acceptance, is the service of the practical interest from the interpretative paradigm, relying on the communication of perceptions and consensus forming.

The key to the value of critical systems thinking to e-banking rests on the value of an approach based on critical pluralist method. This is admirably summarised by Jackson (2000, p. 364-367), and the following section seeks to build this into an e-banking framework.

A CRITICAL SYSTEMS FRAMEWORK FOR KNOWLEDGE MANAGEMENT IN E-BUSINESS

As has been argued, the foundations of a critical systems approach to organisational studies owes much to the work of Churchman (1968), which was built on foundations laid by Singer, and has been continued by Ackoff and other adherents to the systems school (Britton & McCallion, 1994). In the rest of this chapter we will attempt to draw together the issues from organisational theory, systems theory, social theory and philosophy, and critical theory, to provide a foundation for e-banking based on

Figure 10.4. The social validity of hard, soft and critical approaches

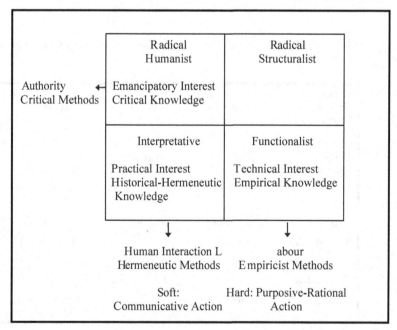

systems thinking and KM. In short, the objective is to construct a critical systems framework for e-banking.

The route we have chosen to this is a review of the progress in critical systems thinking within the domain of management. As the objective is an *action* framework, the initial approach is to assess the various means by which critical systems has been applied in management settings, before drawing this together at the end to form a framework for action.

The work of Jackson and Keys (1984) proved a major turning point in the development of a critical framework which is true to the commitments of critical systems thinking. By looking at the range of problem contexts and at the systems methodologies available for addressing these contexts, Jackson and Keys provided a unified approach which draws on the strengths of the relevant methodologies, rather than debating which method is best, and argued for a reconciliation focusing on which method to use in which context, controlled by a 'system of systems methodologies'. From this point, we then, in the following sections, the development of action approaches to KM, culminating in a recommendation within the discussion section to ground this, for e-banking, on communicative action.

The System of Systems Methodologies

A convenient starting point is to be found in the work of Jackson and Keys (1984), and the 'system of systems methodologies' (SOSM: Figure 10.5).

The SOSM (Figure 10.5) is used as the basis for an argument that organisational intervention can be understood through determination of the problem contexts within which it is conducted. The SOSM is therefore, first and foremost, a problem context classification, through which it is argued that problem contexts can be categorised according to the extent to which they exhibit a 'people complexity', from unitary to coercive, and a 'systems complexity', from simple to complex. So, for example, a 'problem' may be seen as 'simple-unitary': 'simple' in the sense that it has few elements and few interactions between elements; 'unitary' in terms of people complexity in that there is only one agreed viewpoint. Such 'problems', it is argued, do not require discussion, and can be 'solved' using hard, scientific, 'design-based' methods. By contrast, a 'complex-coercive' context not only exhibits system characteristics of high complexity (many elements, many interactions), but also cannot be progressed until the power issues (hence high 'people complexity') dominating the context are resolved (for a more detailed analysis applying the use of the SOSM, (see Clarke & Lehaney, 1999).

In use, this problem context classification forms a basis for determining the methodology to be used in the intervention. So, for example, a 'simple-unitary' problem context will demand the use of a methodology which focuses on design issues, and does not seek to address multiple viewpoints, since these are seen not to

Figure 10.5. The system of systems methodologies (Adapted from Jackson and Keys, 1984; Jackson, 1990; Jackson, 1995)

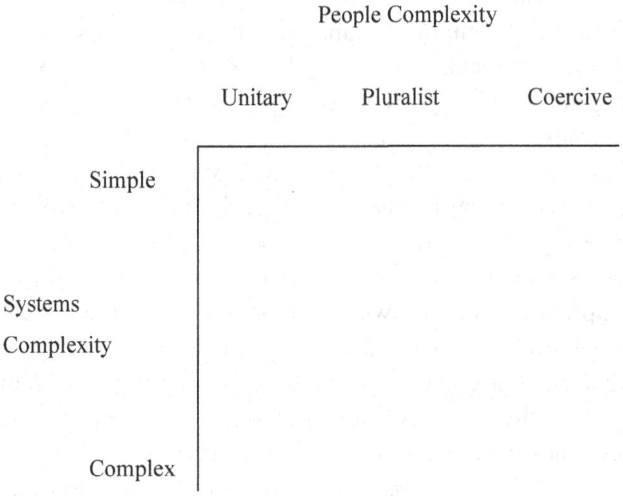

People Complexity

	Unitary	Pluralist	Coercive
Simple			
Systems Complexity			
Complex			

exist within the context identified. For e-banking, our earlier analysis would seem to place it at complex – pluralist / coercive on this classification.

TOTAL SYSTEMS INTERVENTION AND THE COMPLEMENTARIST FRAMEWORK

In the early development of total systems intervention (TSI), the paradigm position taken by the SOSM was core to the approaches recommended. That is to say, it was accepted that different problem contexts 'inhabited' different paradigms, and further that communication across paradigms was difficult if not impossible. So, for example, a problem context characterised by high levels of disagreement among participants, in which debate might be seen as a way forward, might prove difficult to combine with a requirement to produce a technical system, where focus is on design, and agreement as to means and ends is typically assumed.

Whilst 'paradigm incommensurability' was the normal view in these approaches, a way out of the problem, which was proposed through Habermas' theory of knowledge constitutive interests. In essence, this theory was that, at a fundamental level, human beings, in carrying out any task, seek to satisfy three interests: technical, practical and emancipatory. If this could be shown to be so, then the incommensurability of paradigms becomes a human construction, rather than something fundamental to human activity, and by acceding to approaches which take account of Habermas' interest constitution theory, such incommensurability could be overcome.

By the early 1990s, the most comprehensive attempt at applying this theory to organisations was undertaken through total systems intervention (TSI: Flood, 1995), where 'complementarism' was promoted as a way forward, enabling methodologies from different paradigms to be used together in a single intervention, applied to the same problem situation (for an example of TSI in use, see Clarke and Lehaney 2000).

Total systems intervention (TSI), offered a 'critical complementarist' approach which was seen to be capable of resolving both the theoretical and practical difficulties. This Habermasian perspective sees the functionalist view of organisations as an insufficient basis, serving only the technical interest. What is needed in addition is social science, to service the practical (hermeneutic) interest in achieving communication and consensus, together with critical science to deal with issues of power and domination, serving the emancipatory interest. Critique is applied in a Kantian (Kant, 1787) sense, aiming to: (i) free participants from purely instrumental reason; (ii) enable practical reason, to examine and re-examine assumptions made; and (iii) inform the choice and mix of methodologies in relation to the changing nature of the problem contexts and the strengths and weaknesses of the available methodologies.

The process of TSI is shown in Figure 10.6 below, and described in summary in the following text. TSI is iterative and recursive. Iteration implies that the process is continuous, rather than a start-end method. The TSI ideology explicitly recognises the part played by both technical and human activities in organisations, and the extent to which human interpretation may in some instances so distort the so called 'real world' that study of the latter may become meaningless.

TSI provides a critical framework within which choice and implementation of methodologies in an intervention can be managed pluralistically. The problem context is viewed as a 'mess' within which creativity (e.g. brainstorming, metaphor) is used to surface the issues to be managed (Figure 10.6); reflection on creativity then seeks to critically determine whether an adequate appreciation of the 'mess' has been gained.

Originally (Flood & Jackson, 1991), the SOSM was used to inform methodological choice. Latterly, it has been recommended (Flood, 1995) that this be replaced by the complementarist framework. In this, first metaphor is used to determine whether the key concern is one of design (technical), debate (practical) or disimprisonment (emancipation); then a methodology or mix of methodologies may be chosen to address the problem context, with critical reflection on whether these methodologies are indeed the most suitable being carried out prior to implementation.

The Creative Design of Methods

Midgley and Ulrich (Ulrich, 1983; Midgley, 1997) focus on boundary critique as the key to mixing methods. Boundary critique has a long history, but it is from Ulrich

Figure 10.6. The process of total systems intervention (TSI) (Adapted from Flood, 1995)

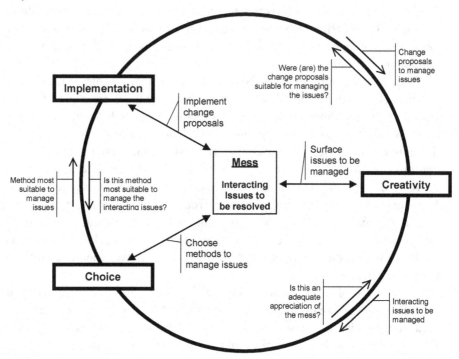

(1983; 1996) and Midgley (1992) that the recommendation to critically challenge what should or should not be considered part of any system is drawn. Midgley's approach is to begin with a boundary definition which is accepted as arbitrary, and progress by " … looking for grey areas in which marginal elements lie that are neither fully included in, nor excluded from, the system definition."

The critical choices made at the boundary are of truth and rightness: truth being represented by questions of what is, and rightness by questions of what ought to be. Critical assessment of the system boundary should be undertaken by a representative sample of participants in the system. Typically, an arbitrary system definition is presented for discussion in, for example, a brainstorming session (de Bono, 1977). Critique can be informed by a combination of Midgley's and Ulrich's approaches to boundary critique: Midgley's (1992) approach to examining what is in the margin for elements which support the secondary boundary or the primary boundary; Ulrich's (Midgley, 1996) approach to challenging system boundaries through twelve 'critically heuristic boundary questions' which address issues of motivation, power, knowledge and legitimisation (see Clarke & Lehaney 2000) for an example of the use of boundary critique).

Boundary critique has led to Midgley's promotion of the creative design of methods (Midgley, 1997), which was originally conceived as an improvement to SOSM, but is now promoted as addressing issues which SOSM deals with insufficiently. For example, whilst SOSM promotes the idea that there is only one interpretation of each method, creative design of methods sees methods as subject to multiple interpretations. Also, importantly, Midgley argues that SOSM restricts boundary judgement to simple coercive problem contexts, whereas it is a primary concern of creative design of methods to free up boundary judgement for use in all contexts.

Applying the creative design of methods requires that the interventionist maintain a multiplicity of participant viewpoints, together with the potential mix of methods or parts of methods required to address them, within an ongoing critical framework. The boundaries must be critically challenged throughout an intervention, and the approach will be continually changing in response to this and participant feedback.

Diversity Management

Flood and Romm (1996) promote diversity management and triple loop learning as an improved way to deal with mixing methods. In essence, triple loop learning is seen as a way to manage the diversity of methodologies and theories available, in addressing the diversity of issues to be found in organisational intervention.

In application, diversity management is about managing design, debate, and might-right issues, and so is a complementarist approach to the perceived hard, soft and critical factors which Flood and Romm see as pervading organisational problem contexts. The overall objective of diversity management might be seen as the enhancement of emancipatory practice.

Critical Systems Practice

In his most recent work, Jackson (1999; 2000) continues to promote critical pluralism, but now sees this in terms of developing TSI into critical systems practice. Pluralism in the use of methodology is advocated: ".. to make the best use of the methodologies, methods, models and techniques ... to tackle diverse and difficult problem situations while ... ensuring their continual improvement through research" (Jackson 2000 p. 382). This pluralism must: encourage flexibility in the use of methodologies, enabling practitioners to decompose approaches and tailor them, within a critical framework; encourage paradigm diversity: using methodologies from different paradigms in the same intervention (for a critique of a range of methodologies, see Clarke, Lehaney et al., 1998).

What is clear in Jackson's recommendations is his view that it is no longer possible to rely on Habermas, but, rather, pluralism calls for a meta-methodology, for which Jackson lays out nine "constitutive rules", (Jackson, 2000 p. 393). This "critical systems meta-methodology" is seen by Jackson as a "structured way of thinking which understands and respects the uniqueness of the functionalists, interpretative, emancipatory and post-modern theoretical rationales, and draws upon them to improve real-world problem situations." It is recommended that methods for enhancing creativity are applied, at least, from these perspectives, and that methodologies are used as appropriate.

Critical systems practice, Jackson recommends, should be embedded within a systems and action research approach; should ensure a pluralism of 'clients', theoretical and methodological pluralism, pluralism in the modes of representation employed, and pluralism in the facilitation process; and should be sensitive to the organisational context in which it is operating.

Further, the claim to be using a generic system methodology, according to the particular theoretical rationale it is designed to serve, must be justified according to the principles and guidelines established for the use of each generic systems methodology.

In essence, critical systems practice calls for an improved version of TSI, but it is as yet unclear how these ideas are to be applied. In essence, a set of constitutive rules are provided, but a framework within which these might be operationalised is not given.

Critical Pluralism

In critical pluralism, Mingers (Mingers & Gill, 1997) promotes what he sees to be missing in critical approaches to the use of a mix of methodologies: multi-paradigm multimethodology. From a discussion of current dilemmas in critical systems thinking, Mingers promotes emphasis on engagement with agents in a social context as the basis for his approach. The focus, he suggests, should be on the relationship between three notional systems seen to form the multimethodological context: the problem content system, or real world situation of concern; the intellectual resources system, or available theories and methodologies; and the intervention system, or agents undertaking the intervention.

In theoretical terms, the work is strongly grounded on Habermas' theory of communicative action (Habermas, 1987), but with the added consideration of knowledge being linked to power.

Mingers uses this thinking to develop a framework for mapping methodologies against the four phases of appreciation, analysis, assessment and action, based on Habermas' three worlds (Mingers & Gill, 1997, p. 431). The actual process of critical multimethodology, he argues, "will be a continual cycle of reflection, judgement, and action" (p 437).

Pragmatic Pluralism

Taket and White (1996) offer pragmatic pluralism as a means of mixing methods from an essentially postmodernist perspective. Their approach is strongly grounded theoretically, with the suggestion that guidelines, examples, stories and metaphors are of more value than prescribed frameworks for action. The approach is expressly holistic, and sees pluralism as a means of addressing diversity. Pluralism , they argue, should be applied to the roles of the interventionist, modes of representation, and the nature of the client. It is explicit that work with the disempowered should be seen as fundamental within any intervention context.

In application, it is argued that, in any intervention, there will be multiple rationalities to be managed, and that, whilst guidelines may be offered for addressing these, there is little to be gained from a prescriptive approach. The approach is therefore largely left open to the practitioner, who should follow a strategy of mix and match, operationalising what feels good in accordance with the guidelines provided: the interventionist should recognise differences in methodologies and match these with variety in the local context. Triangulation, the use of parts of methodologies in combination, a flexible and adaptive stance, and critical reflection, are all fundamental to the application of this approach.

This completes the review of perspectives on KM. In the following section, discussion and critique is conducted, reflecting the issues raised by these theoretical and practical perspectives.

DISCUSSION AND CRITIQUE

Each of the approaches outlined above have in common the aim of addressing diverse (or 'pluralistic') problem contexts with a diversity of methods. The system of systems methodologies originally presented an approach to matching problem context to methodologies seen to be applicable to that context, and was expressly based on Habermas' theory of knowledge constitutive interests (KCI). Total systems intervention initially operationalised SOSM into a process for intervention, similarly based on KCI; arguably, diversity management has continued this theme, being essentially an improved application of KCI. With the creative design of methods came an approach which sought to develop the ideas of SOSM and TSI, enabling the use of parts of methodologies, synthesised to address a unique problem context, within an expressly critical framework. The creative design of methods also introduced the idea of a basis in Habermas' theories of communicative action, rather than the theory of knowledge constitutive interests.

The recent critical systems practice advocated by Jackson also moves away from KCI, recommending instead that any claim to be using a methodology according to its theoretical rationale must be justified "according to the principles and guidelines established for the use of each … methodology." (Jackson, 2000, p. 393). In this, Jackson might be seen as returning to the need to recognise the distinctive background and theory of each methodology (see, for example, Jackson & Keys, 1984; Flood & Jackson, 1991; Brocklesby, 1995).

Pragmatic pluralism draws on a very broad theoretical range, but much is premised on critical social theory. Finally, critical pluralism provides a framework for intervention grounded on Habermas' theory of communicative action.

If we seek to summarise much of the work in KM in terms of theoretical development, the primary basis is to be found in critical social theory, with the main theories being applied in determining intervention approaches having been Habermas' theory of knowledge constitutive interests, and his theory of communicative action. Of these, communicative action seems the most promising arena in which to ground future development of the domain, and to apply KM to e-banking. An outline of the arguments in this respect might be as presented below.

A FUTURE FOR KNOWLEDGE MANAGEMENT AND E-BANKING

The ability to communicate by use of language is something that human beings bring to the world by nature of their existence: that is to say, it is not developed empirically, but is a priori. To the extent that any theoretical position can be grounded on such an a priori ability, then such a position may be seen as fundamental to us as communicative human actors.

In so far as communication, at least partially, may be oriented toward mutual understanding, it might be argued as the foundation of knowledge creation and sharing. In these terms, knowledge is not reducible (as is so often seen in scientific or pseudo-scientific study) to the properties of an objective world, but can be defined both objectively and according to the a priori concepts that the knowing subject brings to the act of perception. This knowing subject, being social, mediates all knowledge through social action and experience: subject and object are linked in the acts of cognition and social interaction, and the so-called subjective and objective 'paradigms' may be represented as just a convenient tool for understanding, which has been accorded too much primacy as a form of reality.

Rather, then, than relying on the concept of paradigms, this concept, and particularly the idea of paradigm incommensurability, should be opened up to challenge. Consider the so-called subjective / objective dichotomy. According to the paradigm argument, viewed (say) from an epistemological perspective, one who sees a problem context as positivistic, and seeks, for example, a technological solution, will be unable to communicate and share knowledge with another who views the same problem context as existing in the views and opinions of those participants involved in and affected by the system of concern. There are at least two fundamental difficulties with this:

1.   It contradicts common human practice, and, dare it be suggested, common sense. Human participants in social groups commonly combine technical ('posi-

tivistic') and interpretative ('anti-positivistic') activity, seemingly denying the paradigm incommensurability thesis from an epistemological standpoint.

2.   Theoretically, the paradigm incommensurability view seems to have dubious support. At its most basic level, it derives from the idea that technical, scientific, functionalist activity cannot be conducted together with interpretivistic, subjective activity. But if, theoretically, subjective and objective are inseparable, paradigm incommensurability becomes much less compelling.

In essence, then, it is the argument of this chapter that these difficulties disappear once a scientific basis for our thinking is denied. For example, suppose science (as is suggested by Kant and Habermas) is seen as just one form of knowledge, which in any case is simply a convenient human perception of how the world works. Now, all human endeavour becomes mediated through subjective understanding, and the paradigms as impenetrable barriers disappear. So, the problem of interest constitution theory being no longer defensible is resolved, since it is no longer being relied on. However, this problem has been replaced with another, which may be stated as follows:

1.   Accepting all human actions as mediated through subjective understanding leads to the possibility of a basis for KM in the universal characteristics of language.
2.   The dichotomy between subject and object has gone, and with it, paradigm incommensurability.
3.   Organisational intervention is recast as an entirely communicative issue. For example, the so-called technical interest of knowledge constitution theory becomes instead an question of how technology may further enable human interaction, all within a framework of human intercommunication.
4.   The difficulty which now arises is essentially a practical one, of how to incorporate these ideas into e-banking practice.

Work by Habermas (1976; 1987) on communicative action presents a universal theory of language which suggests that all language is oriented toward three fundamental validity claims: truth, rightness and sincerity. What is most compelling about this theory, however, is that all three validity claims are communicatively mediated. This viewpoint is most radically seen in respect of the truth claim, where it is proposed that such a claim results not from the content of descriptive statements, but from the Wittgenstinian approach casting them as arising in language games which are linked to culture: truth claims are socially contextual.

'Truth', can therefore be assessed by reference to communication. Rightness is about norms of behaviour, which are culturally relevant, and are therefore to be determined by reference to that which is acceptable to those involved and affected in the system of concern as a cultural group. Finally, sincerity is about the speaker's internal world: his/her internal subjectivity.

These ideas can now be taken forward to provide a KM approach to e-banking which is theoretically grounded, and closer to that which is experienced in action. The conclusions below begin this process.

CONCLUSION

The issues raised in this chapter can now be used to design a critical action framework for KM intervention in e-banking, based on critical theory.

The review of KM undertaken in this chapter indicates the potential for approaches to e-banking explicitly grounded in critical social theory, and points to a possible future direction through a Critical Action Framework for Knowledge Management (Figure 10.7). The research project of which this is part is now moving on to apply this framework and report on its use in action.

Figure 10.7. A critical action framework for knowledge management

Investigation Of	Investigation Through	Outcome – Knowledge to be Managed
Knowledge as:	Subject and Object investigated through Participative Analysis	"Manage" as a systemic process of participative inquiry
Memory	Tests of Communicative Rationality:	Outcomes in the form of:
Introspection	Truth	Systems Descriptions
Reflection	Rightness	Process
Testimony	Sincerity	Content
Inference		
	Involves Application of:	Leads to Understanding of:
	Methodologies for Problem Context Analysis	Context in which KM is to be Applied
	Methodologies for Participative Analysis	Processes for Knowledge Exchange to be embedded within the organisation
	Critical Method for Tests of Communicative Rationality	Knowledge Explicated to be Recorded for Shared Use
		Knowledge for which dissemination is to be Restricted

REFERENCES

Alavi, M. & D. E. Leidner (2001). Review: Knowledge Management and Knowledge Management Systems: Conceptual Foundations and Research Issues. *MIS Quarterly*, 25(1), 107-136.

Audi, R. (1998). *Epistemology: a contemporary introduction to the theory of knowledge*. London: Routledge.

Britton, G. A. and H. McCallion (1994). An Overview of the Singer/Churchman/Ackoff school of thought. *Systems Practice*, 7(5), 487-522.

Brocklesby, J. (1995). Intervening in the Cultural Constitution of Systems - Methodological Complementarism and other Visions for Systems Research. *Journal of the Operational Research Society*, 46(11), 1285-1298.

Burrell, G. and G. Morgan (1979). *Sociological Paradigms and Organisational Analysis*. London: Heinemann.

Churchman, C. W. (1968). *The Systems Approach*. New York: Dell.

Clarke, S. and B. Lehaney (1999). Organisational Intervention and the Problems of Coercion. *Systemist*, 21(December), 40-52.

Clarke, S. A. (2000). From Socio-Technical to Critical Complementarist: A New Direction for Information Systems Development. In Coakes, E., Lloyd-Jones, R. & Willis, D., *The New SocioTech: Graffiti on the Long Wall*, (pp. 61-72). London: Springer.

Clarke, S. A. & B. Lehaney (2000). Mixing Methodologies for Information Systems Development and Strategy: A Higher Education Case Study. *Journal of the Operational Research Society*, 51(5), 542-556.

Clarke, S. A. & B. Lehaney (2002). Human-Centred Methods in Information Systems: Boundary Setting and Methodological Choice. In Szewczak, E. & Snodgrass, C. *Human Factors in Information Systems*, (pp. 20-30). Hershey, P.A.: IRM Press:

Clarke, S. A., B. Lehaney, et al. (1998). A Theoretical Framework for Facilitating Methodological Choice. *Systemic Practice and Action Research*, 11(3), 295-318.

Coakes, E., S. A. Clarke, et al., Eds. (2001). *Knowledge Management in the Socio-Technical World: The Graffiti Continues*. London: Springer.

de Bono, E. (1977). *Lateral Thinking*. Aylesbury, U.K.: Pelican Books, Hazell Watson & Viney Ltd.

Earl, M. (2001). Knowledge Management Strategies: Toward a Taxonomy. *Journal of Management Information Systems,* 18(1), 215-233.

Fayol, H. (1949). *General and Industrial Management.* London: Pitman.

Flood, R. L. (1995). Total Systems Intervention (TSI): A Reconstitution. *Journal of the Operational Research Society, 46,* 174-191.

Flood, R. L. & M. C. Jackson (1991). *Creative Problem Solving: Total Systems Intervention.* Chichester UK: Wiley.

Flood, R. L. & N. R. A. Romm (1996). *Diversity Management: Triple Loop Learning.* Chichester UK: Wiley.

Gerth, H. H. and C. W. Mills (1970). *From Max Weber.* London: Routledge & Kegan Paul.

Habermas, J. (1971). *Knowledge and Human Interests.* Boston: Beacon Press.

Habermas, J. (1976). On Systematically Distorted Communication. *Inquiry,13,:* 205-218.

Habermas, J. (1987). *Lifeworld and System: A Critique of Functionalist Reason.* Boston: Beacon Press.

Hirschheim, R. and H. K. Klein (1989). Four Paradigms of Information Systems Development. *Communications of the ACM 32*(10), 1199-1216.

Hirschheim, R. A. (1986). Understanding the Office: A Social - Analytic Perspective. *ACM 4*(4), 331-344.

Jackson, M. C. (1982). The Nature of Soft Systems Thinking: The Work of Churchman, Ackoff and Checkland. *Applied Systems Analysis 9,* 17-28.

Jackson, M. C. (1985). Social Systems Theory and Practice: The Need for a Critical Approach. *International Journal of General Systems 10,* 135-151.

Jackson, M. C. (1990). Beyond a System of Systems Methodologies. *Journal of the Operational Research Societ,y 41*(8), 657-668.

Jackson, M. C. (1993). Social Theory and Operational Research Practice. *Journal of the Operational Research Society, 44*(6), 563-577.

Jackson, M. C. (1995). Beyond the Fads: Systems Thinking for Managers. *Systems Research* 12(1), 25-42.

Jackson, M. C. (1999). Towards Coherent Pluralism in Management Science. *Journal of the Operational Research Society 50*(1), 12-22.

Jackson, M. C. (2000). *Systems Approaches to Management.* New York: Kluwer/ Plenum.

Jackson, M. C. & P. Keys (1984). Towards a System of Systems Methodologies. *Journal of the Operational Research Society* 35(6), 473-486.

Kant, I. (1787). *Critique of Pure Reason.* Basingstoke, Hampshire (2003), Palgrave Macmillan.

Katz, D. & R. L. Kahn (1978). *The Social Psychology of Organisations.* New York, Wiley.

Lawrence, P. R. & J. W. Lorsch (1969). *Developing Organisations: Diagnosis and Action.* Reading, Mass., Addison-Wesley.

Lyytinen, K. & R. Hirschheim (1989). Information Systems and Emancipation: Promise or Threat? In Klein, H. K., & Kumar, K. (Eds.), *Systems Development for Human Progress,* (pp. 115-139). Amsterdam, The Netherlands: North Holland.

Midgley, G. (1992). The sacred and profane in critical systems thinking. *Systems Practice* 5(1), 5-16.

Midgley, G. (1996). The ideal of unity and the practice of pluralism in systems science. In Flood, R. L. & Romm, N. R. A. (Eds.) *Critical Systems Thinking: Current Research and Practice* (pp. 25-36). New York: Plenum.

Midgley, G. (1997). Dealing with coercion: critical systems heuristics and beyond. *Systems Practice* 10(1), 37-57.

Midgley, G. (1997). Developing the methodology of tsi: from the oblique use of methods to their creative design. *Systems Practice* 10(3), 305-319.

Mingers, J. & A. Gill, Eds. (1997). *Multi Methodology.* Chichester UK: Wiley.

Oliga, J. C. (1991). Methodological Foundations of Systems Methodologies. In Flood, R.L., & Jackson, M.C., (Eds.) *Critical Systems Thinking: Directed Readings* (pp. 159-184). Chichester, UK: Wiley.

Pasmore, W. A. & J. J. Sherwood (1978). *Socio-Technical Systems: A Sourcebook.* San Diego, CA: University Associates.

Selznick, P. (1948). Foundations of the Theory of Organisations. *American Sociological Review, 13,* 25-35.

Sutton, D. C. (2001). What is knowledge and can it be managed? *European Journal of Information Systems,* 10, 80-88.

Taket, A. & L. White (1996). Pragmatic Pluralism: An Explication. *Systems Practice. 9*(6), 571-586.

Taylor, F. W. (1947). *The Principles of Scientific Management*. New York: Harper and Row.

Ulrich, W. (1983). *Critical Heuristics of Social Planning: A New Approach to Practical Philosophy.* Berne, Switzerland: Haupt.

Ulrich, W. (1996). *A Primer to Critical Systems Heuristics for Action Researchers.* Forum One: Action Research and Critical Systems Thinking, Centre for Systems Studies, University of Hull, Hull, UK.

Williams, T. M. & J. M. Wilson, Eds. (2003). Special Issue: Knowledge Management and Intellectual Capital. *Journal of the Operational Research Society..* Birmingham,UK: Palgrave.

Chapter XI
Strategy Development for E-Banking

INTRODUCTION

Whilst e-banking is a relatively recent phenomenon, the strategic issues relating to it are well documented and may be drawn from existing studies. In essence, it will be shown that the key strategic problem in e-banking derives from a number of clearly definable factors:

1. As with all banking, but arguably in a more critical sense, e-banking is highly dependent on technological development. Any strategy has to combine often unknown technological improvements into the strategic process.
2. E-banking links customers to suppliers in a much "looser" relationship than traditional banking, giving rise to security issues which must be addressed strategically.
3. With "counter based" banking, it is much easier for the bank to set up rules and procedures which include elements of customer behaviour. E-banking offers opportunities for enhancement of the customer experience, through which banks are able to leverage competitive advantage.

All of this requires a strategic approach which differs from that taken to traditional banking, but which has a wealth of other strategy experience on which to draw.

Key to understanding this is the extent to which the *scope* of information systems (IS) analysis (and hence e-banking analysis) is often seen to be problematic: IS 'problems' are frequently 'solved' by redefining organisational and human issues in technical terms, and developing the necessary technical solution. Significant questions have been raised regarding such approaches, exposing many IS developments as not susceptible to a technical solution, but exhibiting complexities stemming from high levels of human activity. Arguably, such findings are of particular importance in e-business applications, depending as they do on the understanding and commitment of users who are often remote from and external to the organisation. A clue to how such complex, human-centred issues may be dealt with is to be found in the scoping of these studies which, in systems terms, implies a need to assess the system boundary. In Chapter VI, boundary setting was discussed as an issue to be settled before further progress can be made. This does not need to be repeated in detail here, but it must be kept in mind that determining the boundaries of any e-business implementations is an essential part of their management. A view of information systems as a purely technological domain reduces the complexity of the system of study, and attempts to define it in terms of rules and procedures by which given inputs can be turned into predictable outputs: a so-called deterministic system. A human-centred approach is quite different. Human activity systems are 'complex' and 'adaptive', and cannot be fully described in terms of rules and procedures: to understand such systems requires recourse to social theory.

Furthermore, such a conclusion demonstrates the relevance of this debate to e-banking. In the last twenty years or so, information systems have become more fragmented and distributed, 'user' issues have grown in importance. Arguably, all forms of e-business represent the most distributed form of technology-enabled information, in which a disparate user base needs to be catered for. In effect, the social system to be 'served' is gaining ascendancy over the technical system: this latter has the task of facilitating or enabling – technology has finally ceased to be an end in itself!

To address these issues this chapter focuses predominantly on the development of a toolset for e-banking strategic planning. But before moving on to this, the following section briefly outlines some of the relevant issues drawn from the domain of corporate strategy.

CORPORATE STRATEGY AS PLANS OR PATTERNS

Is it possible, in an IS domain such as e-banking, to write objective strategic plans, agreed on by all concerned, and forming the basis of future development? Or are IS strategies just patterns of activity which, whilst evident subsequent to their emergence, cannot be seen in any prior plans of action?

The planning approaches to strategy may be seen as highly design oriented, whereby plans are drawn up which the organisation then uses as a framework for development over the following planning period. This traditional view of strategy as a planning activity, it has been argued, is particularly ill suited to information systems, where both the human centred nature of the domain, and its reliance on ever changing technologies, makes planning difficult.

Further, it has been argued, after Mintzberg, that strategy has been almost universally depicted as a deliberate process, whilst the evidence shows this not to be the case, with strategies emerging from the organisation without there having been any deliberate plan. This gives support to the logical incrementalist view, which appears as a way to combine the planning and behavioural approaches to strategy.

A summary of the planning (design) and patterning (discovery) approaches is presented below, echoing the hard-soft dichotomy found in information systems.

Alternative Views of Corporate Strategy	
Design	*Discovery*
Plans	Patterns
Planning	Emergent
Design	Debate/Disclosure
How	What
Structured	Unstructured
Hard	Soft
Functional	Interpretative
Systematic	Systemic
Reductionist	Holistic

Strategy is divided under two headings: strategy by design and strategy by discovery. Strategy by design encompasses systematic approaches, whereby plans are derived through objective, reductionist methods. Strategy by discovery, by contrast, requires a systemic (or holistic – concentrating on the whole as sub-systems in interaction rather than the parts or components in isolation) approaches, favouring participative methods covering the whole system of concern. Contextual issues within the organisation will be at least a partial determinant of the approach taken: a planning method, for example, arguably suiting a mechanistic organisation; incrementalism being more suited to professional adhocracies.

As with IS, both views have a place, with a perceived need for a mixture of approaches, premised, at least in part, on the organisational context encountered. Furthermore, in respect of corporate strategy as applied to e-banking management, strategy by discovery may be seen as long term, concerned with planning for the unknown, or forecasting discontinuities; whilst the design approach may be seen as short term, and concerned with carrying out the IS strategy through the application of information technology. Corporate strategy cannot therefore rely on any one approach, but must craft a combination of strategic methods to fit the organisational form and context.

STRATEGY DEVELOPMENT TOOLS: STRATEGIC ALIGNMENT

For the rest of this chapter, a number of tools for strategic management will be presented and described. Each is a key contributor to e-banking strategy, and at the end of the chapter all of these tools are brought together in a single implementation model.

This section is concerned with the alignment of corporate strategic management and e-banking strategic management, which is seen to be more than a simple problem of selecting information *technology* to support the e-banking strategy.

A strategic alignment model is presented as a framework for the process, which then progresses by means of determining the current status of an organisation's IS and IT planning (the 'IS Map'), and analysing the business (e-banking) and IS domains of the organisation in *continuous alignment*. Four strategic alignment perspectives are then discussed, from which an organisation's strategic context may be determined, based on the type of organisation. Finally, a strategic action framework is presented, drawing together the strands of the strategic alignment problem in an action process, based on information needs analysis, and supported by techniques to model the business (i.e. e-banking) and information system domains.

The Alignment Problem

It is often assumed that the purpose of strategic alignment is to align information *technology* with an organisation's corporate and/or business unit strategies (in the case of e-business, this might be seen as the "business unit" to be addressed). However, such an approach has been challenged in recent years, and cannot any longer be taken for granted. Firstly, it cannot be assumed that all organisations *have* a corporate or business strategy, and if they do not – or at least if such a strategy is not written down – there is little with which to strategically align information technology.

Furthermore, information technology cannot be viewed as distinct from the rest of the business, assuming that once corporate strategy is detailed, a strategy for e-business can be formulated to 'fit' the corporate strategy, without regard to any other issues. Such an approach assumes a model of the organisation in which the corporate strategic thrust 'pulls' information technology support in its wake. But such a model will not fit all organisations. What of the technology-based organisation, where new technologies not only provide the new products, but also become ingrained in the processes used to make those products? Arguably, in such companies, technology, including information technology, drives the organisation's strategy.

What is proposed as an alternative is a strategic model (Figure 11.1) in which all the elements of corporate and information systems strategy are aligned, so that an organisation's information resource is placed to support that organisation's strategic and, ultimately, operational activity. Figure 11.1 illustrates this position.

Baets puts strategic alignment '… in a broader framework of information needs analysis (before even attempting the process of alignment) and not just {attempting} to align IS strategy into corporate strategy, but {defining} them in parallel.' Similarly, Venkatraman *et al.* (Venkatraman, Henderson et al., 1993) argue that the strategic issues related to information systems have focussed strongly on IT strategy and have seen it as 'a functional strategy that responds to the chosen business strategy'. This leads to a focus on internal issues such as the information architecture (dominated by types and configurations of computer equipment), processes and skills, and fails to deal the opportunities which exist in the market place and may be exploited through IS strategy.

Figure 11.1. Extended strategic alignment model (Adapted from: (Baets, 1992; Venkatraman, Henderson et al., 1993)

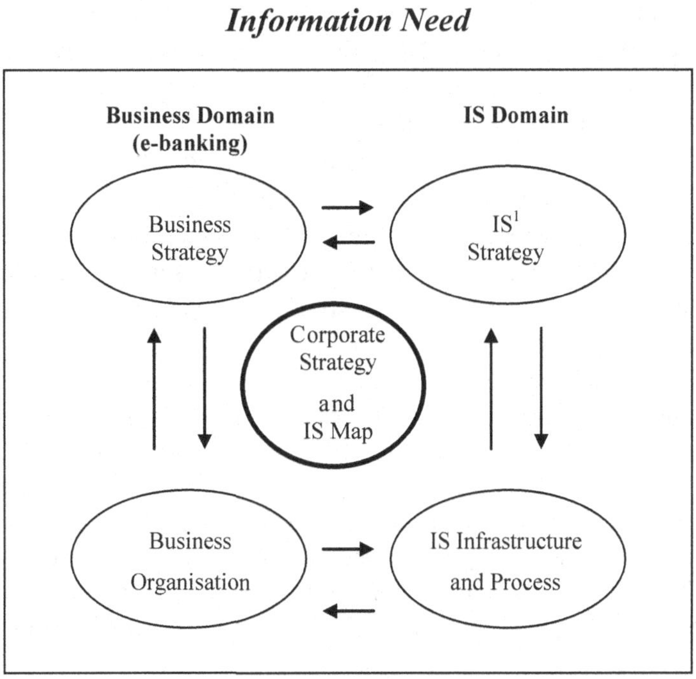

Information Need

As is illustrated in Figure 11.1, the information need drives the process, whilst central to that process is the organisation's corporate strategy, together with the IS map: the framework of information systems currently used to support organisational activity. Information needs are met through the business domain (business strategy and business organisation) and IS domain (IS strategy and IS infrastructure and processes) interacting to support the organisation.

So, the alignment process may be visualized in terms of four essential elements: corporate strategy; business (e-business) strategy; information systems strategy; and information technology strategy – all of which need to be kept in continuous alignment in service of an overall information requirement. This is essentially the approach recommended in two separate studies first by Baets and later by Venkatraman (Baets 1992; Venkatraman, Henderson et al. 1993), and which is represented by the composite model in Figure 11.1.

However, whilst this is a useful framework, it does not guide the process of strategic alignment. For this, a more detailed approach, based on this framework, is outlined in the following sections.

Determining the Current Status of IS and Corporate Planning in the Organisation: The IS Map

Earl (Table 11.1) argues that organisations exhibit five stages of planning for IS, starting with a mapping of IT and IS resources to assess the coverage and quality of the technology and applications. Once the organisation gains confidence with this, attention moves on to an analysis of business needs in order to better direct the IS efforts. However, this stage often serves only to emphasise the poor quality of business planning, and thereby stunt the development of IS strategic plans. The third stage, Earl sees as ' … messy {involving} a mix of detailed planning and investigation.' Essentially this involves bringing together the first two stages in a coherent planning approach. Stage 4, competitive advantage, is one which most organisations aspire to, but few attain: and even if attained, few are able to sustain (see Chapter VI). Finally, the most successful organisations, argues Earl, reach a position where IS, IT and corporate strategy are integrated within a participative environment, encompassing users and managers within the organisation.

This approach can be used by an organisation to determine its current position in relation to corporate strategy, business unit (e-business) strategy, and IS. As with all classifications, it is important to realise that this presents 'ideal types', useful as an aid to thinking about the strategy process, but not to be seen as a pick list from which an organisation can choose its strategic position. For example, a too literal reading of Earl's work might lead the reader to the erroneous conclusion that different businesses or business units will be able to identify their position as 'Stage 1' or 'Stage 4', but this is not the case. In any organisation, the IS map, at any given

Table 11.1. Planning in stages (Adapted from Earl, 1989)

Timeframe/ Factor	Stage 1	Stage 2	Stage 3	Stage 4	Stage 5
Task	IS/IT mapping	Business direction	Detailed planning	Competitive advantage	IT strategy connection
Objective	Management understanding	Agreeing priorities	Firming up the IS strategic plan	Finding opportunities	Integrating IS and business strategies
Direction/ Involvement	DP/IT lead	Senior management drive	Users and IS mainly involved	Executive management and users	Partnership of users, general management and IS
Methodological Emphasis	Bottom up survey	Top down analysis	Matching top down and bottom up plus investigations and prototypes	Inside out processes	Multiple methods accepted

time, will be a complex mixture of the above stages: the purpose of mapping is to attempt to map this complexity.

The E-Business and Information Systems Domain

Once the IS map is determined, attention can be given to other elements of the model (Figure 11.1), which is divided into business and IS domains. The business domain consists of business strategy and the business organisation or infrastructure (and is the part of the model where e-business will be specifically detailed), whilst the IS domain comprises IS infrastructure and processes and IS strategy. The arrows indicate the need for all elements of the model to be continuously aligned around corporate strategy and the IS map, and in satisfaction of the overall information need: it must be *continuously aligned,* since all the elements are ever changing. The strategic alignment process consists of two stages: firstly, determining an alignment perspective; secondly, undertaking the alignment process.

The IS map indicates the stage of planning that an organisation has reached, and rests on the idea that there is little point in, for example, expecting an organisation to strive for seeking competitive advantage from IS if it has not achieved the understanding implicit in the previous three stages. The alignment perspective builds from the position determined by the map, and looks more at how strategic alignment can be pursued in the light of a particular organisational context.

The Alignment Perspective

The first difficulty facing an organisation is therefore that of determining the alignment perspective relevant to the business. Venkatraman *et al* (Venkatraman, Henderson et al. 1993) refer to four perspectives: strategy execution; technology potential; competitive potential; and service level, each of which focuses on a different section of the model (Figure 11.1). Strategy execution as a perspective (Figure 11.2) sees business strategy as the main driving force.

Strategy is formulated by management, and both organisational design and IS and IT are adapted to the changing e-business strategic needs. This is a very common approach to IS planning, but one which may be disastrous if used inappropriately. The current organisational design and the available choices of IS infrastructure to support the proposed strategies may, for instance, be so constrained that the strategic vision promoted by management may be simply unattainable.

Technology potential (Figure 11.3) focuses on available technologies and the infrastructure necessary to their success, with business organisation and e-business strategy following the technological lead.

This is similar to the perspective above, but without the same constraining factors. The aim is to identify the best IS and organisational configurations needed to implement the chosen strategies, and the implication is that the organisation will have the necessary flexibility to achieve these.

Competitive potential (Figure 11.4) seeks to exploit emerging IT capabilities to generate competitive advantage, either by enhancing products or improving processes, with e-business strategy being modified to take advantage of new IT opportunities.

Figure 11.2. A strategy execution perspective (Clarke, 2007, p. 85)

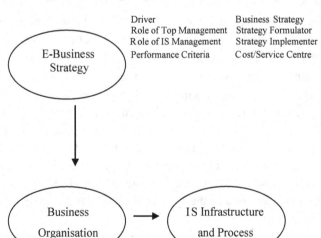

Driver	Business Strategy
Role of Top Management	Strategy Formulator
Role of IS Management	Strategy Implementer
Performance Criteria	Cost/Service Centre

E-Business Strategy

Business Organisation → IS Infrastructure and Process

Figure 11.3. A technology potential perspective (Clarke, 2007, p. 85)

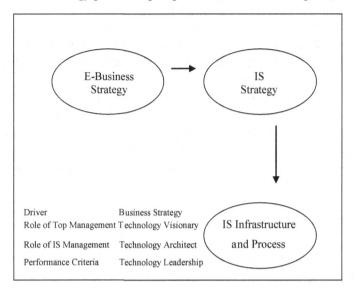

Figure 11.4. A competitive potential perspective (Clarke, 2007, p. 86)

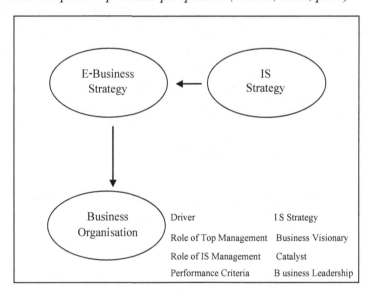

This approach, whilst appealing, may often fail to deliver the anticipated benefits, particularly if the concentration is on IT rather that the information resource as a whole (see Chapter VI). The service level perspective (Figure 11.5) concentrates on IS strategy and IS infrastructure to produce an improved organisation. The danger here lies in becoming detached from the business strategy and losing focus.

The empirical and theoretical evidence therefore strongly supports the view that strategy in the 'information systems' domain should begin with a perception of the information needs of an organisation, and that information systems and information technology should be seen as supporting or supplying that need. Alignment of IT, IS, information, and corporate strategies, the framework for which is encapsulated in Figure 11.1, then becomes a continuous process of aligning the business domain (business strategy and business organisation) with the IS domain (IS infrastructure and processes and IS strategy) in accordance with corporate strategy and the organisation's IS map. It has been argued that the alignment perspective relevant to the organisation must be determined, and that only then is the organisation is ready to move on to implementing strategic alignment. This implementation is the subject of the next section.

Strategic Action

Once IS mapping has been used to determine an organization's alignment perspective, the strategic alignment model (Figure 11.6) lays out a framework for translating this into action. The stages of this process are iterative and the model enables that iterative process.

In principle, the process of strategic alignment consists of determining information needs for the organization, and aligning the business and information systems domains in satisfaction of those needs. Whilst, as with any iterative model, the order of the activities is not prescribed, unless the organization already has a clear definition of its information needs, the process would begin here.

Figure 11.5. A service level perspective (Clarke, 2007, p. 87)

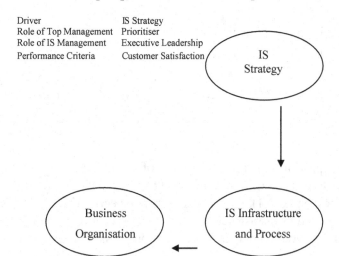

Driver	IS Strategy
Role of Top Management	Prioritiser
Role of IS Management	Executive Leadership
Performance Criteria	Customer Satisfaction

IS Strategy

Business Organisation

IS Infrastructure and Process

Information need is the basis of the whole process, and great care must be taken to determine those needs in relation to the organisation, its market, and the wider environment. Since information to support this must be drawn from various parts of the organisation, the determination of information needs will be a highly participative process, demanding a human-centred approach.

The Business Domain

The second part of the process of strategic alignment involves gaining improved understanding of the business domain (see Figure 11.6). The primary tool for analyzing a company's internal business domain is Porter's value chain. Care should be taken with this, however, to incorporate more recent ideas which cast the value chain as an integrated model, rather than as a collection of functional areas. Viewed in this way, information systems provide the links between the primary activities (inbound logistics, operations, outbound logistics, marketing and service), and the means of ensuring support activities (infrastructure, human resources, technology development and procurement) are used to their full advantage. Increasingly, for example, in organizations using just-in-time manufacturing systems, procurement, inbound logistics, and operations are linked by technology-based systems which ultimately control the whole manufacturing process.

In e-banking, the key will be to focus on the items in bold above – but there is a deeper issue here. Porter's value chain sees an organization from an essentially process-based perspective, with the flow from inbound logistics to service as an ongoing repetitive process supported by infrastructure, technology and so on. The perspective on strategy development for e-banking presented in this chapter

Figure 11.6. The process of strategic alignment (Clarke, 2007, p. 88)

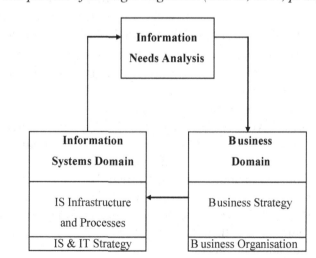

Figure 11.7. The value chain (Adapted from Porter, 1990)

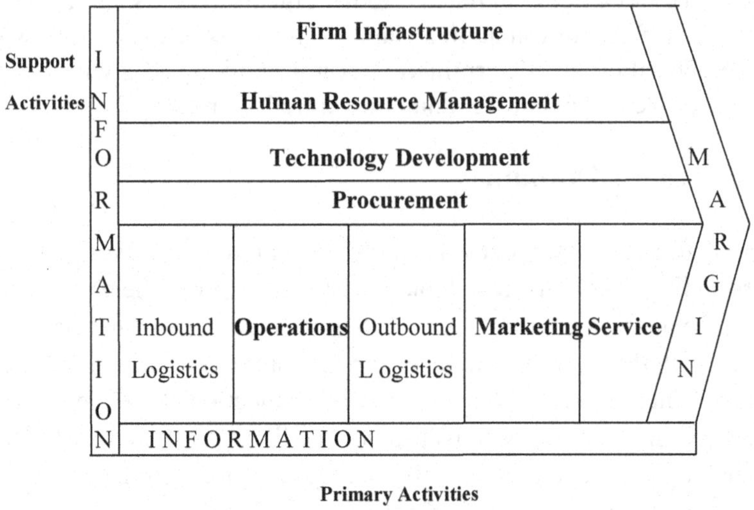

Primary Activities

promotes a view in which technology, human resource and infrastructure are all integrated into the firm's operations.

The Information Systems Domain

Analysis of IS infrastructure and processes commences with an internal and external environmental audit, using the strategic grid (Figure 11.8) to summarise the current position. The strategic grid is a means by which the organisation's current and potential applications may be categorised according to their current or potential value. In practice, our research has demonstrated that this analysis is more powerful if it is conducted in two modes: the 'is' mode, detailing where on the grid applications are currently seen to rest; and the 'ought' mode, assessing where the same applications *should be*. The power of this approach derives from a perceived weakness in analysing where applications *are*, in that this can serve to constrain their potential. By assessing where they *ought to be* an organisation is immediately beginning to define necessary changes.

Analysis using the strategic grid has been developed within our research and consultancy team over a number of years. The first stage of this analysis involves listing an organization's relevant IS applications, and positioning them on the grid. New applications are becoming available all the time, and organizations should be aware of those which are new and untried, but which they should be at least reviewing and perhaps even sampling in use. These are the 'high potential' applications: they may succeed or they may fail, but the key for any organization is to gain understanding of them but, unless following a very high risk strategy, not betting your business on them.

Figure 11.8. The strategic grid (Adapted from McFarlan, 1989)

STRATEGIC	HIGH POTENTIAL
Are or should be critical to the Business and of the Greatest potential value	Have or ought to have A value to the Organization which is high, but this is not yet Confirmed
Are or should be viewed as Essential for primary processes	Are or should be seen as needed to support the Business but of little strategic value
FACTORY	SUPPORT

From the applications entering at the top right of the grid, those which prove successful will begin to move around in an anti-clockwise direction. Initially they enter the strategic segment, where any company not beginning to use a given application will be initially left behind by its competitors. This happened in the U.K. insurance industry in the 1990s, when Direct Line pioneered telephone-based insurance, cutting out the intermediary brokers. Though competitors have extensively copied this approach, Direct Line still maintains its market lead today.

Arguably, the IS used to support Direct Line's activities, which was initially a strategic use of an emerging technology, has now moved to the 'factory' quadrant: the take up has been so great that all major players in the market depend on it for their primary processes and would therefore not survive without it. Lastly, as applications age and lose their value as a strategic weapon, they may continue for a time in a support capacity, but should be selectively divested and replaced by systems selected from the emerging and pacing quadrants. It is here that many organizations are most at fault, hanging on to dying systems often through fear of change: perhaps even Direct Line should be considering the possibility that one day the systems which are now such a fundamental part of their business will be no more than support applications?

So much for the IS, but what of the IT so often used to enable it? Technology which is used to support IS typically will have a finite life. This begins with the emergence of an as yet untried technology, moves through a phase where major competitors are sampling it, to a position where an organisation will not survive without it, and a final scenario where keeping the technology too long makes the company uncompetitive. In effect, the technology life cycle mirrors the application life cycle outlined above.

Figure 11.9. The technology life cycle

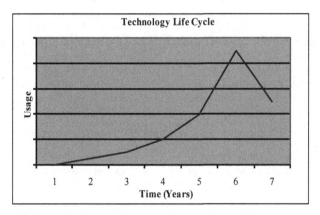

In any given industry, it is essential to be aware of currently used technologies in these terms. Figure 11.11 shows the life cycle of a typical technology, where the first year is one of emergence, followed by periods in which a company in the industry must increasingly commit to the new technology in order to compete, before moving out of it and into newer technologies as its impact declines. Of course, many technologies, after early promise, will fail to make an impact, so companies must be equally ready to dispose of these once their potential proves unrealisable.

Little (1981) provides an approach to monitoring new technologies by superimposing them on the strategic grid. Information technologies support strategy as enabling mechanisms, the aim being to find the correct technologies to enable the required IS and corporate strategies to be achieved.

The grid can be used to match existing technologies against applications and to plan the introduction of future technologies. As with applications, technologies enter the grid at top right, and proceed around in an anti-clockwise direction. The principle of this analysis is that emerging technologies need to be used for systems with high potential but which are not critical to the business, and must be carefully monitored until a decision to utilise them can be made; pacing technologies should be invested in selectively, for applications in which competitors are investing. Primarily the aim is to decide which are likely to become key, at which point they must be used in building strategic / factory systems; base technologies should be selectively divested.

External monitoring feeds this process, which will not succeed unless the organisation has a clear view of what technologies are relevant to its operations in any of the quadrants at a particular time. A generic view of IT at the present might see, for example: internet and multi-media technologies as emerging; wide area networks as pacing; local distributed systems as key; and central computers with terminal access as base. Finally, as with the strategic grid, it is important to review

Figure 11.10. Technology implementation (Adapted from Little, 1981)

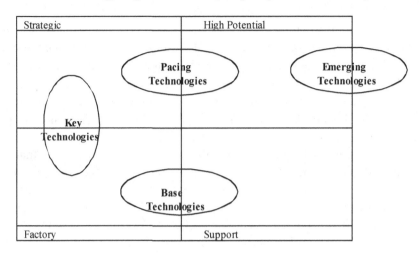

technology usage in terms of what *is* happening and what *ought to be* happening, with the normative (ought) position being of primary importance in planning future systems.

In summary, the objectives of application portfolio and technology management are to:

- Conduct internal and external audit to determine the current position regarding applications used and the technology used to support them.
- Use the audits to determine the applications and technologies available to the organisation.
- Classify applications according to the strategic grid (Fig 5.5). This should be done for both current and intended or available applications.
- Determine the available technologies, categorised as emerging, pacing, key or base (Fig 5.7).
- Match current applications and technologies to those available.

New technologies fundamental to the development of information systems are emerging all the time, and one factor which must not be overlooked in setting IS strategies is the extent to which such strategies are dependent on this emergence. Internal and external environmental scanning must therefore be a continuous process.

COMPETITIVE ADVANTAGE

The idea that information systems can be used to give an organisation an advantage over its competitors came to the fore in the 1980s, and spawned a number of studies purporting to show how new and developing computer technologies such as databases and networks could be applied to give an organisation a competitive edge.

The foremost author in the field of competitive or 'strategic' advantage is undoubtedly Michael Porter, and initially his ideas on how to generate competitive advantage will be used as a basis for this section. As these ideas are developed however, using contributions from other authors, it becomes clear that the idea of competitive advantage from information is a far from simple one. The first question to emerge concerns whether competitive advantage can be generated from information technology, or whether, primarily because the concern at this level is with the *use* of the technology, focus should be on information systems, or even more generally simply on information. Secondly, studies in this domain seek to determine *sustainable* competitive advantage, and questions have been raised concerning the sustainability of a competitive advantage based on information. Finally, there is the question of whether such competitive advantage could ever be systematically planned, or whether it is, at the extreme, just the product of chance.

Porter's Three Generic Strategies

Michael Porter is probably the best known author in the field of competitive strategy. In terms of its relevance to information systems, one of Porter's key notions is that of generic strategies. He proposes (Porter 1990) p. 39) that competitive advantage is to be gained from one of three generic strategies: differentiation; cost leadership; and focus. Differentiation means making your product or service in some way different from that of your competitors; cost leadership generates an advantage by producing at a lower cost, and thereby increasing profit margins; focus is the concentration on a particular area of the market where the organisation aims to outperform competitors by its increased knowledge and skills.

In attempting to generate competitive advantage from information systems (IS) – and hence from e-business, a number of authors have concentrated on these generic strategies, with cost leadership and differentiation being the most favoured approaches. Cost leadership, for example, has been the dominant use of technology by the UK banking sector, using such approaches as automated banking to reduce the overall cost base, largely consisting of personnel costs. The use of information to differentiate has been applied, for example, by insurance companies to differentiate the offering of an essentially service based product. In the UK this has resulted, in the ten years leading to the new millennium, in an increasing migration away from high street based insurance agencies toward telephone based organisations such as Direct Line. However, before looking at examples and theoretical evidence based on the work of Porter and others, it might be helpful to discuss competitive advantage in relation to IT, IS or just information.

Competitive Advantage from Information Technology, Information Systems or Information?

It is important to distinguish between IT, IS and information, the difference between them being illustrated in Figure 11.11. This is particularly relevant in e-banking, where the technology, the system(s) and the use of these as information will often overlap.

Information passes between individuals and groups in a given social environment. In terms of e-banking, the social environment will constitute all or part of the business organisation and its customers. Information within and outside the organisation may therefore be seen as the 'superset' which information systems and information technology are used to support. An information system then may be seen as any system which better enables information to be passed within this environment. The relevance of such a view is that such a system is not necessarily a technological one, but may take many forms.

The impact of this view of an information system should not be underestimated. Firstly, its purpose is to support the information needs of the organisation (see Chapter V), and it is therefore cast as a 'soft' or human-centred issue. Secondly, the conceptual or theoretical background underpinning this study is not technological, but is based on theories of social systems.

Figure 11.11. The nature of information technology, information systems and information

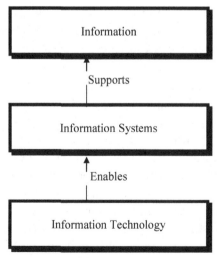

Organisations as Systems

Organisational or business systems are open, human activity systems, which display the properties of: boundary; emergence; holism; interdependence; hierarchy; transformation; and communication and control.

Firstly, why are they open systems? Well, 'open' means open to the environment, and the alternative is to see them as closed, or not affected by the outside environment. Since a business system must be impacted by events beyond its own boundary (political decisions, competitors, and so on), it cannot be viewed as closed.

Secondly, why human activity systems? This question is fundamental to an understanding of the role of information technology, and relates back to the 'hard/ soft' debate discussed earlier in the book. A business is a collection of individuals, or a social group, gathered together for a purpose. The activities within a business are therefore carried out in support of this human activity, and whilst the technology (whatever it may be) can be seen as in support of this activity, it can never be viewed as an end in itself.

The place of information technology is now clear. It may be used to better enable the information system to function, which in turn assists with information planning within the organisation. However, by itself IT serves little purpose.

How, then is competitive advantage to be generated from the use of IT? Practical and theoretical evidence from the literature will now be assessed to determine this.

Information Technology

The concept of competitive advantage from information technology is an appealing one. In a common sense way, it seems obvious that, if your organisation can get its hands on some relevant new technology ahead of its rivals, it must gain a competitive edge. From the earliest studies of competitive advantage from information technology, however, doubt has been cast on this concept. Clemons (Clemons, 1986), for example, follows the generic categories of Porter (cost leadership, differentiation and focus) to throw light on these issues. His view is that, by concentrating on internally or externally focused applications, an organisation can gain advantage by means of reduced costs, or by differentiating the product through improved delivery times and the speed of servicing customers.

Weill (Weill 1990), however, argues that such advantages are not simply IT-based, but derive from the way in which an organisation *uses* the technology, and cites claimed examples of competitive advantage from IT, primary among which is the SABRE booking system of American Airlines and the similar APOLLO system of United Airlines. Weill argues that these are examples of strategic advantage being gained from IT investment, but that such gains will not necessarily follow from all such investments. Weill's research is indicative of the train of thought which developed through the 1980s, which increasingly pointed toward a concept of competitive advantage which is not simply IT focused, but which was seen to depend on the use of the technology within the overall strategic and operational aims of the organisation. As will be seen below, this development has continued into the new millennium, often citing the same or similar practical examples.

Information Systems

Adcock *et al* (Adcock, Helms et al. 1993) refute the suggestion that competitive advantage may be obtained from information technology:

Max Hopper, vice-president of information systems at American Airlines refutes the view that SABRE increased American Airlines' marketing edge over rival airlines. American Airlines doesn't worry whether the competition has access to the technology because American thinks it can be smarter in how it uses the technology.

This argument is supported by the fact that both American Airlines and Baxter Healthcare, another major example of IT use for competitive advantage, were happy to sell their IT applications to competitors, thereby gaining revenue from the sale whilst maintaining their competitive advantage by better use of the technology through superior product and service offerings. From these, and other examples of the use of IT in enabling competitive information systems, Adcock *et al* conclude that, although short-term competitive advantage from IT is possible, in the longer term the impact of IT is on industry structure rather than the competitive position of any particular organisation within that industry.

Information

It seems clear that, through the twenty years leading up to the new millennium, the focus for competitive advantage has moved away from IT and towards IS, highlighting the use made of the technology within a given organisation rather than just the technology itself. It appears that both IT and IS need to be integrated into an organisation, and that it is the organisational system which should be the focus of attention. In citing Baxter's Healthcare (Adcock, Helms et al. 1993) as gaining advantage from the ' ... service behind the system', Adcock *et al* argue that competitive advantage does not come from IT or IS, but from the 'underlying management processes' which make use of them. These are human activity processes, and need to be seen in terms of systems, including the information system to be implemented, and its place in the wider organisational system of which it is a part. The purpose is to facilitate the use of information within an organisation, if necessary through the use of an IT-enabled information system.

The Sustainability of Competitive Advantage from Information

The question of competitive advantage sustainability can now be placed in perspective. Any such sustainability is essentially short-term in nature, and related to such issues as the time taken to 'harvest' the results, and switching costs (costs incurred by competitors switching to the new technology, or customers switching from one supplier to another) (Clemons 1986). In so far as competitive advantage is derived mainly from the technology used, its sustainability will depend on continuing innovation, in order to stay ahead of the competition as they imitate the organisation's lead, or innovate to move ahead themselves. This innovative use of IT is therefore, in the long term, unsustainable, and will soon be lost (Adcock, Helms et al. 1993). Competitors are quick to respond, and what happens is that the industry structure as a whole changes, as was evidenced, for example, with the switch of the banking system to automated teller machines.

The greatest promise of sustainability comes from human advantages. If the system of concern is seen in terms of a human activity system, then sustainability perhaps depends on a holistic view of interdependent sub-systems which, when functioning together, give rise to advantages which competitors find hard to emulate. Such advantages may be intangible, relying on such things as the skill base of the organisation, experience of those involved, adaptability and so on.

Frameworks for the Analysis of Competitive Advantage

Regardless of the view taken concerning the sustainability of competitive advantage, or its attainability from IT, IS or information, any organisation needs to understand its competitive position. Porter (Porter, 1991) mounts a convincing argument to support the view that an organisation's success depends on its competitive position relative to others in the same industry or sector, and offers a number of frameworks to help assess this. Although these frameworks are geared to competitive advantage overall, rather than just competitive advantage from information, they can be adapted for the latter purpose. Similarly, Earl (Earl, 1989) p.54) discusses the use of business strategy frameworks. These approaches are adapted here to provide an overall method for analysing and managing an organisation's competitive position in respect of information.

Although competitive advantage is not seen to be derived from IS or IT in isolation, nevertheless there is a need to determine what information systems and technology are being used by competitors, what is available, how these systems are used, and when they should be changed. The importance of human-centred issues in this process makes this even more critical: human activity systems take time to adapt and change, giving rise to a need to manage the process of IT and IS infusion in an organisation.

Three key approaches may be seen as supporting the monitoring and management of competitive advantage from information in an organisation: industry or sector analysis; positioning the organisation within the industry or sector; and internal analysis of the organisation.

Industry or Sector Analysis

In terms of the information it uses, a firm needs to position itself within its industry or sector. Porter and Millar (Porter & Millar 1985) have devised a framework for assessing this (Figure 11.12).

The impact of information is greatest in the top right segment, and least in the bottom left. The importance of this analysis is that the value of information management to an industry needs to be assessed, and competitive advantage from information is more critical in companies in the upper half of this grid, and particularly in the upper right quadrant.

E-banking therefore emerges as a sector most clearly dependent on the use of information.

Positioning the Organisation within the Industry

The position of an organisation within its industry will also help determine its approach to information management. Where rivalry is strong, organisations can use information to keep pace with or ahead of competitors, as is the case with the

Figure 11.12. The information intensity matrix (Adapted from Porter & Millar, 1985)

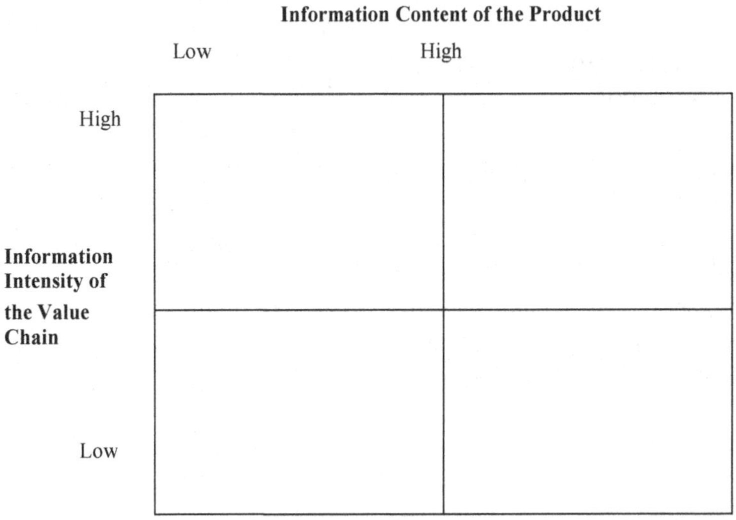

Information Content of the Product

	Low	High
Information Intensity of the Value Chain — High		
Low		

earlier cited airline booking systems, now used by all major airlines. The threat of new entrants can be reduced by barriers to entry such as the high cost of acquiring and using the necessary information systems: the lower the cost of acquisition, the greater the need to be better at using them. The threat of substitutes implies a need for information about the nature of substitute products or services, and indicates an area where information management is likely to be crucial. Suppliers and buyers positions are best managed through information on the supply and customer chains, a strategy adopted by all the major car manufacturers.

The value chain has been discussed earlier, and in relation to the issues of this section becomes a valuable technique for assessing the importance of information to the organisation. Information may be seen as pervading and linking all of the activities in the value chain, with culture (HRM) and structure as important elements, enabled by available technologies. These linkages require co-ordination: the whole must be managed as a system.

By combining the information intensity matrix, the five forces model, and the value chain, an organisation can therefore assess the relevance of information to its operations; the need for enhanced use of information to combat the external forces to which its operations are exposed; and the value of information in linking and enhancing internal activities.

In terms of its information resource, e-banking clearly stands to gain from the strategic use of *information*. Focus on IT alone, or even on IS, seems unhelpful: the real competitive advantage comes from the *use* of technology and systems. There is clear evidence from empirical studies that, even where a number of major players within an industry have access to the same technology, some succeed by using that technology better, while others fail. To quote from Max Hopper, American Airlines succeed by being smarter in the use of the same technology. Sustainability comes from the interaction of interdependent sub-systems within a system of human activity: this kind of competitive advantage is not 'planned for' in any instrumental sense, but is the natural outcome of information which is strategically managed.

The greatest promise of sustainability comes from human interaction. In terms of its information resource, an organisation clearly stands to gain from the strategic use of *information*. Focus on IT alone, or even on IS, seems unhelpful: the real competitive advantage comes from the *use* of technology and systems. There is clear evidence from empirical studies that, even where a number of major players within an industry have access to the same technology, some succeed by using that technology better, while others fail. Sustainability comes from the interaction of interdependent sub-systems within a system of human activity: this kind of competitive advantage is not 'planned for' in any instrumental sense, but is the natural outcome of information which is strategically managed.

Figure 11.13. A framework for information systems strategic management (Clarke, 2007, p. 168)

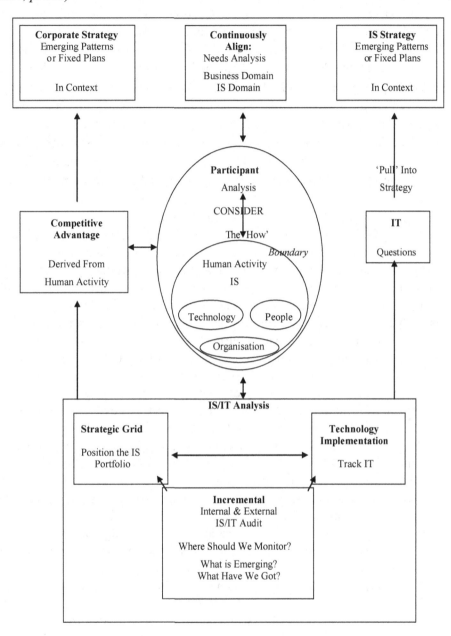

STITCHING IT TOGETHER

Figure 11.13 presents the core of information systems strategic management (ISSM) as analysis of an e-banking system by participants: those involved in and affected by the system. Firstly a holistic view of the system must be formed. This, represented by the Participant circle at the centre of Figure 11.13, will be a human activity system, informed by boundary critique, and will include organisational and technological subsystems. The importance of this part of the analysis cannot be overstated: e-banking strategic management is not something to be conducted by a privileged group of experts or managers; the necessary knowledge on which an organisation must build is held by the members of that organisation, all of whom must be represented in the strategy process. A number of methodologies or techniques are available to assist with this process, including a wide range of soft methods (see Clarke & Lehaney, 1998 for a summary).

The rest of the analysis must be carried out with participants at the centre of the activity. This is shown in Figure 11.13 as a number of interdependent strands to be considered in managing the information systems strategy process. Firstly, the present position in relation to corporate and IS strategy must be determined. The form this takes will depend on the context of the system, but in most organisations is likely to be a matter of determining patterns of activity, past and emerging, rather than looking at some plan which purports to be the organisation's strategy. The ISSM process then commences proper with an information needs analysis, from which the corporate and IS strategies can be developed interdependently, stressing either the e-business or IS domain, depending on the 'planning perspective' taken. Focus on information needs throughout the ISSM process enables alignment of corporate and IS strategies to be continuously monitored, and followed according to the relevant alignment perspective. Information needs analysis combined with continuous strategic alignment is the primary process which drives ISSM.

Simultaneously with this primary activity, there will also need to be ongoing participant analysis of the organisation's competitive position, its strategic use of information systems, and the availability and implementation of IT solutions. Many participant groups within an organisation have knowledge of and a view on its competitive position, and all should be drawn into the discussion of 'competitive advantage'. Similarly, there will be identifiable groups who can contribute to the IS/IT analysis. The use of Porter and Millar's 'Information Intensity Matrix' and Porter's 'Five Forces Model' (see Chapter VI) could be employed here. These activities feed the strategic study, the IS/IT analysis doing so partly through competitive positioning of the IS portfolio, and partly by strategy 'pulling in' IT solutions.

CHAPTER SUMMARY

The argument in this chapter has been for an approach to strategic development and management of e-banking grounded on corporate, IS and IT strategy within a common framework, based on participant analysis.

All of the evidence drawn from IS, corporate strategy, and the strategic domains of IS such as competitive advantage and strategic alignment, points to participant analysis being at the centre of both the corporate and IS strategy domains. This is complicated, however, by the need, of primary concern in e-banking, to utilise technology to support the strategy process, which requires technology-based and human-centred analysis to be used together within ISSM.

The solution is presented as a strategic ISS process to be followed (Figure 11.2). Two key factors drive the process and must be identified:

1.   What is the system of concern?
2.   Who are the participants to be involved in the analysis?

Strategic issues of corporate / IS strategic alignment, competitive advantage, and IS and IT analysis, are then all considered through the participants' view of the system of concern.

- Information systems should be seen as a human-centred domain, enabled by technology, and therefore requiring a mixture of human-centred and technology-based methods.
- Corporate strategy is similarly and predominantly a human-centred domain, in which planning/design issues should not be allowed to dominate.
- Information systems strategic issues further support the domain as being human-centred.
- The overall conclusion is that e-banking strategy needs to be approached from a perspective informed by participative analysis, and a framework has been presented to achieve this.

REFERENCES

Adcock, K., Helms, M. M., et al. (1993). Information Technology: Can it provide a sustainable competitive advantage? *Information Strategy: The Executive's Journal, 9*(3), 10-15.

Baets, W. (1992). Aligning information systems with business strategy. *Journal of Strategic Information Systems 1*(4), 205-213.

Clarke, S. A. (2007). *Information Systems Strategic Management: An Integrated Approach.* London: Routledge.

Clarke, S. A. & Lehaney, B. (1998). Intervention Methodologies in Coercive Situations. *Analytical Approaches to Studying Power and Influence in Contemporary Political/Military Affairs.* Farnborough, UK: Defence Evaluation Research Agency, Farnborough.

Clemons, E. K. (1986). Information Systems for Sustainable Competitive Advantage. *Information and Management, 11,* 131-136.

Earl, M. J. (1989). *Management Strategies for Information Technology.* London: Prentice Hall.

Little, A. D. (1981). Technology Implementation. *Strategic Planning for Information Systems.* J. Ward and P. Griffiths. Chichester, UK: Wiley.

McFarlan, F. W. (1989). Portfolio Approach to Information Systems. In Boehm, B. W., *Software Risk Management,* (pp. 17-25). Washington, D.C.: IEEE Computer Society Press.

Porter, M. E. (1990). *The Competitive Advantage of Nations.* London: Macmillan.

Porter, M. E. (1991). Towards a Dynamic Theory of Strategy. *Strategic Management Journal* 12(Winter), 95-117.

Porter, M. E. & Millar, V. E. (1985). How information gives you competitive advantage. *Harvard Business Review,* (July/August).

Venkatraman, N., Henderson, J. C., et al. (1993). Continuous Strategic Alignment: Exploiting Information Technology Capabilities for Competitive Success. *European Management Journal, 11*(2), 139-49.

Weill, P. (1990). Strategic Investment in Information Technology: An Empirical Study. *Information Age, 12*(3), 141-147.

Chapter XII
E-Banking:
A Fuller Picture

INTRODUCTION

This last chapter is a summary of previous chapters. Whereas previous chapters focused on specific issues in e-banking, this chapter presents a summarised full picture along with recommendations about good practice in the domain. We defined e-banking as provision of information about a bank and its services via a home page on the World Wide Web (WWW). More sophisticated e-banking services provide customers access to accounts, the ability to move their money between different accounts, and making payments or applying for financial products via e-Channels.

E-banking started in the form of PC banking in the early 1990s, through which a user could use a PC and dial up modem to login to their bank's system without connecting to the Internet. Owing to various reasons such as lack of functionality, call costs and so on, this approach didn't quite gain wide acceptance. With the arrival of the Internet, interest in e-banking re-emerged and many banks started offering e-banking in the late 1990s. During the last decade or so, new players such as Internet only banks as well as other organizations such as supermarkets or clothing retailers have also started offering e-banking. While large banks still hold the major market share, these new arrivals are winning noticeable market share. The importance of services distribution channels is also changing at a rapid pace.

In the past the main source of retail banking services distribution was 'bricks and mortar' branches. With the arrival of other channels such as telephone banking and e-banking, the number of branches is steadily declining, a trend also fuelled by mergers and takeovers. Now, most banks choose to deliver their products and services through multiple channels, including the Internet and telephone.

Often the main goal of e-banking is to provide most, if not all, of the services offered at a branch. This may include transactions as well as information, advice, administration, and even cross-selling. However, the interactive nature of the Internet not only allows banks to enhance these core services, but also enables banks to communicate more effectively and enrich customers relationships. When combined with the improving analytical capabilities of data mining, customers relationships management and other related technologies, the potential for enriching the relationship with customers is huge.

In the context of e-banking, many challenges lie ahead in the banking sector. First of all banks need to satisfy customers needs that are complex and difficult to manage. Second, they need to face up to increased competition from within the sector and from new entrants coming into the market. Third, they must continually invest in new products and services in the light of the changes described above. Central to meeting these challenges is the development of strategies to exploit existing markets and explore new ones using new delivery channels such as the Internet or mobile banking. However these new delivery channels bring their own sets of organizational and external challenges, which need to be managed in order to achieve success. This chapter presents a summary of these issues, are covered in detail in previous chapters.

REASONS FOR IMPLEMENTING E-BANKING

E-banking is a significant investment, so the question must be answered as to what motivates banks to participate and deal with the associated problems and risk. This section summarises some of the reasons often cited by banks to be their primary motive for implementing e-banking.

Customers Demands

With the emergence of the digital economy the balance of power seems to be shifting to customers. Customers are increasingly demanding more value, 24 hours availability, with goods customised to their exact needs, at less cost, and as quickly as possible. To meet these demands, banks need to develop innovative ways of creating value, and e-banking is seen as one of those innovative ways to meet customers' expectations.

Selling More to Existing Customers

The financial services markets in most developed countries have matured considerably and there is very limited scope for creation of new markets. This means that the most common route to growth is to sell more products to existing customers. Early indications are encouraging as both the volume and value of new business generated from the Internet channel are growing for the banks which have implemented e-banking. In some cases, such as Woolwich in the UK (See Chapter VIII for details) each e-banking customer holds four financial products on average, which is a considerably higher figure than for traditional banking customers.

Changes in the Environment

There have been some significant shifts in the importance of different sectors of the economy. In most western countries, primary (such as mining, agricultural) and secondary (manufacturing) have been steadily declining, whilst the service (e.g. financial services) sector is growing in importance. This has increased the prominence of service sector organizations, resulting in more pressure on them to diversify their offerings and look beyond their immediate markets to create value. They see new technologies such as the Internet and mobile telecommunications as a key enabler in accessing new markets and the creation of value.

Social changes are also forcing banks to change the way they interact with their customers. Customers are increasingly mobile (they move or travel more often), and this, coupled with the rise of single person households, means that demand for flexible services is rising at rapid pace.

E-Banking is a Hygiene Factor

Some banks are offering e-banking because their competitors have done it, and not doing so will mean losing an important customer segment to traditional competitors as well as new entrants to the financial sector. If this is their sole reason for doing so, they often drag behind their competitors and lack of enthusiasm prevents them from using e-banking to boost other sources of innovation, which are often enabled by the new technologies.

Achieving Competitive Advantage

Most organisations aspire to achieve competitive advantage, but few attain truly succeed, and even if attained, few are able to sustain this(see Chapter VI). As Internet banking has spread widely, it is no longer a source of competitive advantage on its own, at least in developed world. E-banking with the help of other technologies such as data mining can however help in other sources of competitive advantage such as faster product development, superior customers service and cross selling. To gain competitive advantage, banks must continually develop new and innovative services to differentiate themselves from the competition, as having a large branch network or even e-banking is no longer seen as a main source of competitive advantage. Innovative products and state of the art customer service are the key differentiating factors and e-banking could play a central role in achieving both.

New types of interactions enabled by the Internet and other communication technologies create innovative relationships between consumers, marketers and suppliers of products and services. These relationships can enable exchange of an unprecedented flow of information in all directions (Talha et al., 2004). Effective exploitation of this information and its flow might be another main source of competitive advantage in future. This could be true especially of financial services owing to fast changing customers' needs, high diversification of products and leadership in technological innovations.

To Achieve Efficiencies

Some banks look at e-banking from a cost savings point of view, as it is widely reported in e-commerce literature (Shah et al., 2007) that cost per transaction is much lower than for other service delivery channels. Banks may fail if they are thinking only of providing low cost transactions, as these costs only become lower once a bank exceeds a critical mass of online customers, owing to the large upfront costs of implementing e-banking. Conducting cost/benefit analysis on a regular basis often gives a clearer picture in this regard, enabling the analysis of feasible alternatives in terms of the major costs involved together with the major benefits that are expected to accrue.

E-banking can also help lower operational costs since, to offer e-banking, banks have to fine tune their business processes, systems and the ways in which employees communicate with one another. This may be seen as an unnecessary and costly exercise initially, but in the long run can prove immensely valuable, and may even enable a bank to survive the economic pressures and down-turns.

BENEFITS OF E-BANKING

E-banking has helped many banks to realise benefits, which are summarised in this section.

Choice and Convenience for Customers

The nature of e-banking means that personal contact between customers and banks is eroded. Harden (2002) suggests that e-channels erode a direct relationship with customers as compared with traditional over-the-counter banking: e-banking does not offer face-to-face contact in what is essentially a one-to-one service relationship. To compensate, e-banks must deliver higher quality services in order to compete with other service delivery channels (Liao & Cheung, 2005). Another factor in the loss of personal relationships is the convenience of Internet shopping: it is much easier now to compare products and switch between different providers. This creates the need for offering high value products and to cut operational costs to remain competitive, which in turn may further erode the avenues for building personal relationships with customers. The solution to these problems appears to be offering a multi channel experience which is better than direct competitors.

In the fierce battle over customers, providing a unique experience is the compelling element that will retain customers. A 'customer first' approach is critical for success in e-banking. Customers hold the key to success and companies must find out what different customers want and provide it using the best available technology, ensuring that they are acting on the latest, most up-to-date information. Consumer needs continue to change all the time. These shifts represent a significant problem for banks that can't change themselves quickly, but, on the other hand, they also represent an enormous opportunity for banks that can (Temkin, 2007).

Customers want the traditional range of banking services, augmented with online capabilities and a stronger focus on personal relationships. Avkiran (1999) stressed the importance of the human touch in customer services. Politeness and neatness, recognition in terms of greeting, willingness to provide prompt service, ability to apologise and express concern for a mistake are all important for bank customers. Most of these aspects of customer service cannot be automated. The adequacy of staff members serving customers can be expected to directly influence customer satisfaction.

Offering extra service delivery channels means wider choice and convenience for customers, which itself is an improvement in customer service. E-banking can be made available 24 hours a day throughout the year, and a widespread availability of the Internet, even on mobile phones, means that customers can conduct many of their financial tasks virtually anywhere and anytime. This is especially true of developed countries, but increasingly in developing countries, in both of which the spread of wireless communications means that services such as e-banking are becoming accessible.

Attracting High Value Customers

E-banking often attracts high profit customers with higher than average income and education levels, which helps to increase the size of revenue streams. For a retail bank, e-banking customers are therefore of particular interest, and such customers are likely to have a higher demand for banking products and an interest in more complex (and even riskier) products. Most of them are using online channels regularly for a variety of purposes, and for some there is no need for regular personal contacts with the bank's branch network, which in turn is an expensive channel to run (Berger & Gensler, 2007).

Some research suggests that adding the Internet delivery channel to an existing portfolio of service delivery channels results in nontrivial increases in bank profitability (Young, 2007). These extra revenues mainly come from increases in non-interest income from service charges on deposit/current accounts. This may be due to the idea that the added convenience of e-banking has encouraged some customers to purchase additional fee-based services and/or to willingly pay extra for the services they used to buy almost free of charge. These customers also tend to be high income earners with greater profit potential for the bank.

Accounts Aggregation

Another benefit of e-banking from a customer's point of view is that most banks provide accounts aggregation services, at least internally. Accounts aggregation enables a consumer to be presented with all his or her account details (current account, saving account, mortgage account) on a single page. Customers can have their financial data from many banks on one page but it currently requires consumers to provide their account passwords to the aggregator (usually a bank). The aggregator uses the passwords to access automatically the consumer's accounts. The information is then provided to the consumer on a consolidated basis on a single page so the customer has a full view of his/her financial portfolio (Engen, 2000).

Banks are also concerned about the idea that a third party might play the middleman between them and their customers. They complain of privacy issues that come up when customers hand over passwords and user IDs to third parties. the legal position is not clear, leaving banks potentially incurring losses in the event of a security breach caused by a third party. Bankers also fear losing part of the customer relationship to the third party aggregators (Engen, 2000). There are many other security and privacy issues associated with accounts aggregation and a comprehensive aggregation service (summary of all financial products regardless of the organization from which they are purchased) is still rarely offered by banks.

Enhanced Image

E-banking helps to enhance the image of the organization as a customer focused innovative organization. This was especially true in the early days when only the most innovative organizations were implementing this channel. Despite its common availability today, an attractive banking website with a large portfolio of innovative products still enhances a bank's image. This image also helps in becoming effective at e-marketing and attracting a young/professional customer base.

Increased Revenues

Increased revenues as a result of offering e-channels are often reported, because of possible increases in the number of customers, retention of existing customers, and cross selling opportunities. Whether these revenues are enough for reasonable return on investment (ROI) from these channels is an ongoing debate. This has also allowed banks to diversify their value creation activities. E-banking has changed the traditional retail banking business model in many ways, for example by making it possible for banks to allow the production and delivery of financial services to be separated into different businesses. This means that banks can sell and manage services offered by other banks (often foreign banks) to increase their revenues. This is an especially attractive possibility for smaller banks with a limited product range.

E-banking has also resulted in increased credit card lending, since this type of transactional loan is most easily deliverable over the Internet. Electronic bill payment is also rapidly rising (Young, 2007), which suggests that electronic bill payment and other related capabilities of e-banking have a real impact on retail banking practices and rapid expansion of revenue streams.

Easier Expansion

Traditionally, when a bank wanted to expand geographically it had to open new branches, thereby incurring high start up and maintenance costs. E-channels, such as the Internet, have made this unnecessary in many circumstances. Now banks with a traditional customer base in one part of the country or world can attract customers from other parts, as most of the financial transaction do not require a physical presence near a customer's living/working place. In one case study presented in

Chapter VIII, a bank based in the southern part of the UK was attracting customers from northern England, where it had no branches. In many countries banks share their resources such as ATMs or use post offices as their main interaction points, with customers for services such as cash and cheques deposits.

Load Reduction on Other Channels

E-Channels are largely automatic, and most of the routine activity such as account checking or bill payment may be carried out using these channels. This usually results in load reduction on other delivery channels, such as branches or call centres. This trend is likely to continue as more sophisticated services such as mortgages or asset finance are offered using e-Banking channels. In some countries, routine branch transactions such as cash/cheque deposit related activities are also being automated, further reducing the workload of branch staff, and enabling the time to be used for providing better quality customer services.

Cost Reduction

The main economic argument of e-banking so far has been reduction of overhead costs of other channels such as branches, which require expensive buildings and a staff presence. It also seems that the cost per transaction of e-banking often falls more rapidly than that of traditional banks once a critical mass of customers is achieved. The research in this area is still inconclusive, and often contradicting reports appear in different parts the world. The general consensus is that the fixed costs of e-banking are much greater than variable costs, so the larger the customer base of a bank, the lower the cost per transaction would be. Whilst this implies that cost per transaction for smaller banks would in most cases be greater than those of larger banks, even in small banks it is seen as likely that the cost per transaction will be below that of other banking channels.

However, some sources of research in this area suggest that banks so far have made little savings from introducing e-banking (Young, 2007). The implication is that any efficiency related savings are offset by above average wages and benefits per worker, owing to the need for a more skilled labor force to run the more sophisticated delivery system. Other costs such as systems integration and extra security measures also take their toll.

Organizational Efficiency

To implement e-banking, organizations often have to re-engineer their business processes, integrate systems and promote agile working practices. These steps, which are often pushed to the top of the agenda by the desire to achieve e-banking, often result in greater efficiency and agility in organizations. However, radical organizational changes are also often linked to risks such as low employee morale, or the collapse of traditional services or the customer base.

E-Marketing

E-marketing in the financial services sector (which is covered later) was made possible by the arrival of e-banking. E-marketing builds on the e-channel's ability to provide detailed data about customers' financial profiles and purchasing behaviour. Detailed understanding of customers enables customised advertising, customised products (called mass customization) and enrichment of the relationship with customers through such activities as cross selling.

Mass customisation enables manufacturers of the products or service providers to create a specific product for each customer, based on his or her exact needs. For example, Motorola gathers customer needs through their website for a mobile phone, transmits them electronically to the manufacturing plant where they are manufactured, according to the customers' specification, i.e. colours, features, and then sends the product to the customer within a day (Turban et al., 2000). Similarly, Dell Computers and Levi use this approach. Using online tools, customers can design or configure products for themselves. For example, customers can configure a PC to their exact needs (in case of Dell) or design their T-shirts, furniture, cars and even a Swatch watch.

The nature of financial products and the process of product/service development is changing rapidly due to the dynamic nature of online trade. Now it is possible to create so much flexibility in a product/service that customers can customise it, within pre-defined limits, to meet their exact needs. Advanced databases/data mining tools, internet cookies which provide detailed insights into a customer's behaviour when they conduct their financial activities, and new communication technologies make it easy and cost–efficient to mass market personalized services, because the whole process of personalization can be automated.

Other potential benefits of e-banking to organizations may include: improved use of IT resources and business processes; better relationships with suppliers/ customers; quick delivery of products and services; and a reduction in data entry and customer services related errors.

It is important to note that e-channels do not automatically bring these benefits, as other organizational issues ,must also be dealt with. There are only a few examples reported in the literature where e-banking is realising its promised potential. One such example is the Royal Bank of Canada, where its number of online relationships was 340,000 and was growing at a rate of almost 700 new enrolments a day during the year 2002-2003. Another example of realisation of the above benefits is the Woolwich Building Society in the U.K., which is described in Chapter VIII. The number of its online customer was growing so fast that it was cited as one of the main reasons for its takeover by a much bigger bank, Barclays. Not only did the number of its online customer grow very quickly, but the new customer base was also very profitable. According to Woolwich's own figures, its online customers bought four financial products each - much higher than its 'branch banking only' customers.

BARRIERS TO E-BANKING

The following factors demonstrate why e-banking may be difficult to implement, or why a bank may not realise the full benefits from it.

Access to the Internet

Although the growth of the Internet has been very fast, there is still a large population not connected to the Internet. Lack of computer literacy, high cost of hardware and call charges and various other social and economic factors are some of the reasons cited for this (Walczuch et al., 2000). This is changing fast as more and more people connect to the Internet, and numbers are expected to grow even faster with the maturity of mobile communications (Samuals, 2002). However, this is still more of a problem in some developing countries, where the telecommunications infrastructure is less developed.

Consumer Behaviour

A large number of consumers of financial services are still reluctant to conduct their financial management online. A study of consumer habits in 10 countries found that two-thirds of consumers do not consider online services important and that almost 30 percent do not know whether their bank offers Web-base services (Regan & Macaluso, 2000). Changing consumer behaviour takes many years, as was the case with the 10-year adoption cycle of the ATM. This process can be accelerated with aggressive marketing and high value-added features, two things that are lacking in today's online banking market (Franco & Klein, 1999). This can also be true for some businesses, which may be even slower than consumers in adopting new technologies. Factors such as security, perceived difficulties of use, perceived usefulness, functionality and lack of promotion (such as availability of cheaper products on new channels) are most commonly cited factors which are hindering the widespread adoption of new technologies (Cheng et al., 2006).

Language and Culture Issues

These play a major role in global e-Commerce. Although English is accepted as the primary language of the Internet worldwide, in some cases a website has to be designed specifically to suit the market that it is trying to reach. The main problems associated with this are speed and cost. It takes a human translator up to a week to translate a small website into just one language (Turban et al., 2000). Financial services related websites are usually very large and consume large resources in the translation process. The problem does not end with the translation of a website, it also need be adapted to the local culture to attract visitors. Banks around the world would do well to learn from Swiss banks, which successfully offer their services in several different languages.

Adverse Industry Trends

The financial services industry worldwide is in the middle of dealing with a number of significant developments, which usually means that e-banking is low on their priority list. These developments include the recent 'credit crunch', conversion to the Euro, and various mergers. These require sizeable resources to deal with resulting costs and to upgrade and integrate various systems, distracting the attention from e-banking development and advancements.

Fear of Competition

Some banks have been hesitant to promote e-banking systems, fearing that their costs will become too high and that it will be difficult for them to match the prices of competing Internet only banks. These fears have proven to be significant in most developed markets. Mols (1998) also stresses this point but suggests that not offering e-Services is not an option, instead companies should focus on other means such as product differentiation to protect themselves from excessive competition. Traditional banks could also use their well established brand names and product development expertise to manage competition from new entrants.

Security Issues

Internet security is still one of the major issues hindering the growth of Internet related trade. Since the Internet is an open network, high security risks are involved with financial transactions (Han & Noh, 1999-2000). Internet fraud is common, and related stories get immediate media attention, making people hesitant to bank online. Different security methods (including hardware and software) are being tested and employed currently but there is still some way to go to win the trust of a large majority of customers (Mols, 1999).

Project Management (Discussed in Detail in Chapter VIII)

Project management is a vital part of an e-Commerce implementation strategy, and lack of project management skills with some banks is considered to be a major barrier to the implementation of e-banking. E-commerce projects must be carefully planned and executed. There are some factors which relate specifically to software projects but can be applied to e-Commerce projects. Appleton (1997) recognises that the important skills needed for a software systems implementation are team building and communication skills, which she refers to as 'soft skills'. Projects need to be business driven with a cross-functional project team, and a rapid decision making process to help ensure that the project does not fall behind schedule (Martin, 1998).

Availability of Resources

For some banks, lack of financial and human resources will be a problem because offering the sophisticated Internet based services is an expensive project requiring major changes in IT infrastructure (Mols, 1998). Similarly, Walczuch et. al. (2000) reported that the primary deterrents for businesses establishing a Web presence is start up costs and the costs associated with major organisational changes required for such moves. Mols (1998) suggests strategic partnerships between banks to share such costs. These partnerships could combine to develop e-banking related systems. However, finding suitable partners in very competitive environments may prove difficult.

Return on Investment

E-banking should be considered more as a business project rather than a techno-logical initiative. In this context, cost benefit analysis may be very useful. Offering e-banking is expensive because of initial technological, human and marketing costs. A detailed investment appraisal may save a company from costly mistakes. Internet banking should be considered in terms of how it can achieve business objectives. Moreover, a number of studies may be needed to find out:

- To what extent will business strategy be affected?
- To what degree this transformation of business strategy will impact the competitive advantage of the company?
- How the enterprise strategy is changing against the competitors?
- What will be the Return on Investment (ROI)?

Lack of Promotion of E-Banking within Banks

As the Internet is a relatively new delivery channel, customers need a great deal of persuasion to switch to this new channel. Incentives, such as higher interest rates on savings or low cost services (for example insurance) are often used for this purpose. This can be costly and success uncertain, with any decision regarding backed up by concrete marketing information. Promotion of e-banking to employees is also important. Change resulting from e-Commerce implementation affects many people in organisations. Uncertainties resulting from changes are usually addressed by getting as many employees involved as possible at all stages of a project life cycle. This may lengthen the project duration but the benefit can be immense. It is also important to keep communication going and keep all stakeholders, including users, informed of the progress for the entire duration of the project. Some organisations such as the Woolwich also use incentives such as free WAP phones and bonuses for e-banking promotion within organisation (see Chapter VIII).

TECHNICAL ISSUES IN E-BANKING

Advancements in information and communication technologies (ICTs) have been the primary drivers behind the rise of e-banking. According to Consoli (2003), the historical paradigm of IT provides useful insights into the 'learning opportunities' that opened the way to radical changes in the banking industry. These changes are evident in offering of new services distribution channels and innovative services. Banks rely heavily on ICT for their internal operations and their interaction with individual as well as business customers. To deliver services via the e-banking channel, a bank needs Internet technologies for universal connectivity, back end applications such as account systems, support applications such as Customer Relationship Management (CRM systems), communication technologies to link e-banking to the payment systems such as LINK, and middleware to integrate all these often different type of systems.

Backend systems include data processing systems, accounts management systems and management information systems. These systems form the backbone of e-banking. Most of these systems were developed before the arrival of e-banking (thus

268 Shah & Clarke

the term legacy systems used for them) so they often lack connectivity, meaning they are difficult to connect to each other or with new systems. E-banking often requires rapid modification in systems to respond to changes in the market, and because of lack of flexibility in these systems they are very difficult of modify swiftly.

Integration with other systems which support different service delivery channels such as branches or the internet is also key to ensuring efficient enterprise-wide work flow information and to giving the bank a uniform look and feel. Lack of integration with other systems is one of the most common reasons for the failures of e-banking projects. There are many ways of tackling the problem of integration, such as re-coding parts of existing systems or replacing them altogether, but one method, the use of middleware, has been implemented widely. These technologies enable different types of systems to interact with each other, and make it easier to integrate new systems which a company may implement in the future into the existing infrastructure. There are many types of middleware technologies (some examples are described in case studies included in the Chapter VIII) but one which is becoming increasingly dominant is Services Oriented Architecture (SOA). Potential benefits, such as reduced IT costs, systems integration and greater business agility have persuaded many organizations to adopt SOA (Knorr & Rist, 2005).

According to O'Donnel (2005) the advantages of SOA over other integration and software development technologies is that by externalizing functionality into reusable components and organising them into a logical framework, it minimizes two of the greatest causes of delay - the need for exhaustive communication between the business and IT, and the need for IT to write code. In addition, unlike other IT paradigms, organizations can also re-use their legacy systems as SOA enables legacy systems to communicate with other systems. Often viewed as a methodology, the SOA can be implemented across multiple projects, both internally and externally, eliminating the need to rebuild similar services for each project. Many vendors now offer SOA related products such as messaging solutions or business process management tools (BPM) that help implement SOA.

In e-banking, a bank's website acts as a bank branch or front end. The main difference is that when customers login they do most of the work themselves without any assistance. Therefore developing a user friendly and functionality rich website is critical in the e-banking environment. To create a positive experience, a great deal of planning, resources and expertise needs to be invested in the development and ongoing maintenance of websites.

Website development related issues are growing in complexity giving rise to a debate about technical versus social approaches to the development. As usual in any type of technology, technical views take higher priority in the beginning and related social issues gain a slower acceptance. The main challenge here is *not* to see web development and management as a problem for technical people. A framework (for example, of user groups) needs to be developed, from which the contribution from representatives of all stakeholders including customers should be sought. Membership of participating groups or committees should not be fixed, and, of course, should not be limited to managers or those in authority.

Some banks are making significant investments in mobile systems to deliver their services. A factor that has contributed to this development has been the extended availability and capacity of mobile communications infrastructure around the world. The number of mobile devices has been increasing rapidly, there are many times more mobile devices in use than personal computers, and their functionality is also improving all the time.

There are two main types of technologies available for use in mobile banking: Wireless Application Protocol (WAP) and Wireless Internet Gateway (WIG).

WAP is an application environment and set of communication protocols for wireless devices designed to enable manufacturer, vendor, and platform independent access to the Internet and advanced telephony services. WIG is a Short Message Service (SMS)-based service, in which a menu of available banking options is initially downloaded from the bank to the phone device (Brown et al., 2003). This enables users to browse bank accounts and conduct other banking related tasks.

E-banking systems are complex, large-scale systems with demanding requirements for performance, scalability, and availability, and even the most technologically sophisticated organizations are struggling to manage them. Success in e-banking requires far more than a Web server, a storefront and transaction processor or a database. It requires a comprehensive approach to address integration and scaleablity, and dynamic responses to changes in requirements and technologies. E-banking, like other electronic business systems is complex, large-scale, and mission-critical. Organizations should start with new Web technologies and e-commerce functionality and combine them with the design, development and implementation of management practices that have been proven successful for other types of large-scale, complex, mission-critical systems.

TOOLS FOR MANAGING E-BANKING

There are many ICT based tools (computer applications) which are employed to support e-banking operations such as data warehousing systems and customer relationships management systems. These tools help to manage information which can be used for product development and marketing purposes.

Data warehouse technology can be described as collecting data from several dispersed sources to build a central data storage, so that users can use appropriate data-analyzing tools to analyze and convert this data into meaningful aids for decision making. Banking activities are highly information intensive, hence the need for data warehousing is greater in this industry than most others. Data warehouse tools can collect daily transaction data both internally and externally, and then accumulate, categorize, and store data for further analysis. Many such systems also have analysis tools, and analyzed information is distributed to relevant parties such as managers and CRM systems.

CRM systems are technology enabled management tools which help manage an organization's relationships with its customers. CRM systems help gather and store customer data, analyze this data to enable customised marketing, and are often used to semi-automate customer services. The main purpose of CRM is often stated as 'enriching relationships' with customers to gain greater loyalty, but at times they are used to cut the costs of customer services processes. In an e-banking context, CRM software can help move customers from expensive branch or phone-based services to self-help services over the internet.

Knowledge management (KM) systems can also be a great aid to maximize benefits from e-banking. The key to understanding KM systems is that not all knowledge can be codified and maintained in data or information management systems. Much of the knowledge we use on a daily basis is part of what we do as social beings – in KM terms, it is implicit rather than explicit. As banks seek to move more toward e-banking solutions, the computerised information systems will perhaps be able to cope with explicit knowledge, but the incorporation of implicit knowledge requires systems which combine technology with human expertise. The review of KM undertaken in this book (Chapter X) indicates the potential for approaches to e-banking explicitly grounded in critical social theory, and points to a possible future direction through a Critical Action Framework for Knowledge Management (see Chapter X).

SOCIAL ISSUES

E-banking literature is dominated by technical issues and human issues get little attention. We have argued that human activity is more fundamental to the success of e-banking, so the investigation of approaches underpinned by theories of social interaction are outlined in this book. From research in the social domain, a foundation in critical social theory emerges as a promising direction (see Chapter VI for details). Within such an approach, the first issue to be addressed is that of *understanding* the problem context. For this, critical social theory points to the use of critical systems heuristics and critical boundary judgements to critique and determine the system boundary. Boundary critique further informs intervention strategy. The methods required must embrace functionalist (technological), interpretivist (human-centered), and radical humanist (emancipatory, participatory, 'social inclusion') issues. In any future work, the ongoing research in the application of critical theory to management issues must be considered, and a brief outline of this is provided.

Given these findings, how might a manager seek to action them? He or she should:

- Determine the initial scope of the system of concern, identify the social group(s) involved in and affected by that system and form representative samples from these groups. In terms of management action, the challenge here is *not* to see e-banking development and management as a problem to be solved by an expert group of developers. A framework (for example, of user groups) needs to be established, from which the contribution from those participating in web usage can be drawn. Managers should also:
- Conduct boundary critique to initially determine the system of concern and continue this throughout the project.
- Use participative forums to discuss all issues of web design, development and implementation.
- Choose and implement the relevant methodological approaches in a critical framework.

Initially, formal boundary setting sessions will be needed to set the scene. Quite quickly, groups will form their own clear views about the scope of e-banking developments within a particular organisational context (it will become 'culturally' ingrained), and less time will be necessary in formal sessions to discuss this. The particular forums can then be used to surface the issues, the only primary requirement in terms of expertise will be a facilitator who can assist with guidance on the process and lead the forum.

We argue that e-banking management is a task to be conducted within a social framework. A purely technical approach or even a technical approach, even where informed from participative analysis, is insufficient to address the complexity of the problem contexts encountered. It is essential to recognise that what is being dealt with is a social system, albeit enabled by technology, and, this being so, it is difficult to envisage how such an undertaking could be informed from anywhere other than social theory.

PROJECT MANAGEMENT ISSUES

E-banking is often treated like a large scale project and broken into several small scale projects to manage various different aspects (called project portfolios), ranging from BPR to make the organization ready for online operations, to actual implementation of e-banking technologies. Project management is defined by the Project Management Institute (PMI, 2008) as the application of knowledge, skills, tools and techniques to a broad range of activities in order to meet the objectives of a project. Another relevant concept in this context is Programme Management. PMI (2008) defines Programme Management as the coordinated management of a portfolio of projects to achieve a related set of business objectives.

A project may involve a number of steps such as feasibility study, determination of objectives, planning, execution as well as end of project evaluation. A number of project management methodologies/tools such as MS Project or PRINCE 2 are available to support these steps. These project management methodologies offer a systematic approach to all stages of a project by providing guidance as well as monitoring facilities so that every step is carefully planned, monitored, and measured.

In this book we recommended a "Systems Approach" to Project Management. It has been argued earlier that banking is a complex domain and the management of systems might be seen as attempts to control variety and complexity through a reductionist approach. Reductionism seeks to understand systems in terms of their constituent parts, assuming that these parts operate independently. This approach, which sees organizations as rigid structures, with departments working in an isolated manner, is not suitable for the banking industry, with its mix of professionals working toward common objectives but often within fairly loose forms of organization. This approach is especially undesirable in e-business environment where systems and organizational integration is vital for success. Here, a more holistic and systemic approach might be seen as more likely to be successful, and such an approach is fundamental to systems approaches to project management.

The key idea behind systems thinking is that organizations are constituted of sub-systems, or elements, that are in interrelationships with one another, and which exist within a boundary. What are important are not the elements per se, but the interrelationships between them, because it is the nature of the interrelationships that give character to the system. Inputs to the system are transformed within it, and go out as output, which in turn informs further input with feedback. Systems thinking promotes the understanding that departments may contain boundaries, but not barriers. Whereas boundaries allow permeation of ideas and opinion, and facilitate team working, barriers do not. Hence, whereas boundaries can be facilitative, barriers are prohibitive.

STITCHING IT TOGETHER: RECOMMENDATIONS

This section summarizes some of the key recommendations of this book to deal with a variety of e-banking related issues.

Strategy Development

Companies involved in e-banking are dealing with continuous uncertainty about the future of their business models and how this impacts their business as a whole. This uncertainty requires proper strategic planning in order to fully utilise opportunities and minimise threats. Strategic planning often requires a methodological approach (Julta et al., 2001). All major banks have been struggling with the formation of winning strategies that will enable them to maintain their current positions in the face of competition from new Internet enabled banks and other non-banking organisations offering banking services (Dewan & Seidmann, 2001).

In a corporate environment, strategy is a an organized decision-making process which enables organizations to match resources with opportunities which surface from the competitive environment. External environment has a strong influence on the strategy-making processes, as has the availability of resources to the organization. The main aim of a business strategy is often to maximize the performance of an organization by improving its competitive position.

Strategy can be divided under two headings: strategy by design and strategy by discovery. Strategy by design encompasses systematic approaches, whereby plans are derived through objective, reductionist methods. Strategy by discovery, by contrast, requires a systemic (or holistic – concentrating on the whole as sub-systems in interaction rather than the parts or components in isolation) approach, favouring participative methods covering the whole system of concern. Contextual issues within the organisation will be at least a partial determinant of the approach taken: a planning method, for example, arguably suiting a mechanistic organisation; incrementalism being more suited to professional adhocracies.

In context of e-banking, both views have a place, with a perceived need for a mixture of approaches, premised, at least in part, on the organisational context encountered. Furthermore, in respect of corporate strategy as applied to e-banking management, strategy by discovery may be seen as long term, concerned with planning for the unknown, or forecasting discontinuities; whilst the design approach may be seen as short term, and concerned with carrying out the IS strategy through the application of information technology. Corporate strategy cannot therefore rely on any one approach, but must craft a combination of strategic methods to fit the organisational form and context.

Chesher and Kaura (1998) suggest a number of key factors that an organisation needs to consider when developing a strategy towards e-Commerce and these also apply to e-banking. First, e-Commerce initiatives should be business driven and not technology or trend driven. Second, the project should be customer focused, that is, making it easier than competitors to conduct business. Third, e-Economy partnerships with other organisations are more important than ever. A group of companies is better placed to offer competitive goods under one roof than an individual company. Fourth, integration of technology and business processes from suppliers to customers to provide real-time (or close to it) business decisions. Finally, management of information and knowledge is the key to understanding customers and offering customised products/services according to individual needs.

The argument in this chapter has been for an approach to strategic development and management of e-banking grounded on corporate, IS and IT strategy within a common framework, based on participant analysis. All of the evidence drawn from IS, corporate strategy, and the strategic domains of IS such as competitive advantage and strategic alignment, points to participant analysis being at the centre of both the corporate and IS strategy domains. This is complicated, however, by the need, of primary concern in e-banking, to utilise technology to support the strategy process, which requires technology-based and human-centred analysis to be used together within Information Systems Strategic Management (ISSM).

Under the ISSM approach, firstly a holistic view of the system must be formed. This includes a human activity system, informed by boundary critique, and will include organisational and technological subsystems. The importance of this part of the analysis cannot be overstated: e-banking strategic management is not something to be conducted by a privileged group of experts or managers; the necessary knowledge on which an organisation must build is held by the members of that organisation, all of whom must be represented in the strategy process. A number of methodologies or techniques are available to assist with this process, including a wide range of soft methods (see Clarke & Lehaney 1998 for a summary).

Channel Integration

Services distribution channels for banks have evolved over a long time driven primarily by need, changes in regulations, market environment and technological advances. Before the arrival of e-banking, the need for channel integration was rarely on top of the management agenda. But now that financial institutions are juggling numerous channels and ways in which they communicate with customers, banks need to integrate these channels in a more pro-active way. Furthermore, banks need to invest in a consistent and seamless customer experience across all channels, which requires integration of real-time cross-channel communications.

Many banks need to build integrated channels that facilitate customer information and process flows which will enable them to achieve the operational efficiencies they expected from the implementation of e-banking. But most banks need to deal with the problem of legacy architectures which are not easy to integrate. Legacy systems are very inflexible so maintaining them is also time-consuming, prone to error, and expensive.

Change Management

When considering the implementation of e-banking, an important question to think about concerns both structure and organisational culture (Jayawardhena & Foley, 2000). This requires focusing on an organisation's business structure and business processes with the existing IT systems, as well as examining new processes designed specifically for e-Commerce. Existing processes often have to be re-engineered in order to align them with the new processes. Therefore, companies should be ready to face this challenge (Kalakota & Robinson, 1999) and strategic planning is required to manage ongoing changes. Change management is the process of planning, controlling, coordinating, executing and monitoring changes that affect business (IBM Global Services, 2001).

Change management projects have very poor success rates and the literature is full of failure examples. To prevent these failures, it is important to understand that organizational change is a dynamic process encompassing different but interrelated forms of diversity. This diversity might be related to several dimensions such as organizational structure and culture, or the interactions between different dimensions of an organization. Causes of failures can often be found in inefficient interactions of technical and human activities, the organization with its environment, or organizational design and management style. Lack of systematic change management methodologies or problems in their implementation is another commonly cited problem (Clarke, 2007). Most of the change management methodologies focus on four common dimensions of an organization (process, design, culture and politics).

Process change may involve changing services development process (from market research to actual roll out) cash flow (from investments to profits), human resource input, and information flow. Structural change involves changes to organizational functions, their organization, co-ordination and control, such as changes in horizontal and vertical structures; in the decision systems or policy and resource allocation mechanisms; and in the processes used for recruitment, appraisal, compensation and career development. Culture encompasses such issues as values, beliefs and human behaviour in terms of mutual relationships and social norms.

Change management requires considerable emphasis on the management of change skills and responsibilities (Morton & Chester, 1997). They proposed three main steps in managing change:

- Use of the initial, vision-creating phase to unfreeze the organisation and to make employees 'change prone'. At the same time, attention should be paid to the potential causes of resistance and dissent and these are eliminated or minimised.
- Placing of duty on all staff for appropriate aspects of change.
- Placing of specific responsibility on one or more senior executives to facilitate the process of change.

Core to successful change management is commitment from the work force. It is important to keep communication going and to consult on the meaning of change for their job (Chesher & Kaura, 1998). It is not appropriate to go in to the further details of the change management process here, but the importance of change management when implementing e-banking cannot be over emphasised and it may dramatically influence the outcome of and e-banking project.

Adaptable Flexible Organizational Model to Compete with Start-Ups

Physical companies often have a great deal more experience and knowledge of their products and how to sell them than new Internet traders, and usually also have established brands and a large customer base. However, Owens and Robertson (2000) contend that it takes longer for physical organizations to develop an integrated e-commerce structure than it does for virtual traders to commence trading. This is due to the reduced, simple physical structure of virtual organizations. They argue that a structure of similar efficiency must be adopted by physical organizations for the provision of Internet services.

Promote Innovation Culture

A key strategy for the success of e-banking is to promote innovation in organizations. There are many ways in which innovation can be promoted in an organization including: creating room for experiments, tolerance to failure of good ideas, implementing a reward system to encourage individuals as well as teams to innovate. Some concepts such as 'absorptive capacity' and 'complexity studies' see knowledge as the key enabler in organizational innovation. Absorptive capacity is about measuring an organization's ability to value, assimilate, and apply new knowledge.

Measuring is done at multiple levels (individual, group, firm, and national level) (Zahra & George, 2002). 'Complexity studies' are derived from general systems theory and regard innovation as the continuity and transformation of patterns of interaction, understood as complex responses of humans relating to one another in local situations (Fonseca, 2001). These frameworks help organizations to understand the usefulness of information, assimilate it through systematic interactions, and apply it to achieve success at innovation through technology.

There are also many barriers to innovation, including: short term results culture, resistance to change, low acceptance rates of new ideas. In an online environment, the speed of new innovations may overwhelm many employees or consumers, and proper change management strategies become more important than in conventional situations.

Effects of these barriers can be minimized by promotion of an innovation culture in organizations and careful change management.

Leverage Existing Brand to Deliver New Services

Due to perceived lack of security and fraud threats, many customers only deal with trusted brands in online environments. For this reason, well established banks often outperform new Internet only banks. For new entrants to the e-banking market, building a trusted brand may therefore require considerable effort and resources. To build a new e-brand, an appropriate logo & key message would have to be developed. Building an e-brand is not just a management challenge, all levels of the organizations, its customers and intermediaries need to be involved in this process. Owing to these difficulties, the use of existing brands in online environment would be a preferable course of action.

Reinforce "Trust Relationships"

Traditionally, trust in an online environment generally meant a secure website, but according to Chankar et al (2002) perceptions of online trust have steadily evolved from being a construct involving security and privacy issues on the Internet, to a multidimensional, complex construct that includes reliability and credibility, emotional comfort and quality for multiple stakeholders such as employees, suppliers, distributors and regulators, in addition to customers.

Kim et al (2003) conducted a study into the determinants of online trust and found that the following six elements or dimensions play a key role in formation of online trust. These are information content, product, transaction, technology, institutional, and consumer-behavioral dimensions. These elements, which were further broken down into many sub-categories, formed a theoretical framework of online trust, covering the different stages that a consumer went through to complete an online transaction. Many customers seem to face a usage barrier because they perceive e-banking to be unsuitable for them. This usage barrier arises from the thinking that there is no relative advantage in switching from branch banking or ATMs to Internet and prefer the old routine of ATM use or consider Internet an unsafe, inefficient or inconvenient channel. Fear of costly mistakes due to pressing wrong key, security fears also play a role in deterring customers from use of e-banking.

The issue of online trust building can be addressed in a number of ways. To start with a professional customer advisor in a dedicated call centre can do a lot to inspire confidence. When a stakeholder knows that somebody will be there to speak to if anything goes wrong in an online environment, he/she will have confidence in conducting financial transactions online. Other factors such as keeping product/ delivery promises, providing unbiased comparisons with competitor's products, giving detailed product information, and providing tools such as financial calculators to enable a customer to play what-if type scenarios also helps. Customers need assurances that their liability in the event of things going wrong would be limited. Approval by third parties such as governments, financial service authorities, and professional associations or by other trusted brands also plays a big part. In addition, banks need to take active steps to further promote trust in e-banking. These steps may include:

- Purchase of similar web domain names so it becomes difficult for fraudulent traders to set up similar websites.
- Being pro-active in combating online crimes and cooperating with other banks and other regulatory/professional bodies to detect and prevent crimes.
- Taking proper care in protecting consumer's data and taking particular care in using it for marketing purposes.
- Providing appropriate guarantees against consumer losses in the event of fraud.

Website design can incorporate a number of features discussed above which contribute to the formation of online trust. Professional feel and look as well as a phone number to call if in doubt about anything, inspires confidence. Simple things such as choice of background color could be used by consumers to decide whether to trust this trader or not. Generally speaking, orange color website indicates a cheap/ no frills operation whereas use of light blue may be taken as a high-end trustworthy business. Most consumers like a simple and easy to navigate structure as it creates a smooth and positive experience which is a key dimension in winning trust.

Universal Product Offerings (Not Just Own Products)

Changes in basic business models resulting from the rise of the Internet have affected information intensive industries like the financial services industry a great deal. Customers now have access to a wider range of financial services, but on the other hand, they are obviously burdened by the huge amount of information which has to be analyzed and applied to customers' needs. This need has given rise to new kinds of intermediaries offering their services to assist the customers in designing the appropriate bundle of services according to their respective needs (Zimmermann & Koerner, 1999).

The following example will illustrate the difference between a traditional bank and these new intermediaries. A typical individualised package in the retail banking business could be composed of a saving and a current account, a loan, credit cards, life insurance and a portfolio of different investments. While a typical bank will offer these services based on their own products, an intermediary such as VirginMoney.com, is able to combine service modules from different suppliers in order to create a solution that maximises the customer's satisfaction. This trend is likely to force many banks to bundle products from their own products as well as from their partners to be competitive resulting in a greater need for alliances and partnerships across industry sectors (Zimmermann & Koerner, 1999).

In addition, a considerable number of applications for various financial products are rejected because a bank doesn't have a product suitable for that customer or on the ground of the low credit score of the applicants. Low credit scoring is typical of the Internet enthusiastic customers segment as they tend to be younger than average applicants with perhaps a bit less careful attitude to their financial management aspects resulting in their low credit scores. With some flexibility in product differentiation, banks can sell its products to them at higher prices or with payment protection plans, instead of rejecting these applications altogether. Another possibility is to sell other providers' products who may be willing to take higher risks and earn commission for referrals. This may be a too radical departure from current business models which means that most banks focused on selling only their own products. Changing this mind set might be the biggest challenge in implementing this strategy.

Highly Secure, Robust Environment

Security related issues are a major source of concern for everyone both inside and outside the banking industry. E-banking increases security risks for banks, potentially exposing traditionally isolated systems to the open and risky world of the Internet. According to McDougall (2007) security problems can mainly be categorized as; hacking with criminal intent (e.g. fraud), hacking by 'casual hackers' (e.g. defacement of web sites or 'denial of service' - causing web sites to slow or crash), and flaws in systems providing opportunities for security breaches (e.g. a user is able to transact on other users' accounts). These threats have potentially serious financial, legal and reputational risks associated with them. Luckily actual financial losses from these breaches have been very low in comparison to (say) credit card frauds.

Robustness of e-banking systems is another complex and challenging issue to mange. It is difficult to predict the usage of e-banking on an hourly or daily basis. These 'scalability problems' can give rise to a slowing down of the website, or even a website crash (temporary unavailability). This can cause many reputation problems and financial damage. This was the case at Northern Rock Bank in UK. This bank ran into credit problems, and when news spread that the bank was in trouble, thousands of people rushed to the bank website to transfer their money elsewhere which resulted in numerous technical problems in their e-banking system for many days. Some of the ways of addressing this problem according to Seargeant (2000) are:

- Undertake market research to predict demand,
- Adopt systems with adequate capacity and scalability,
- Undertake proportionate advertising campaigns, and
- Ensure adequate staff coverage and develop a suitable business continuity plan which not only helps coping with scalability problems but with other causes of systems failure.

A number of other technical solutions are also available to address this problem but owing to the high cost associated with them, banks often do not implement them.

Manage Resistance to Change

An e-banking system will be used by a number of different types of people including customers, executives, management staff as well as other interested parties such as trade partners and even competitors. Many systems fail simply because one or more type of user refuses to use a system or uses stealth tactics to undermine the new system. This phenomenon is often referred to as user resistance. Resistance to change can be defined as implicit or explicit negative reactions against change, or restrictive forces opposed to any reorganization of work process and new competences acquisition (Bareil, 2002) To minimise user resistance it is important to understand what are the main causes of user's resistance. Generally speaking, user acceptance is often linked to two outcome variables: system quality and system acceptance.

But underlying these are the more complex issues of cognitive and motivational factors which give rise to improved quality or improved acceptance.

Manage Technological Issues with Care

There are numerous technological issues with regard to e-banking. Lack of unified messaging standards is one of them. While messaging standards are fast evolving towards unification, the problem of legacy systems still remains one of the main obstacles in the way of e-banking. Many banks still operate on large mainframe based legacy systems for their core processing functions. While for most functions this is fine, e-banking will increasingly require capabilities that these systems are ill equipped to provide (Franco & Klein, 1999). Being at the forefront of technology adoption for many years, the financial services industry faces cutting-edge technological issues before other industries encounter similar issues (Dewan & Seidmann, 2001). E-banking systems are complex, large-scale systems with demanding requirements for performance, scalability, and availability and even the most technologically sophisticated organisations are struggling to manage them.

Success requires far more than a Web server, a storefront and transaction processor or a database. It requires a comprehensive approach to predict future demands and building systems to handle quick surges in use. According to Kramer (2000) because electronic business systems are complex, large-scale, mission-critical systems, businesses should start with new Web technologies and e-Commerce functionality and combine them with the design, development, implementation, management disciplines and practices that have been widely proven for other types of large-scale, complex, mission-critical systems.

E-Commerce is about how an organisation has to re-shape itself to enable commerce online. An organisation needs to have process oriented and fully integrated information systems (IS) to achieve the true vision of e-Commerce (Kalakota & Robinson, 1999). Even in cases of disparate applications, or in cases where the company does not abandon existing applications (e.g. legacy systems), there is a way to solve the problem. There are several alternatives available for increasing the level of systems integration. Data warehousing, a bundle of technologies that integrate data from multiple source systems for query and analysis, provide a cheaper alternative for data integration. Other technologies, such as Enterprise Applications Integration (EAI), may turn the legacy systems (as well as the rest of business applications) into strategic assets at a much lower cost. EAI is a new class of software that aims to provide an integration infrastructure for all business applications. A similar approach is the development of a middleware software for integration of all systems in the organisations. This approach is used by the banks like Bank B and the Woolwich (see Chapter VIII).

Kramer (2000) points out that systems must scale to accommodate business growth. Maintaining excellent performance across growing workload is imperative. There is no greater customer annoyance than a poor, unpredictable response, and competitors are only one click away. The requirement for scalability goes beyond the ability to use more powerful servers, to distribute workload across a few server platforms, or to balance communications traffic across multiple Web servers. New, pioneering approaches to system architecture, software structure, and workload distribution are needed.

E-Channels Specific Marketing

As mentioned before electronic distribution channels such as the Internet are shifting the balance of power from financial services providers to customers. This is due to the increasing number of choices available to customers and declining switching barriers (Mols, 1998). For these reasons, enrichment of relationships with customers has become an important issue. Greenland (1994) was one of the earliest to suggest this in his work about rationalisation and restructuring in the Financial Sector in the UK. He argued that personal relationship building is highly desirable for financial services institutions as they can be actively cultivated to promote image and stimulate cross selling. Greenland's (1994) work was focused on using branch banking for this purpose. Modern data mining and customer relationships management software has added another dimension to this proposition, which may now also change the e-channels to personalise financial services to the individual or a segment level.

Human Resources

Human resources (HR) is a key support function in implementation of e-banking. They need to identify employees with skills different from those found in more traditional organizations. People working in e-banking often are doing jobs that did not exist before and are working in an organization or division that did not exist before. Therefore, basic human resource problems are exaggerated for e-banking environment. For a typical e-banking project, HR often need to recruit employees with a wide range of skills, such as: technical staff like Web architects and designers, infrastructure specialists, Web developers, Web site managers, Internet security experts, and a team administrator, business-focused staff like content experts for marketing or sales and specialists like Web graphics designers, IT staff such as programmers and analysts and managerial staff for strategic planning, relationships management, project management, content creation/management, and process integration.

In addition to above specific skills, knowledge, aptitudes, and other charac-teristics (KSAO's) are desirable and combined in a proper way so they can work together to accomplish the desired goals. Since e-banking staff are in short supply, skills that are in short supply must be used most efficiently (Mitchell, 2001). For example, some non-IT tasks (such as report writing, routine coding, and systems administration) can be shifted to non-IT staff so that the IT staff can have more time to use the skills efficiently. A good understanding of these job roles, skills and issues would be required to recruit, retain, organize and develop an e-banking department or team.

Mobile Banking

A widespread use of mobile communications and their improving functionality means that stage is set for wider mobile banking adoption. There are still many hurdles in the way of mobile banking such as call costs, security and user's resis-tance, but need for mobile banking, to support an increasingly mobile life style is such that many users will adopt it. Mobile banking also promises to be an answer to Internet connectivity problems in some rural areas and developing countries. We presented an example of a mobile banking application earlier in this book and similar approaches could prove to be useful and profitable for banks.

"Bricks & Mortar" Mixed Business Model will Win

Many people see the development of e-Banking as a revolutionary development, but, broadly speaking, e-banking could be seen as another step in banking evolution. Just like ATMs, it gives consumers another medium for conducting their banking. Many analysts in late 1990s predicted that e-banks, having the advantage of a low cost base, would win deposits and loans by offering superior rates, and that many existing providers of those products would be driven out of the market. In the US, large banks targeted affluent customers using this medium. For example, in 2000, HSBC and Merrill Lynch committed to spend $1bn on a joint venture that would combine online premium banking and share dealing. Within a few months, sev-eral other banks had followed suit (Larsen, 2004). But the response was generally disappointing. Banks found customers reluctant to give up their bricks and mortar branches, and the take up was much lower than expected. The fears that this channel will completely replace existing channels may not be realistic, and experience so far shows that the future is a mixture of "clicks (e-banking) and mortar (branches)". There is another advantage for established banks to implement e-banking, as they can leverage their core competencies in primary activities. Physical banks often have a great deal more experience and knowledge of their products and how to sell them than new Internet- only banks and they usually also have established brands and a large customer base.

Early experience showed that even the most keen e-banking customers also wanted the convenience of branches and phone banking. This led to an argument that e-banking just adds another layer of complexity and unjustifiable costs. The growth of 'phishing', where fraudsters use spam e-mails and bogus websites to encourage people to reveal their account details, together with other security concerns, were also used to argue against the very existence of e-banking. Nevertheless, in spite of some scepticism, given the real and promised benefits of the e-banking it continues to grow rapidly in most parts of the developed world.

Brand name plays an important role in formation of trust and as customers use a brand, if their experience is positive, they tend to come back for repeat purchase. Their recommendations as well as carefully crafted marketing campaigns play a vital role too. Having some sort of physical presence (bricks) or having an already established brand name often proves to be an invaluable asset in inspiring consumer trust. Consequently, banks with well trusted brand names which also keep high street branches are performing better in e-banking than their rival virtual banks.

Another advantage of using mixed channels strategy is that, although start up costs for an internet banking channel can be high, it can quickly become profitable once a critical mass of customers is achieved. Moving some of the existing branch banking customers to the cost-effective e-channel is much easier than winning new ones. Low Return on Investment (ROI) from e-banking initially meant that some traditional retail banks which used e-banking as just another channel rather than replacing branches or call centres are benefiting most.

Another important strategic distribution channel decision faces banks. Whether to target the branch banking segment or the Internet banking segment (Mols, 1998). Arrival of new e-Channels has offered organisations new opportunities as well as new dilemmas about which channels offer the best return on investment in the long run, in an increasingly volatile business environment. There has been a steady reduction in the number of branches even before the arrival of new e-Channels. As Greenland (1994) notes, before the late 1970s the branches network of the largest financial institutions had grown steadily. Since then however, the trend has been large-scale reduction because of greater industry competition and economic hardship. Recession in the early 1990s dictated that distribution channels should function much more efficiently. Arrival of e-Channels may cause further downsizing of the branch networks. However, the question remains whether these new channels will make the old channels redundant? The most likely strategy for banks is to pursue a dual strategy offering both old channels and new e-Channels (Mols, 1998). Branch-networks are likely to survive for a long time as banks are likely to change their role from routine transaction driven to customer service centres (Greenland, 1994).

At first sight the advantages of establishing new distribution channels with respect to costs, market-reach and potential penetration seem to be promising. However, a 'blind' investment in novel forms of distribution can also have severe disadvantages. A traditional branch-based bank establishing a separate direct banking firm and lower margins could suffer negative externalities by cannibalising their traditional market and jeopardising overall profits. On the other hand, competitors will also consider how to make best use of various distribution channels including the question of whether or not it might be advantageous to combine innovative forms of distribution channels with traditional ones (Buhl & Will, 1998).

CONCLUDING REMARKS

e-banking is making significant progress in terms of customers' adoption, functionality and profitability for banks. However it still faces a number of threats including security and privacy issues which will have to be dealt with to ensure long term survival. It is difficult to predict the future, but some remarks can be made based on the experience so far. In our view, the next developments in e-banking will involve new products and services that were not feasible in traditional banking models. This could involve making instant payments (possibly using mobile phones), or tools to help people manage their multi-bank financial portfolio. Internet only banking may also become more viable as the functionality of e-banking grows, and customers adapt to the new ways of conducting their financial activities. International banking might become a reality for ordinary consumers as banking payments systems are increasingly harmonised. For example, in Europe, new measures are being introduced by the European Union to allow cross-border provision of e-commerce services by providing a single payment system.

Some companies such as IBM have expressed their vision of the future of financial services, complete with biometrics, state-of-the-art branch offices, enterprise risk-management systems, and advanced customer interaction (Marlin, 2005). Some of the technologies associated with such a vision are already in use but the feasibility of industry-wide use is still difficult to predict. Schneider (2005) predicted that in fifty years customers will carry a translucent plastic bank card displaying a talking head with artificial intelligence. Cash and checks will have been eliminated in favour of the new electronic currency of "credits," which will be much easier to transfer, maybe using mobile phones. The early signs are that it is already started to happen. Developments in biometric technologies may help to deal with the most persistent security issues as well as dealing with customers' difficulties in remembering many different login keys.

REFERENCES

Appleton, E. L. (1997). How to Survive ERP, *Datamation*, March, 50-53.

Bareil, C. (2002). *Managing Resistance to Change or Readiness to Change?* http://web.hec.ca/sites/ceto/fichiers/04_02.pdf

Berger, S. C., & Gensler, S. (2007 April). Online banking customers: insights from Germany. *Journal of Internet Banking and Commerce, 12*(1). http://www.arraydev.com/commerce/jibc/2007-04/SvenBergerFinal_PDFVersion.pdf

Birch, D., & Young, M. A. (1997). Financial Services and the Internet - What does Cyber-Space Mean for the Financial Services Industry?, *Internet Research: Electronic Networking Applications and Policy, 7*(2), 120-128.

Brown, I., Cajee, Z., Davies, D. & Stroebel, S. (2003). Cell phone banking: predictors of adoption on South Africa. An exploratory study. *International Journal of Information Management, 23*(5), 381-394.

Buhl, H. U., & Will, A. (1998). Economic Aspects of Electronic Commerce in Financial Services and Advantageous Steps to Extended Offers in Internet Banking. In Blanning, R. W., King, D. R. (Eds.) *Proceedings of 31st Annual Hawaii International Conference on System Sciences*, Internet and Digital Economy Track, IEEE Computer Society, Hawaii, USA.

Chankar, V., Urban, G. L., & Sultan, F. (2002). Online trust: a stakeholder perspective, concepts, implications, and future directions. *The Journal of Strategic Information Systems, 11*(3-4), 325-344.

Clarke, S. A. (2007). *Information Systems Strategic Management: An Integrated Approach*, (2nd Ed.). London: Routledge.

Clarke, S. A. & B. Lehaney (1998). Intervention Methodologies in Coercive Situations. *Analytical Approaches to Studying Power and Influence in Contemporary Political/Military Affairs*. Farnborough, UK: Defence Evaluation Research Agency, Farnborough.

Cheng, T. C. E. Lam, D. Y. C. & Yeung, A. C. L. (2006). Adoption of internet banking: An empirical study in Hong Kong. *Decision Support Systems, 42*, 1558–1572.

Chesher, M., & Kaura, R. (1998). *Electronic Commerce and Business Communications*. Springer, London, UK.

Consoli, D. (2003, September). *The evolution of retail banking services in United Kingdom: a retrospective analysis.*(CRIC Working Paper No 13, ISBN: 1 84052 011 6). http://129.3.20.41/eps/io/papers/0310/0310002.pdf

Dewan, R., Seidmann, A. (2001, June). Current Issues in e-Banking. *Communications of the ACM,* 44(5), 31-32.

Engen, J. (2000). Financial Funnel. *Banking Strategies, 76*(6), 64–72.

Fonseca, J. (2001). *Complexity and Innovation in Organisations.* Routledge: London.

Franco, S. C., Klein, T. (1999). *Online banking report.* Piper Jaffray Equity Research., www.pjc.com/ec-ie01.asp?team=2

Greenland, S. J. (1994). Rationalization and Restructuring in the Financial Services Sector. *International Journal of Retail & Distribution Management,* 22(6) 21-28.

Han, K. S., & Noh, M. H. (1999-2000). Critical Failure Factors That Discourage the Growth of Electronic Commerce. *International Journal of Electronic Commerce,* Winter, 4(2), 25-43.

Harden, G. (2002). E-banking Comes to Town: Exploring how Traditional UK High Street Banks are Meeting the Challenge of Technology and Virtual Relationships. *Journal of Financial Services Marketing,* 6(4), 323-332.

IBM Global Services (2001). *E-business Strategies for Conventional Insurers.* IBM White Paper. http://www-5.ibm.com/services/uk/pdf/e-bus-strat.pdf

Jayawardhena, C., & Foley, P. (2000). Changes in the banking sector: The case of Internet banking in the UK. *Internet Research: Electronic Networking Applications and Policy,* 10(1), 19-30.

Julta, D. N., Craig, J., & Bodorik, P. (2001 January 3-6). A Methodology for Creating e-Business Strategy. In Sprague, R. H. J. (Ed.), *Proceedings of the 34th Hawaii International Conference on System Sciences: Minitrack Infrastructure for e-Business on the Internet,* Maui, Hawaii, USA.

Kalakota, R., & Robinson, M. (1999) *e-Business, Roadmap for Success.* , Reading, MA: Addison-Wesley.

Kim, D. J., Ferrin, D. L., & Rao, H. R. (2003). A Study of the Effect of Consumer Trust on Consumer Expectations and Satisfaction: the Korean Experience. In *Proceedings of the 5th international conference on ElectronicA literature review of online trust in business to consumer e-commerce transactions, 2001-2006 Volume 8(2), Issues in Information Systems commerce,* 310-315

Knorr, E., Rist, O. (2005, Nov 7). 10 Steps SOA. *InfoWorld, 27*(45), 23-35. San Mateo, CA http://proquest.umi.com/pqdweb?did=930819081&sid=7&Fmt=3&clientId=3224&RQT=309&VName=PQD.

Kramer, M. I. (2000). *How to Succeed @ e-business.* IBM White Paper. http://www-3.ibm.com/e-business/resource/pdf/16768.pdf

Larsen, L. B. (2004, November). The Automatic Pool Trainer - a Platform for Experiments with Multi Modal User Interaction. In *Proceedings of the Fourth Danish HCI Research Symposium,* Aalborg University, Denmark.

Liao, Z. & Cheung, M. T. (2005, March 29-31). Service Quality in Internet E-banking: A User-based Core Framework. In *Proceedings of the 2005 IEEE International Conference on E-technology, E-commerce and E-service,* (pp. 628-631).

Marlin, S. (2005, July 01). Banking for the 21st Century. *Bank Systems & Technology.*

Martin, M. H. (1998, February 2). An ERP Strategy, *Fortune,* 95-97.

McDougall, P. (2007, February 13). Credit Suisse Outsources to BT in Deal Worth $1.1 Billion. *Information Week.*

Mitchell, M.E. (2001). Human resource issues and challenges for e-business. *American International College Journal of Business.* http://www.encyclopedia.com/doc/1G1-82256136.html

Mols, N. P. (1999). The Internet and the Banks' Strategic Distribution Channel Decisions. *International Journal of Bank Marketing, 17*(6) 295-300.

Mols, N. P. (1998). The Behavioural Consequences of PC Banking. *International Journal of Bank Marketing, 16*(5) 195-201.

Morton, R., & Chester, M. (1997). *Transforming the Business: the IT Contribution.* London: McGraw-Hill.

O, Donnell, T. (2007 March). Addressing SOA's Vulnerability.*Visual Studio Magazine.* Retrieved June 22, 2008 from http://visualstudiomagazine.com/features/article.aspx? editorialsid=2311

Owens, I., & Robertson, D. (2000, April 26-28). Aligning e-Commerce with Business Strategy: The Case of the Bank of Scotland. In *Proceedings of the 5th UKAIS Conference* (pp. 67-75), University of Wales Institute, Cardiff, UK.

Regan, K., & Macaluso, N. (2000, October 3). Report: Consumers Cool to Net Banking. *E-Commerce Times.* http://www.ecommercetimes.com/news/articles2000/001003-4.shtml

Samuals, M. (2002, May 16). More Europeans are Logging On. *Computing,* 33-34.

Schneider, I. (2005, May 26). Citibank, Daring to Dream of the Year 2054, Warns of Lessons of History. *Bank Systems & Technology.*

Sergeant, C. (2000). *E banking: risks and responses.* Financial Services Authority, London. http://www.fsa.gov.uk/Pages/Library/Communication/Speeches/2000/sp46.shtml

Shah, M. H. Braganza, A., & Morabito, V. (2007). A Survey of Critical Success Factors in e-Banking: An Organisational Perspective. *European Journal of Information Systems,* 16(4), 511-524. http://www.palgrave-journals.com/ejis/journal/v16/n4/index.html

Talha, M., Shrivastva, D., Kabra, P., Sallehhuddin, A., & Salim, A. (2004). Problems and Prospects of Internet Marketing. *Journal of Internet Banking and Commerce,* 9(1), http://www.doaj.org/doaj?func=abstract&id=169650&toc=y

Temkin, D. (2007, June 26) Banks Prepare For Customer Experience Wars. *Forester Report.* Retrieved October 30, 2008 from www.forrester.com

Turban, E., Lee, J., King, D., & Shung, H. M. (2000). *Electronic Commerce, a Managerial Perspective.* London: Prentice Hall.

Walczuch, R., Braven, G. D., & Lundgren, H. (2000, August 10-13). Internet Adoption Barriers for Small Firms in the Netherlands. In Chung, H. M. (Ed.) *Proceedings of the Americas Conference on Information Systems: Organisation Track,* 2, (pp. 672-680). Long Beach, CA.

Young, R. D., Lang, W. W., Nolle, D. L., (2007). How the Internet affects output and performance at community banks. *Journal of Banking & Finance, 31,* 1033–1060.

Zahra, A.A., & George, G. (2002) Absorptive Capacity: A Review Re-conceptualisation and Extension. *Academy of Management Review, 27*(2), 185-203.

Zimmermann, H., & Koerner, V. (1999, August 13-15). Emerging Industrial Structures in the Digital Economy - the Case of the Financial Industry. In Haseman, W. D. (Ed.), *Proceedings of the 5th American Conference on Information Systems,* (pp. 115-117). Milwaukee, WI.

Glossary

Account Aggregation: A service that gathers account information from many different sources, presents that information to the customer in a consolidated format and often allows the customer to conduct their financial management related task on a single page.

Account Management: Activities such as balance inquiry, statement balancing, transfers between the customer's accounts at the same financial institution, maintenance of personal information, etc.

Application Service Provider (ASP): Also known as "apps-on-tap," an ASP is a company that offers access to software and/or network applications, typically via an Internet connection. ASP services provide an attractive option to companies wishing to minimize up front costs and reduce internal support requirements.

Automated Clearing House (ACH): A computerized facility used by member depository institutions to electronically combine, sort, and distribute inter-bank credits and debits. ACHs process electronic transfers of government securities and provided customer services, such as direct deposit of customers' salaries and government benefit payments (i.e., social security, welfare, and veterans' entitlements), and preauthorized transfers.

Automated Teller Machine (ATM): A machine, activated by a magnetically encoded card or other medium, that can process a variety of banking transactions. These may include accepting deposits and loan payments, providing withdrawals, and transferring funds between accounts.

Authentication: Verification of identify by a computer system based on presentation of unique identifiers.

Bank Statement: Periodically the bank provides a statement of a customer's deposit account. It shows all deposits made, all checks paid, and other debits posted during the period (usually one month), as well as the current balance.

Bill Presentment: An e-banking service whereby a business submits an electronic bill or invoice directly to the customer's financial institution. The customer can view the bill/invoice on-line and, if needed, pay the bill through an electronic payment facility.

Biometrics: The method of verifying a person's identify by analyzing a unique physical attribute of the individual (e.g., fingerprint, retinal scanning etc).

Certificate Authority (CA): The entity or organization that attests using a digital certificate that a particular electronic message comes from a specific individual or an organization.

Checking Account: Also called current account. A demand deposit account subject to withdrawal of funds by check.

Current Account: Also called checking account. A demand deposit account subject to withdrawal of funds by check.

Customer Relationship Management: The strategies, processes, people and technologies used by companies to successfully attract and retain customers for maximum corporate growth and profit. CRM initiatives are designed with the goal of meeting customer expectations and needs in order to achieve maximum customer lifetime value and return to the enterprise. As a primary sales, service and retention touch point for many companies, the Contact Center is a critical component of a successful CRM strategy.

Data Mining: Data mining entails analyzing information for previously undiscovered correlations between two markets. Data mining connections can be made through associations (baseball fans also watch football), sequences (buying wood and then buying paint), forecasting (based on patterns found), and clustering (grouping information in a new way).

Debit Card: A debit card allows the account holders to access their funds in a current/check account electronically. Debit cards may be used to obtain cash from automated teller machines or purchase goods or services using point-of-sale systems. The use of a debit card often involves immediate debiting and crediting of consumers' accounts.

Digital Certificate: The electronic equivalent of an ID card that authenticates the source of a digital signature.

Digital Signatures: A security option that uses two keys, one public and one private, which are used to encrypt messages before transmission and to decrypt them on receipt.

E-Banking: In its very basic form, e-banking can mean the provision of information about a bank and its services via a home page on the World Wide Web (WWW). More sophisticated e-banking services provide customer access to accounts, the ability to move their money between different accounts, and making payments or applying for loans via e-Channels.

Electronic Bill Payment: An e-banking application whereby customers direct the financial institution to transfer funds to the account of another person or business. Payment is typically made by ACH credit or by the institution (or bill payment servicer) sending a paper check on the customer's behalf.

Encryption: A data security technique used to protect information from unauthorized inspection or alteration. Information is encoded so that it appears as a meaningless string of letters and symbols during delivery or transmission. Upon receipt, the information is decoded using an encryption key.

Firewall: A hardware or software link in a network that relays only data packets clearly intended and authorized to reach the other side.

HTML: Abbreviation for "Hypertext Markup Language." A set of codes that can be inserted into text files to indicate special typefaces, inserted images, and links to other hypertext documents.

Hyperlink: An item on a webpage that, when selected, transfers the user directly to another location in a hypertext document or to another webpage, perhaps on a different machine. Also simply called a "link."

Information Management: Describes the measures required for the effective collection, storage, access, use and disposal of information to support agency business processes. The core of these measures is the management of the definition, ownership, sensitivity, quality and accessibility of information. These measures are addressed at appropriate stages in the strategic planning lifecycle and applied at appropriate stages in the operational lifecycle of the information itself.

Information Systems (IS): Organised collections of hardware, software, supplies, policies, procedures and people, which store, process and provide *access* to information.

Interest: The term interest is used to describe the cost of using money, a right, share, or title in property.

Interest Rate: The amount paid by a borrower to a lender in exchange for the use of the lender's money for a certain period of time. Interest is paid on loans or on debt instruments, such as notes or bonds, either at regular intervals or as part of a lump sum payment when the issue matures.

Internet: A cooperative message-forwarding system linking computer networks all over the world.

Legacy Systems: A term commonly used to refer to existing computers systems and applications with which new systems or applications must exchange information.

Mortgage: A debt instrument used in a real estate transaction where the property is the collateral for the loan. A mortgage gives the lender a right to take possession of the property if the borrower fails to pay off the loan.

National Bank: A bank that is subject to the supervision of the Comptroller of the Currency. The Office of the Comptroller of the Currency is a bureau of the U.S. Treasury Department. A national bank can be recognized because it must have "national" or "national association" in its name.

Online Banking: A service that allows an account holder to obtain account information and manage certain banking transactions through a personal computer via the financial institution's web site on the Internet. (This is also known as Internet or e-banking.)

Operating Subsidiary: National banks conduct some of their banking activities through companies called operating subsidiaries. These subsidiaries are companies that are owned or controlled by a national bank and that, among other things, offer banking products and services such as loans, mortgages, and leases.

Outsourcing: The practice of contracting with another entity to perform services that might otherwise be conducted in-house.

Public Key Infrastructure (PKI): Policies, processes, and technologies used to verify, enroll and certify users of a security application. A PKI uses public key cryptography and key certification practices to secure communications.

Screen Scraping: A process used by information aggregators to gather information from a customer's website, whereby the aggregator accesses the target site by logging in as the customer, electronically reads and copies selected information from the displayed webpage(s), then redisplays the information on the aggregator's site. The process is analogous to "scraping" the information off the computer screen.

Service Charge: A charge assessed by a depository institution for processing transactions and maintaining accounts.

Smart Cards: A card with an embedded computer chip on which information can be stored and processed. A smart card may act as a debit card, credit card, access card or for claiming services provided by the state.

Virtual Mall: An Internet website offering products and services from multiple vendors or suppliers.

Wireless Application Protocol (WAP): A data transmission standard to deliver Wireless Mark-up language (WML) content on mobile devices.

Website: The service of providing ongoing support and monitoring of an Internet-addressable computer that stores web pages and processes transactions initiated over the Internet.

About the Authors

Mamood Shah is regional director, Institute of International Business (IIB) & SL at the Lancashire Business School. Previously he has held academic posts at Cranfield University and the University of Hertfordshire, both in the United Kingdom. He has also acted as a consultant to several UK and International banks on e-banking management related issues. He received a PhD in e-banking from Brunel University, a MRes in Innovative Manufacturing from Cranfield University and a BSc (Hons) in Information Systems from University of Bedfordshire, all in the United Kingdom. He has published papers in several high quality journals such as the European Journal of Information Systems and the International Journal of Information Management. His other research interests include mobile government, online security and technology alignment.

Steve Clarke received a BSc in economics from The University of Kingston Upon Hull, an MBA from the Putteridge Bury Management Centre, The University of Luton, and a PhD in human centered approaches to information systems development from Brunel University – all in the United Kingdom. He is professor of Information Systems in the University of Hull Business School. Steve has extensive experience in management systems and information systems consultancy and research, focusing primarily on the identification and satisfaction of user needs and issues connected with knowledge management. His research interests include: social theory and information systems practice; strategic planning; and the impact of user involvement in the development of management systems. Major current research is focused on approaches informed by critical social theory.

Index

D

data warehousing 40, 51
delivery of retail banking services 9–17
DeLone and McLean model 170
demanding customers 15
deregulation 15
digital economy 1
diversity management 219, 226

E

e-banking, barriers 264
e-banking benefits 259
e-banking, defined 2
e-banking evolution 2
e-banking future 25
e-banking is a hygiene factor 257
e-banking management 1–8
e-banking management, problematic issues
    103–129
e-banking overview 18
e-banking project management 167–189
e-banking project, typical steps 179
e-banking, strategy development 229–254
e-banking technologies 30–55
e-channels specific marketing 61
e-commerce to e-banking 21
economic climate change 15
EDI 18, 19, 30
electronic data interchange (EDI) 18, 30
electronic services delivery, models 18
e-marketing 5, 7, 263
epistemology 198, 205, 206, 208, 225
ethical issues 123
external environmental audit 240

F

fear of competition 265
Financial Services Authority (FSA) 112
flexibility in organizations 66
FSA 112, 113

G

GIROMAT 130 26

H

hard systems thinking (HST) 116
HCI 34, 53
high value customers, attracting 260
HRM 250
HST 116, 117
human activity (micro-social) systems 191
human-centered methods 89
human computer interface (HCI) 34
human involvement 86, 87
human involvement and e-banking 86–102
human issues managing 184
human relations model 191
human resources (HR) 282
human resources management 72

I

ICT 12, 13, 14
ICT role in banking 12
implementing e-banking, reasons 256
information needs analysis 232, 233, 252
information systems as social systems 90
information systems domain 240
information systems strategic management
    (ISSM) 252
innovation and sustainable growth 159
innovation culture promotion 276
interactive television (iTV) 31
internal adoption, managing 67
internal communications management 150
internal environmental audit 240
Internet specific marketing 147
ISSM 252, 253

K

Kant and knowledge 201
Kantian critical philosophy 200
KCI 221
key indicator system 130, 131
KMS 41
knowledge constitutive interests (KCI)
    221
knowledge management for e-banking
    190–228

T

U

W